PATRIOTS
IN
DISGUISE

PATRIOTS IN DISGUISE

Women Warriors of the Civil War

RICHARD HALL

PARAGON HOUSE
New York

First edition, 1993

Published in the United States by

Paragon House
90 Fifth Avenue
New York, N.Y. 10011

Library of Congress Cataloging-in-Publication Data
Hall, Richard
Patriots in disguise:
women warriors of the Civil War / Richard Hall.—1st ed.
p.   cm.
Includes bibliographical references and index.
ISBN 1-55778-438-8
1. United States—History—Civil War, 1861–1865—Participation, Female.
2. Women soldiers—United States—History—19th century.
3. Women—United States—History—19th century.   I. Title.
E628.H35   1993
973.7'4'082—dc20
92-17204
CIP

ared in the United States of America

Dedication

I would like to pay tribute to the many women whom I admire for their intelligence, accomplishments, abilities, and humanity within my own extended family, particularly including my sister, my stepmother, my nieces, my cousins, and my sisters-in-law. They have my love and respect. In addition, I dedicate this book to the memory of two very extraordinary, warm, caring, and resourceful women:

Rachel Ernestine Rudd Hall, my mother, whose self-confident political activism in Connecticut town and county politics (long before this was an "accepted" activity for women) and whose loving outreach to less fortunate members of society exemplified important principles to me in my youth.

Sarah Emma Edmonds Seelye, one of the main protagonists in this book, whose memoirs captured my imagination and inspired the entire research project, and whose character I found to be admirable, without qualification.

Contents

Acknowledgments

I am indebted to numerous people for their generous help and advice in my historical quest, chief among them:

Dr. Stuart Sprague, professor of history at Morehead State University, Kentucky, for unselfishly sharing with me his "accumulation" of articles and research notes about Civil War female soldiers, and digging out additional information for me in response to my questions, altogether making a major contribution to the book.

Phil Germann, Executive Director of the Historical Society of Quincy and Adams County, Illinois, for extraordinary help and personal intervention with other repositories (above and beyond the call of duty) in obtaining photographs and documentation relating to "Albert Cashier" (Jennie Hodgers).

Mrs. Mary L. Dalzell, former Reference Librarian at the Flint, Michigan, Public Library, who provided substantial information not only about "Franklin Thompson" and the 2nd Michigan Infantry (organized in Flint), but also about Genesee County history and postwar biographical information about several members of the regiment. Her very responsive and helpful replies to my early inquiries were an important factor in encouraging me to continue my research.

At Lansing and the Michigan State Archives, I am indebted to former archivist Julie K. Bennett who was helpful to me during my original foray into the field; also to John C. Curry and Charles Cusack, archivists, for their later assistance on many important details. Professor Frederick D. Williams, Civil War scholar at Michigan State University's department of history, gave me helpful advice on source materials.

Calvin L. Collier, author of *The War Child's Children* and other books on Arkansas Civil War soldiers, very kindly provided information and advice about Loreta Janeta Velazquez's alleged "Arkansas connection."

For research assistance in cities or towns having significance for one or more female soldier(s), I wish to thank the following people: Lewis H. Averett, research staff, Jones Memorial Library, Lynchburg, Virginia, for considerable help in tracing the Lynchburg and Richmond parts of Loreta Janeta Velazquez's story. Katharine Harbury, genealogist and historical researcher, Williamsburg, Virginia, for research related to Loreta Janeta Velazquez's "Richmond connection." Joanne H. Harvey, genealogist, Lansing, Michigan, for yeoman research efforts on various Michigan female soldiers, and particularly an intensive effort to track down, on the basis of census data, the otherwise unidentified "Emily" from Brooklyn who is reported to have served in a Michigan regiment.

Ruth T. McMahon, Northville, Michigan, for Detroit-area research on various Michigan female soldiers, including successful searches through the Burton Historical Collection for important photographs and copies of contemporary newspaper articles from microform collections. Karan L. Zucal, historical and genealogical researcher, South Lyon, Michigan, for general research on Michigan female soldiers. Patricia Jaques Myers, genealogical and historical researcher, Jefferson City, Missouri, for help in attempting to trace records of Frances Clalin, as well as Kansas City-area aspects of other female soldiers.

Carl P. Curry and Governour D. L. Clements of Concerned Citizens for Washington Cemetery Care, Inc. (CCWCC, Inc.) provided information pertaining to the final resting place of Sarah Emma Edmonds Seelye in Washington Cemetery, Houston, Texas; and Mrs. Leona Zaboroski, member of the CCWCC, Inc. preservation and maintenance committee, who took photographs of the cemetery plot and gravestone.

Frank G. Rankin, Jr., Historian General of the Military Order of the Stars and Bars (Society of Descendants of the Confederate Officer Corps) generously volunteered his time and research skills in an effort to track down the story of a female Confederate spy, purportedly from Kentucky, who may have been Loreta Janeta Velazquez.

Charles Lindquist, curator, Historical Society of Lenawee County, Michigan, provided research assistance on Michigan soldiers and help with photographic research. For other photography, including reproduction of photographs and engravings from old books and journals, I am particularly grateful to Marvel Ireland of Burton, Michigan, and Robert P. Swiatek of Arlington, Virginia.

At my place of employment, Congressional Information Service in Bethesda, Maryland, a publisher of Government-related information, Steven M. Daniel, Director of Congressional and Legal Services, helped me obtain published records relating to Sarah Emma Edmonds Seelye's efforts to obtain a Government pension and he was interested in and supportive of my research; and Debra Turnell, keyboarder *extraordinaire*, not only helped in manuscript preparation, but also gave me valuable "review comments" and feedback, and assisted in analyzing and interpreting some difficult-to-read, hand-written historical documents.

Literary agent John White receives my special gratitude for recognizing the merit of this work and finding a home for it, and standing up for my interests; and I thank my editor, PJ Dempsey, for championing the book despite all sorts of aggravations within the labyrinthine circles of the publishing world.

Introduction

A surprising number of women served in combat on both sides during the American Civil War, some as officers or sergeants. A contemporary author, Dr. L. P. Brockett, wrote: "The number of women who actually bore arms in the war, or who, though generally attending a regiment as nurses and *vivandieres*, at times engaged in the actual conflict was much larger than is generally supposed, and embraces persons of all ranks of society."

Until recently, when barriers crumbled and American women participated significantly in Operation Desert Storm and the Panama invasion as soldiers, it was thought to be a rare—even a freak—occurrence for women to be on the battlefield. A few women, including Deborah Sampson, Margaret Corbin, and Nancy Hart, were known to have fought in the American Revolution, but that was viewed as an aberration. In World War II, women pilots ferried combat aircraft overseas; and WACS and WAVES served in noncombat positions. The roles of women in the military changed only very slowly after that, but in the 1990s, revolutionary change is in the air.

In her 1989 book, *The Warrior Queens*, Antonia Fraser observed: "Almost every culture throughout history has had its Warrior Queen or Queens either in fact or in fiction, or in some combination of them both. The U.S. is so far one of the significant exceptions." Women warriors figure in the history and legends of many nations. Joan of Arc, who led troops in combat during the 15th century, is the most famous. (Several women who elected to fight in the American Civil War professed admiration for her.)

"My imagination fires with a desire to emulate the glorious deeds of Joan of Arc, the Maid of Orleans," wrote Loreta Janeta Velazquez, who served as a Confederate officer while disguised as a man. Others include:

- Matilda of Tuscany who, in the 11th–12th centuries was a woman warrior for Pope Gregory VII, and served in several military engagements in the cause of Alexander II, leading soldiers on horseback and wielding a sword.
- Queen Eleanor of Aquitaine who, in the 12th century, led a force of women dressed as men, mounted on horses and armed with weapons, during the Second Crusade.
- Queen Jinga of Angola (Jinga Mbandi) who, in the 17th century, wore male apparel in leading her people in a sort of guerrilla warfare against Portuguese occupiers. At one point, fighting for independence and to close off slave trading, she conquered the Jaga tribe in the Kingdom of Matamba.
- Lakshmi Bai, the Rani of Jhansi in India, who studied martial arts and, armed with a sword and pistols, led men of the Bengal army in a revolt against British rule shortly before the American Civil War. She met a soldier's end, dying in hand-to-hand combat.

When the American Civil War broke out, the regular U.S. Army numbered fewer than 16,000 men, many of them manning forts on the western frontier. Individual states were obliged to raise volunteer regiments and supply them with arms and equipment. In fact, many volunteer regiments reported for duty without uniforms, poorly trained and with only makeshift weapons and minimal supplies. Eventually, the threat posed to their way of life by a "common enemy" united and "federalized" the North, just as the perceived threat to their way of life "confederated" the southern states.

Both sides scrambled to suppress factional differences and assemble military resources for what each of them viewed as a moral conflict that would decide what form the American government would take. Self-government, individual rights, states' rights, and Federalism were all philosophical factors underlying the dispute, along with the pernicious and pervasive issue of slavery.

This book celebrates the women who, for a variety of motives (including patriotism, adventurism, and a sense of duty), placed their lives on the line from the outset and braved shot and shell on the bloody battlefields of the Civil War. Dr. Brockett, influenced by the prejudices of his era, did not choose to honor the women who fought disguised as men. However, it is impossible today *not* to recognize the raw courage, dedication, and integrity of the women whose true sex was discovered only after they were killed or severely wounded in battle. At Gettysburg, for example, a female Confederate soldier was found dead alongside the body of her husband, both killed during Pickett's charge. Another female Confederate soldier was discovered after losing a leg in combat at Gettysburg. Female Union soldiers also were wounded or killed in action.

Most women who served on or near the battlefield did so as nurses. There were regimental nurses who came along with the soldiers, Catholic sisters who aided in caring for the sick and wounded, and a special category of women known as *vivandieres* (a term from Europe, for female sutlers or canteen women who supplied food and water to soldiers). Many nurses like Clara Barton, Dorothea Dix, and Mary ("Mother") Bickerdyke obtained well-deserved fame and honors for their yeoman service in nursing care and hospital organization. However, they are not the main focus of this book.

Another concept borrowed from European armies was "daughter of the regiment," usually a young female who was intended to be an inspiration to the unit, wearing a colorful uniform and serving an ornamental role by leading the soldiers in parades during camp life, and who was expected to be a nurse and all-purpose supportive person once it came to combat. There were, of course, other women in camp: cooks and laundresses, officers' wives, and sometimes camp followers. But when the soldiers went into combat these women usually stayed behind. Some nurses and daughters of the regiment, on the other hand, went along with the soldiers, staying just behind the lines with their medical supplies.

In the heat of combat, however, artificial distinctions tended to vanish and nurses, daughters of the regiment, and even officers' wives sometimes found themselves caught up in battle. Some, like Anna Etheridge, daughter of the regiment for three Michigan regiments, were frequently on the battlefield assisting fallen soldiers, as bullets and shells whizzed all around them. Etheridge went to war with the 2nd Michigan Infantry Regiment. The 2nd Michigan serves as a microcosm of women in the war. Also with the regiment were Jane Hinsdale, a nurse who went along with her husband and was taken prisoner at 1st Bull Run, and "Franklin Thompson," a female solider.

The two main protagonists in the story of female Civil War soldiers are Loreta Janeta Velazquez, female lieutenant for the Confederacy who used the name "Harry T. Buford," and Sarah Emma Edmonds who served as Private "Franklin Thompson." Both were in combat, and both served as spies. Their stories, although controversial, provide a point-counterpoint for studying the presence of women on both sides of the battlefields of the Civil War.

In addition, the fragmentary records of several dozen other female soldiers for North and South have been retrieved and scrutinized, and studied in comparison with the better known cases. They are reported here as completely as possible to enable a thorough study of the entire phenomenon of women participating in combat during the Civil War. The records strongly suggest that women played a much greater role in Civil War combat than has ever been recognized. This is their story.

Dates of Major Battles and Campaigns

July 21, 1861	1st Bull Run (Manassas)
April 6–7, 1862	Shiloh (Pittsburg Landing)
March–July, 1862	Virginia Peninsula Campaign
August 29–30, 1862	2nd Bull Run
September 17, 1862	Antietam (Sharpsburg)
December 13, 1862	Fredericksburg
December 31, 1862	Stone's River (Murfreesboro)
January 1, 1863	Stone's River (second day)
May 1–4, 1863	Chancellorsville
June–July, 1863	Vicksburg Campaign (final stages)
July 1–3, 1863	Gettysburg
September 19–20, 1863	Chickamauga
May 5–7, 1864	Wilderness
June 1864–April, 1865	Richmond-Petersburg Campaigns
July 22, 1864	Atlanta
November–December, 1864	Nashville Campaign, March to Sea
January–March, 1865	Carolinas Campaign
March–April, 1865	Appomattox Campaign

PATRIOTS
IN
DISGUISE

I

The Half-Soldier Heroines

Women who actually bore arms in the war were "half-soldier heroines . . . who deserve a place in our record."
—DR. L. P. BROCKETT, 1867.

From the earliest call to arms, many women went openly to war. Some, like Anna Etheridge, went as daughter of the regiment; others went as *vivandiere*, colorfully dressed in Zouave uniforms. They were originally thought of as regimental ornaments, guardian angels, nurses, water carriers, cooks, and laundresses—whatever the circumstances required. Some women went along with their enlisted or officer husbands, and they tended to be "mother figures" who also pitched in as nurses and helped with camp chores. Some women adopted semimilitary dress, practiced with weapons, and participated in military drills and marches.

Unlike the ones who disguised themselves as men and fought in the ranks, these women did not particularly crave adventure. Instead, they sought to play some supporting role to help the cause. However, until later in the war when women and all civilians were banned from camp, it was not unusual to see married couples and even children in camp. Usually families stayed behind when the regiments marched off into battle. But often there was no sharp dividing line between camp and battlefield, and these women sometimes found themselves under fire in the midst of combat.

In practice, both *vivandieres* and daughters of the regiment, as well as wives who followed the soldiers and sometimes marched with them, typically served as sort of half-nurses and half-soldiers, taking an active role on or adjacent to the battlefield. Like Anna Etheridge, they not only experienced the rigors of camp life, but also were exposed to shot and shell, and sometimes took up arms

3

and shot back. An early postwar commentator called them "half-soldier heroines."

Along with their sister soldiers, these women were present in the ranks from the first major engagement at Bull Run on July 21, 1861, through the 1864–1865 Atlanta, Richmond, and Petersburg campaigns (see table of dates of major battles and campaigns). Despite occasional bans by military commanders, they managed to circumvent the restrictions imposed on them and performed courageously under combat conditions.

When the war broke out in 1861, Robert S. Brownell, a mechanic in Providence, Rhode Island, enlisted in the 1st Rhode Island Infantry for three months, and was appointed as an orderly sergeant. His wife, Kady, daughter of a Scotsman and soldier in the British army, went with him when the regiment went to camp in Maryland that summer. She had grown up accustomed to camp life, arms, and soldiers from infancy and was not about to be left behind.

"This daughter of the regiment was resolved not to be a mere water-carrier, nor an ornamental appendage," according to biographer Frank Moore. Their company was the eleventh to be formed (a regiment required only ten) and so trained as sharpshooters. Kady took rifle practice with the men, proving skillful at it. She "became one of the quickest and most accurate marksmen in the regiment. Nor was the sergeant's straight sword, which hung at her belt, worn as an idle form. She practised daily with her husband and his friends in camp, till she felt herself as familiar with its uses as with the carbine." Due to her impressive display of martial arts, Kady was appointed color bearer, and when the regiment moved she marched in line beside her husband wearing her sword and carrying the flag.

By the time of the battle of 1st Bull Run, July 21st, the enlistments of several three-month regiments had run out, or were about to do so, but the 1st Rhode Island volunteered to stay on until the conclusion of the campaign in northern Virginia. At least two other units refused to stay.

Early in the conflict, soldiers of Kady's sharpshooter company were deployed as skirmishers in the pinewoods on the left of the Union line. As the men advanced by fours, Kady, proudly carrying the flag, became separated from Robert. Following military procedure, Moore wrote that

> she remained in the line, guarding the colors, and thus giving a definite point on which the men could rally, as the skirmish deepened

4

into a general engagement. There she stood, unmoved and dauntless, under the withering heat, and amid the roar, and blood, and dust of that terrible July day. Shells went screaming over her with the howl of an avenging demon, and the air was thick and hot with deadly singing of the minie balls.

About four o'clock, the far right of the Union line broke. Confusion and panic set in, and the army retreated in disarray toward Washington. As the 1st Rhode Island retreated in the direction of Centreville the panic spread, and they did not rally on their colors and retreat in good order. "She knew her duty better," wrote Moore, "and remained in position till the advancing batteries of the enemy opened within a few hundred yards of where she stood, and were pouring shells into the retreating mass."

Just then a Pennsylvania soldier running past grabbed her hand, and said, "Come, sis, there's no use to stay here just to be killed; let's get into the woods." They started running down a slope toward the pinewoods, but had not gone far before a cannonball struck the soldier in the head, shattering his skull and splattering blood on Kady's uniform. She ran on into the woods and found some members of her company there, but the cannonballs were flying thick and they were forced to flee. Spotting a stray horse, Kady mounted it and made her escape to Centreville.

Throughout the next day Kady heard several rumors to the effect that Robert had either been killed or badly wounded. One such story was that his body had been left in the pinewoods on the edge of the battlefield. Hearing this, she mounted a horse and started out toward the woods to find him. Along the way she came across Colonel Ambrose Burnside (organizer of the 1st Rhode Island and a brigade commander at Bull Run), who assured her that Robert was unhurt and that she should be reunited with him in a few hours.

The Brownells were reunited and, at the conclusion of the campaign, returned to Providence with the regiment and were discharged. They quickly reenlisted in the 5th Rhode Island Infantry. Burnside, now promoted to brigadier general, led an expedition to approach Richmond from the south, including the 5th Rhode Island in his force. In January 1862 they took Roanoke Island, and in March were along the Neuse River advancing on New Bern, North Carolina. Kady, serving in the dual capacity of nurse and daughter of the regiment, marched with the regiment fourteen miles through the mud of the Neuse River.

As the column neared New Bern, Kady asked to carry the regimental colors if they should charge the enemy's works. She was finally granted the privilege, but only with the understanding that she could carry the colors just up to the time when the charge was ordered. While the regiments were moving into position, the 5th Rhode Island was seen by other units advancing through the woods from an unexpected direction, and were mistaken for a force of Confederates. Preparations were quickly made to open fire with both muskets and artillery. Seeing the danger, Kady promptly and courageously dashed to the front into open ground and waved the colors until the advancing regiment was recognized as friendly. Her action no doubt saved dozens of lives that could have been lost due to a battlefield blunder.

Shortly afterwards the battle began in earnest, with shot and shell flying thick. A line of bristling Confederate bayonets and gun barrels could be seen up ahead. Kady again begged to carry the colors in the charge, but the officers refused. Disappointed, she walked slowly to the rear and immediately began caring for the wounded.

After a while word was brought to her that Robert had fallen wounded and was lying bleeding. Rushing to the scene she found him lying there helplessly, his thighbone shattered by a minie ball. Fortunately, no arteries were severed so the wound was not immediately life threatening. Kady retrieved some blankets from a position where the dead and wounded were lying thick along the breastwork, and made Robert and some other wounded soldiers as comfortable as possible. Some of the wounded were lying helplessly in the mud and shallow water; she helped them to reach dryer ground.

For over a month Kady remained in New Bern nursing Robert, who for a time grew worse. During this period she also took soup and coffee to the Confederate hospital every day, handing out servings to the wounded rebel soldiers. Finally, in late April, Robert was well enough to be removed by steamer to New York, where he recuperated for eighteen months. But the surgeons pronounced him unfit for further active service, so his days as a soldier were over.

*　　*　　*

Also at 1st Bull Run was Marie Tebe, a colorful *vivandiere* of the old school. She had married a Philadelphia tailor in 1854 who, in January, 1861—even before Fort Sumter was fired upon—had enlisted for three months in the 27th Pennsylvania Infantry ("Washington Brigade"). After Sumter, the 27th returned to Philadelphia and reorganized for three years, later mustered into service on May 31st. "French Mary," as she was called, insisted on going with her husband. She wore a blue Zouave jacket, short skirt trimmed with red braid over red trousers, boots, and a sailor hat with the rim turned down.

Marie acted as a female sutler in the original sense of the *vivandiere,* selling goods to the soldiers, including contraband whiskey. When the regiment was not in action, she cooked, washed, and mended for the men, and served hospital duty. She was said to have been under fire thirteen times. Sometime before December, 1862 she left the 27th and joined the 114th Pennsylvania, a Zouave regiment. (Her husband may have been transferred; his record has not been determined.)

Several glimpses of Marie appear in a memoir of the 114th Pennsylvania Infantry by Frank Rauscher. In camp near Washington, the 114th on October 27, 1862, received orders to cross the Potomac. They reached the river on the last day of the month. "At first the water proved to be shallow, but on approaching the Virginia side the current brought us into much deeper and rougher obstructions," Rauscher wrote.

> Nearly all the men fell headlong into the channel and stumbled over the large stones, becoming wringing wet. All were in the same predicament, excepting the staff officers, who were on horseback, and Marie, the *vivandiere,* who had the forethought to pick up an old mule, on which she safely crossed the river.

At the battle of Fredericksburg, December 13, 1862, Marie and some soldiers of the 114th helped to establish the field hospital and administer to the wounded. (She herself had been wounded by a bullet in the left ankle.) The following spring in the midst of the major battle at Chancellorsville, Virginia, Marie went among the thirsty troops with a canteen, braving heavy fire. For her courageous exploits, she was awarded a medal for gallantry by Major General David B. Birney. "She would not wear it," Rauscher reported, "remarking that General Birney could keep it, as she did not want the present."

"She was a courageous woman," Rauscher wrote, "and often got within range of the enemy's fire whilst parting with the contents of her canteen among our wounded men. Her skirts were riddled by bullets during the battle of Chancellorsville."

At the end of the war, Marie mustered out with the regiment on May 29, 1865.

✳   ✳   ✳

In the Western Theater, due to her exploits at the battle of Shiloh, April 6–7, 1862, Belle Reynolds was commissioned as a major by the governor of Illinois. In the summer of 1861 her husband had joined the 17th Illinois Infantry as a lieutenant. (His initials may have been J. P., based on indirect evidence.) On August 20th, Belle joined her husband in camp at Bird's Point, Missouri. From then until near the end of the war she kept a journal of her army life and adventures, from which the following extracts are taken.

Throughout the fall and winter of 1861–1862, Belle stayed with the regiment, sometimes riding in an army wagon or ambulance, and sometimes on a mule. At other times she marched in the ranks with the soldiers, carrying a musketoon (a short, large-bore musket) on her shoulder. While in camp along the Mississippi River in southern Missouri, it was a picturesque scene, and a romantic period for the recently married couple. The regiment was involved in the battle of Belmont, Missouri, on November 7, 1861, led by a new brigadier general named Ulysses S. Grant. They wintered over in Cape Girardeu.

In February, 1862 Grant captured Fort Henry and Fort Donelson, opening middle Tennessee to invasion by Union Forces. On April 6th, threatened by Grant's army near Corinth, the Confederates attacked the Union camp at Pittsburg Landing (Shiloh), Tennessee. Belle wrote in her journal for April 4th:

> The long roll has called the regiment out, and we know not what an hour may bring forth. Pickets have been driven in, and skirmishing is going on at the front. Distant musketry and the rumbling of artillery past my tent give the situation a look of reality which I had not dreamed of an hour ago. Although so near the enemy's lines, we feel no fear. Mrs. N. and myself are the only ladies in camp, and our tents are adjoining.

The battle broke full force at daybreak Sunday, April 6th, lasting through the next day after an overnight interruption. A sudden attack in force in the early morning hours caused half-awake Union troops to flee their camps. In her next journal entry dated April

17th, Belle reported her experiences when the Union camps were overrun:

> At sunrise we heard the roll of distant musketry. . . . [About an hour later] while preparing breafast over the campfire, which Mrs. N. and I used in common, we were startled by cannonballs howling over our heads. [The soldiers were ordered to fall in.] Knowing my husband must go, I kept my place before the fire, that he might have his breakfast before leaving; but there was no time for eating, and though shells were flying faster, and musketry coming nearer, compelling me involuntarily to dodge as the missiles shrieked through the air, I still fried my cakes, and rolling them in a napkin, placed them in his haversack, and gave it to him just as he was mounting his horse to assist in forming the regiment.

Lieutenant Reynolds asked her what she would do, but there was no time to think. "Shells were bursting in every direction about us. Tents were torn in shreds, and the enemy, in solid column, was seen coming over the hill in the distance." As they fled, they saw cavalry soldiers forming on the parade ground near the camp. "Balls were flying and shells bursting among the terrified horses and fearless riders."

Before they had gone very far, Belle and Mrs. N. came upon ambulances from which the wounded were being carried out and laid on the ground. "We stopped, took off our bonnets, and prepared to assist in dressing their wounds," she said. But an orderly dashed up, shouting orders to move the wounded immediately to the river. The rebels were closing in, and they were not safe where they were. Making their way to the river, Belle and her friend boarded the *Emerald,* one of the steamers that served as Captain Norton's headquarters. Soon the wounded came pouring in, and they were busy for the next thirty-six hours doing what they could to comfort the soldiers.

By nighttime, the *Emerald* alone had 350 wounded aboard. "I dared not ask the boys if my husband was unharmed," she wrote, "and feared each moment to see him among the almost lifeless forms that were being brought on board the boat."

All day long they heard the thunder of artillery, and spent bullets fell like leaden hail on the deck of the boat. Shells directed at the ammunition ship nearby whirled over their heads. Near sunset the retreating Union army crowded the scene, many seeking shelter on the already crowded boats, some swimming to the opposite shore. Just as it seemed their position would be overrun, the gunboats

Lexington and *Tyler* steamed upriver and unleashed a deadly fire on the Confederates. Union reinforcements could be seen on the opposite shore, approaching at the double-quick. As the transports were pressed into service to ferry the soldiers across the river, officers rushed around trying to rally the dispirited army to join in a counterattack.

"At the Landing it was a scene of terror," Belle reported. "Rations, forage, and ammunition were trampled into the mud by an excited and infuriated crowd. . . . Trains [wagons] were huddled together on the brow of the hill and in sheltered places. Ambulances were conveying their bleeding loads to the different boats, and joined to form a Babel of confusion indescribable. None were calm, and free from distracting anxiety and pain, save the long ranks of dead, ranged for recognition or burial, at the hospital on the hill-side."

Nightfall brought a temporary halt to the infantry clashes, and both sides tried to rest. But throughout the night the gunboat cannonade continued, and the rain came pouring down. The storm increased in fury as the night wore on. Toward morning the *Emerald* slipped downstream to Savannah and unloaded the wounded. Morning found Belle and her friends at work again, dressing the wounds of a new group of soldiers who had just been brought in from the field.

Belle still had no news of her husband. The mud and rain confined them to the boat, but persistent reports reached them that the rebels were retreating. That the Union army, having received strong reinforcement by Major General Don Carlos Buell's army and Major General Lew Wallace's division, was pushing the rebels back. The tide had turned.

About dusk on the second day, Lieutenant Colonel Smith arrived from the regiment with a message to Belle from her husband. Although his horse had been shot out from under him, he was unharmed. "How thankful I was none can know but those who have endured like suspense and anxiety," she wrote. Greatly relieved, Belle loaded Smith's saddlebags with loaves of bread for the regiment, and he dashed off into the dark.

Throughout the night the storm continued to rage, but on Wednesday morning, "the sun came forth upon a scene of blood and carnage such as our fair land had never known." The roads were muddy, but Belle and two friends set out to help at the hospital. "We climbed the steep hill opposite the landing, picked our way through the corrals of horses, past the long lines of trenches which were to receive the dead, and came to an old cabin, where the wounded were being brought," Belle noted in her journal. "Outside lay the bodies of more than a hundred, brought in for recognition and burial—a sight so ghastly that it haunts me now."

Inside they found one room full of wounded, another with surgeons amputating limbs. Belle pitched in to help. "The sight of a woman seemed to cheer the poor fellows, for many a 'God bless you!' greeted me before I had done them a single act of kindness." The soldiers cried out for water, so Belle organized a bucket brigade to fetch water from the river. She bathed and bandaged their wounds, and distributed the small available supply of bread and jelly. Finding a sutler's stand, she bought a supply of gingerbread, which she called "singular food for sick men, but very acceptable."

Side by side on the floor she observed two dying soldiers, one an old man severely wounded in the chest, the other a rebel with both legs taken off below the knees by a cannonball. To one side was a soldier who had been hit in the face by a bullet, near one eye. The bullet had penetrated into his lower brain, and the surgeon had probed unsuccessfully trying to remove the missile. "His breathing," she wrote, "was of that horrible sort which once heard is never forgotten. He, too, was past all cure. And that operating table," she continued, "these scenes come up before me now with all the vividness of reality."

She watched as one soldier after another was brought in and placed on "those bloody boards," and given chloroform. Often before the sedation took hold,

> the operation would begin, and in the midst of shrieks, curses, and wild laughs, the surgeon would wield over his wretched victim the glittering knife and saw; and soon the severed and ghastly limb, white as snow and spattered with blood, would fall upon the floor—one more added to the terrible pile.

Finally, about 3:00 P.M., she could stand no more. One of the surgeons gave her a spoonful of brandy, and she turned to go back to the boat. Just then she felt a hand on her shoulder and turned, startled to see her husband. "I hardly knew him—blackened with powder, begrimed with dust, his clothes in disorder, and his face pale. We thought it must have been years since we parted. It was no time for many words; he told me I must go. There was a silent pressure of hands. I passed on to the boat."

That night, each time she closed her eyes and tried to sleep, vivid images of the dying soldiers and the amputating table caused her to bolt awake and jump out of bed. Repeatedly, she had to convince herself that she was not still there in the hospital. A few days later, sorely in need of rest and a change of scenery, Belle found space on the steamer *Black Hawk* back to Illinois with a delegation of visitors. About twenty members of the regiment also were on board. She said good-bye to her husband, who had to return to camp.

"Each parting seemed harder than the last," she wrote, "for I knew now the dangers and uncertainties to which he was exposed. But my health had been failing . . . and I felt I must recruit now, or I might not be able to spend the summer with him." On board the *Black Hawk* conversation naturally centered on the battle just concluded.

As an eyewitness, Belle was the center of attention and was bombarded with questions.

> The terrible scenes were still before [me] and seemed to be a dreadful part of me, which I was glad to have removed, if relating them might have that effect. I told my story to quite an audience of ladies and gentleman, Governor Yates being of the number. As I was one of the very few ladies who were present at the battle, and had witnessed so large a portion of its scenes, the story seemed to interest all who heard.

Soon one of the party, impressed by her story, suggested that Belle deserved a commission more than some of the officers, and another suggested that it be done. The governor directed his secretary to fill out a commission form giving Belle the rank of major. The document was formally signed, sealed, and handed to her amidst general congratulations.

After a brief period of rest back in Illinois, Belle rejoined her husband in the field and shared the hardships of camp life, seeing service in Mississippi and being an eyewitness to the duel between Confederate shore batteries and Union gunboats at Vicksburg in July, 1863. When Lieutenant Reynolds's period of service expired in the spring of 1864, they gratefully returned to the quiet of home and hearth.

❖   ❖   ❖

An undetermined number of other women also were at the battle of Shiloh in one capacity or another, including at least three with

Confederate regiments, one as a soldier. Agatha Young reports three others on the Union side: Modenia Weston, who served as a nurse on the battlefield and on the hospital boats; Mrs. Jerusha Small, helping the wounded on the battlefield with her husband's 12th Iowa Infantry Regiment; and Lucy Kaiser, a free-lance, tart-tongued nurse who was under fire on the battlefield.

When W. D. Philips joined the 4th Kentucky Infantry Regiment (Confederate) as quartermaster, September, 1861 in Bowling Green, his wife refused to stay behind. Bettie Taylor Philips went with him and shared the fortunes of war, "in camp, on long marches, often under shot and shell of the enemy." She ministered to the sick, wounded, and dying of the famous "Orphan Brigade," so-called because they were not recognized by the state of Kentucky and had to train and organize mainly in Tennessee.

At the battle of Shiloh, Bettie cared for the wounded and dying soldiers. After two years of hardships, her health began to fail and she set out for home to rest. At Nashville she was arrested by Federal soldiers, who started to search her. "Stop where you are!" she cried, drawing her pistol. "I will never submit to the humiliation of being searched by men. Send a woman to me." The soldiers tactfully retreated, bringing a woman to complete the search. Bettie Taylor Philips was sent to Louisville and tried as a spy, but was acquitted and set free. Later she returned to camp and remained with the brigade until the end of the war, afterwards returning home to Uniontown, Kentucky.

*   *   *

Betsy Sullivan joined her husband, John, in Company K of the 1st Tennessee Infantry Regiment (Confederate) when it was organized at Pulaski in May, 1861. She became known as "Mother Sullivan," ministering to sick and wounded soldiers, mending their clothes, and cooking and washing for them. The regiment went first to West Virginia and then to northern Virginia, where it served under Stonewall Jackson. "She marched on foot with her knapsack on her back through the mountains of West Virginia, slept on the frozen ground, under the cold skies, a blanket her only covering, her knapsack, her pillow."

Early in 1862 the regiment was ordered back to Tennessee. Betsy was with the soldiers on the battlefields of Shiloh and Corinth— "Not in the rear, working in a hospital, but on the battleground with her boys, carrying bandages and with canteens of water suspended from her shoulders, she bound up wounds and stanched the life blood of many soldiers, moistened the lips of the dying, and closed the eyes of the dead."

Betsy was serving as a battlefield nurse at Perryville, Kentucky, on October 8, 1862—a bloody and hotly contested fight—when her husband sustained a severe head wound and Lieutenant John H. Wooldridge of the same company lost both eyes. (Federal casualties in the battle were 4,211 and Confederate 3,396.) When General Braxton Bragg retreated from Kentucky, the wounded men were left at Harrodsburg and taken prisoner. Betsy went with them to prison, where she continued to take care of her husband and other members of the company. Her later history is not reported.

As a postscript to Shiloh, some seventy years later a secret was accidentally revealed. A homeowner on the Shiloh battlefield in 1934 was digging a flower bed when he discovered the remains of nine Union soldiers buried on the battlefield. Subsequent examination of the skeletons revealed that one of them was a woman! The circumstances suggested that she had been killed by a minie ball found near her remains. The nine bodies were reburied in the Shiloh National Cemetery. "The identity of the woman and why she was dressed in uniform will never be known, but it is probable she was one of the many, yes many, members of her sex who donned uniform and posed as a man in order to fight for the cause she believed in," according to author Fred Brooks.

*   *   *

On April 19, 1861, one week after the firing on Fort Sumter, Francis C. Barlow, a young lawyer (Harvard graduate, 1855), enlisted as a private in the 12th New York Militia Regiment. The next day he married his sweetheart, Arabella Griffith, a native of New Jersey, and then left with his regiment for Washington, D.C. on April 21st. Arabella followed him within a week, and stayed in camp with him in Washington, and when he was stationed under General Patterson's command at Harper's Ferry. The regiment returned home early in August, 1861. Francis reentered service in November, 1861 as lieutenant colonel of the 61st New York Infantry. The clean-shaven soldier later became known as the "boy general."

Arabella spent the winter of 1861 with her husband in camp at

Alexandria, Virginia. Colonel Barlow and his regiment served under General George B. McClellan in the Virginia Peninsula Campaign in the spring and summer of 1862, the first serious attempt to capture Richmond. After the campaign failed, Arabella joined the Sanitary Commission and helped care for sick and wounded soldiers at Harrison's Landing, until the army withdrew to northern Virginia in August. She then rejoined Barlow in the field during the Maryland campaign, but went north on business and missed the battle of Antietam.

At the battle of Antietam on September 17, 1862, Barlow was badly wounded. Arabella arrived on the field the following day, and nursed her husband over the fall and winter of 1862–1863. Barlow was promoted to brigadier general two days after Antietam, but was unfit for further service until the following spring. He then commanded a brigade in XI Corps in May at Chancellorsville and in July at Gettysburg.

Barlow was again severely wounded at Gettysburg and taken prisoner behind enemy lines, temporarily paralyzed and thought by Confederate General John B. Gordon to be mortally wounded. Accordingly, when Arabella made overtures to rescue her husband, Gordon compassionately gave her a pass to enter the lines and allowed her to transport General Barlow behind the Union lines.

Barlow returned to duty in the spring of 1864 in time for General Grant's Virginia campaign, commanding a division of II Corps. At times, Arabella was with General Barlow in the trenches before Petersburg, and after battles helped care for the sick and wounded. During her unceasing labors on behalf of the soldiers, her health was impaired, and she came down with typhus fever. She died in Washington, D.C., on July 27, 1864. Contemporaries praised her as a society woman who labored in the trenches, careless of her own health, long and faithfully in support of the soldiers.

After the war, Francis Barlow returned to his law practice. He was a founder of the American Bar Association and, as New York State Attorney General, initiated prosecution of the infamous Tweed ring, a corrupt faction of Tammany Hall politicians. He died in New York City, January 11, 1896.

* * *

Mrs. Rose K. Rooney is said to have left New Orleans, Louisiana, in June, 1861 to serve with Company K, 15th Louisiana

Infantry until the end of the war. According to the memoirs of Fannie Beers, "[Rose] served with the undaunted bravery which led her to risk the dangers of every battle-field where the regiment was engaged, unheeding the zip of the minies [bullets], the shock of shells, or the horrible havoc made by the solid shot, so that she might give timely succor to the wounded or comfort the dying." At the end of the war Rose was taken prisoner for a while because of her defiance of Federal authorities. Later, she made her way back to New Orleans, where she served as matron of Camp Nichols Soldiers' Home.

The contributions of Irish and German immigrants to Civil War regiments is well known. Another "minority" of the time (in addition to women and Native Americans, who served on both sides) were Russians. Ivan Vasilovitch Turchinoff was born on January 30, 1822 in the province of Don. He graduated in 1841 from the Imperial Military School in St. Petersburg, served as an ensign in the Czar's horse artillery, and as a colonel of the Imperial Guard. As a captain on the Russian general staff, he fought in Hungary and the Crimea.

Ivan came to America in 1856 along with his wife, the daughter of a Russian officer. They settled in Chicago, where he was employed by the Illinois Central Railroad. When the war broke out, Turchin (now spelling his name without the Russian ending) was commissioned colonel of the 19th Illinois Infantry Regiment in June, 1861. The following spring the regiment marched into Tennessee, with Mrs. Turchin along as an informal nurse and "mother" to the troops.

When Colonel Turchin was taken seriously ill and had to be carried in an ambulance, she assumed command of the regiment and apparently it did not miss a beat. An early postwar book reported, "her commands were obeyed with the utmost promptness. In the battles that followed, she was constantly under fire, now encouraging the men, and anon rescuing some wounded man from the place where he had fallen." After Colonel Turchin returned to command, she continued to serve as a battlefield nurse "always manifesting the most perfect indifference to the shot and shell or the whizzing minie balls that fell around her. She seemed entirely devoid of fear, and though so constantly exposed to the enemy's fire never received even a scratch."

Colonel Turchin's notions of total war later got him in trouble. When he encouraged his soldiers to loot and pillage Athens, Alabama, his commander was enraged. For this offense, and for having his wife with him in the field contrary to orders, he was court-martialed and dismissal was recommended. However, Mrs. Turchin went to Washington and personally lobbied President Lincoln on his behalf. She persuaded Lincoln to set aside the verdict. In addition, the President commissioned Turchin as a brigadier general.

Turchin subsequently performed valiant and meritorious service as a brigade commander at Chickamauga (where he earned the nickname of "Russian Thunderbolt"), at Missionary Ridge, and during the Atlanta campaign. Late in 1864, ill health compelled him to resign.

Little information survives about other *vivandieres* or women in camp. "Dutch Mary" makes a brief appearance in the wartime journal of John Haley, a soldier in the 17th Maine Infantry Regiment. In camp near Fredericksburg, Virginia, in December, 1862, Haley notes that the "frau" of a Zouave is with them, "a woman whose adipose tissue is quite remarkable, as is her agility. . . . She cooks and washes for the officers, thereby earning an honest penny."

Haley writes with wit and insight, showing a grudging respect for "Dutch Mary" despite some unflattering ethnic remarks.

> When a battle rages, she is on hand to minister to the needs of the wounded. When in camp, she sometimes drills with the men, as today, and she can go through it as well as any. The way her legs fly when executing a wheeling operation reminds me of some swift-moving insect. . . . With her tight Zouave suit on, she looks like a man. One private, thinking to have a little sport at her expense, once came up behind her as she was washing some clothes at the brook, and kissed her. She seized a wet shirt and belabored him right and left, pursuing him out of camp, to the great amusement of his comrades and chagrin of himself. When next he felt in a jocose frame of mind, no doubt he didn't take Dutch Mary as the object of his mirth.

Bell Wiley reports a "laundress" (*vivandiere?*) attached to the Irish Brigade who advanced with the soldiers at Antietam, and "swung her bonnet around and cheered on the men." At this stage the Irish Brigade consisted mainly of New York infantry regiments of Catholic Irish (the 63rd, 69th, and 88th regiments). The 39th New York Infantry Regiment ("Garibaldi Guard") reportedly had at least six *vivandieres* who wore colorful costumes, though more than likely not on the battlefield; and Lizzie Jones served with the

6th Massachusetts Infantry Regiment wearing a colorful uniform and silver canteen presented to her by the men. But few if any anecdotes about them are known.

Early Wisconsin regiments apparently included a large number of women, according to contemporary sources, among them:

Hannah Ewbank, with the 7th Wisconsin Infantry, wore a blue Zouave jacket trimmed with military buttons and gold lace, scarlet skirt trimmed with blue and gold lace, white pants and vest, boots, and blue velvet hat with yellow plumes and white kid gloves! The regiment was mustered in on September 2, 1861, and fought at Antietam, Fredericksburg, Chancellorsville, and Gettysburg.

Georgianne Peterman, from Ellenboro, served as a "drummer boy" in the 7th Wisconsin at age 17, for two years. A contemporary newspaper story described her homecoming from the army: "She . . . is about 20 years old, wears soldier clothes, and is quiet and reserved."

Belle Peterson was "a young country girl, who lived near Ellenboro" and is said to have enlisted in a Wisconsin regiment, probably late in 1862. Belle is said to have "served in the army for some time, possibly as a spy or scout. Those who saw her in uniform, say that she made a fair-looking soldier, and that no one would have suspected that she was a woman."

Eliza Wilson of Menomonie, daughter of a wealthy citizen, served as daughter of the regiment for the 5th Wisconsin. She had her own tent and servant, and paid her own way. She wore a "Turkish" (Zouave) costume, including bright brown dress with pantalettes, black hat with plumes, and morocco boots. Her reported duties were classic for the early war period (the regiment was formed on July 12, 1861): "to head the regiment when on parade, and to assuage the thirst of the wounded and dying on the battlefield, where it was hoped that she would be a real guardian angel of the regiment."

Ellen Goodridge reportedly served with her boyfriend, James Hendrick, a lieutenant in an early Wisconsin regiment. She "followed her soldier-lover through four years of active service, and at last closed his eyes in death in a Washington hospital a few days after Lee's surrender." The unidentified regiment was said to have been at 1st Bull Run and in "every great battle that was fought in Virginia. . . . In the intervals she often went with him in skirmishes and raids, and on one such occasion receiving a painful wound in her arm from a minie ball."

Sarah Collins of Lake Mills tried to enlist with her brother, Mason, who helped her adopt male disguise. She was described as "robust," and capable of bearing the hardships of army life. Although her hair was cut short and she dressed like a man, her sex was detected in camp because of female mannerisms and she was sent home.

Unfortunately, very little information can be found to indicate how many or which of these Wisconsin women actually served in combat. Probably the daughters of the regiment dropped out early. The historical record is distressingly incomplete. Yet, the story of Ellen Goodridge, as far as it is known, implies a long-term involvement in the war that is unrecognized by history. Her story, among many others, suggests that our knowledge of the role of women in the Civil War is faulty and incomplete.

How many other "half-soldier heroines" have been lost to history? Possibly others will be discovered and receive long overdue recognition with additional research.

Female Campaigners for the North

*How an Irish lassie, disguised as a man, enlisted in the Union
Army, fought valiantly under General Grant and later spent
nearly a year in the State Soldiers' and Sailors' Home at Quincy
without her sex being discovered, was revealed here today.*
St. Louis *Republic*, dispatch from Quincy, Illinois,
May 3, 1913.

Late in the Civil War, in the Western Theater, a soldier was mortally wounded in a great battle and discovered to be a woman.
Before she died she told her story, which otherwise would have
gone with her to her grave.

It had started several years earlier when one William Fitzpatrick
of western Virginia had enlisted in Company F of the 126th Pennsylvania Infantry Regiment from Juniata County. His "girl friend"
was Frances Day. A few weeks later he fell ill, and on August 24,
1862 died in the hospital at Alexandria, Virginia. That same day,
Sergeant Frank Mayne of Company F "unaccountably deserted"
from camp at Clouds Mills, Virginia. The dying soldier out west
had been Frances Day. She told how she had followed her lover,
William Fitzpatrick, into the army, disguised as a man, and how
she was soon serving so effectively that she was promoted to sergeant. She described how she had deserted when he died, and in
her despair had decided to stay in the army. Other soldiers in the
regiment heard nothing more from Sergeant Mayne until her death-
bed confession.

The record for *documented* length of service by a female soldier
in the Civil War is held by Jennie Hodgers ("Albert Cashier"),
who completed a three-year term of enlistment in the 95th Illinois
Infantry Regiment. Anna Etheridge served with three different regiments for a total of three years, but not as a full-fledged soldier

nor constantly in camp nor at the battlefront. However, many others also served over a period of years, sometimes changing from one regiment to another to avoid detection. Information commonly is lacking to substantiate the records of women who may have campaigned for three years or longer.

"Albert Cashier's" secret was discovered following a freak automobile accident in 1911. Jennie Hodgers's identity had been concealed for more than fifty years. Former State Senator Ira M. Lish regularly employed the old soldier with household chores. One day in 1911, while Cashier was doing yard work, Lish backed up his car and accidentally hit Cashier's leg, breaking it near the hip. He called a doctor, who discovered that "Albert Cashier" was a woman.

Hodgers begged Lish and the doctor not to make her secret public. Compassionately, they helped her gain admission to the Soldiers' and Sailors' Home at Quincy, Illinois, taking the commandant into their confidence. He and the physicians guarded her secret, and she was allowed to continue living there. On the application forms for admission, the physicians cited both "senility" and "weakened mental faculties." At the home, Hodgers enjoyed socializing with the other veterans and recounting her wartime adventures in the 95th Illinois.

The regiment had been formed at Belvidere, Illinois, on August 6, 1862, under the command of Captain Elliott N. Bush. About a month later Albert D. J. Cashier, occupation "farmer," joined the regiment at Rockford. Born in Belfast, Ireland, in 1844, she had arrived in the United States as a shipboard stowaway at an early age in male disguise. She was 18 years-old upon enlistment, and just over five feet tall, with blue eyes and light hair and complexion. In camp Albert tended to sit apart from the others and seemed somewhat aloof.

Embarking on a fleet of fifteen transports headed down the Mississippi River on January 19, 1863, General Thomas Ransom's 2nd Brigade (including the 95th Illinois) headed for Mississippi to join General Ulysses S. Grant's campaign against Vicksburg. The 95th Illinois was aboard the aging steamship *Marie Denning* along with the 11th Iowa, 18th Wisconsin, 2nd Illinois Artillery, plus assorted horses, mules, and wagons. Vulnerable to fire from the shore, the flotilla traveled only by night, arriving at Milliken's Bend fifteen miles above Vicksburg on January 26th, where they disembarked.

In ensuing days the brigade marched to Grand Gulf, skirmishing

with the enemy from there to Vicksburg. During the campaign, Captain Bush often selected the diminutive, slightly built "Albert Cashier" for foraging and skirmishing duty because he was considered very dependable, was in vigorous good health, and was apparently fearless. In one skirmish, Cashier was captured by Confederate soldiers, but seized a gun from the guard, knocked him down, and fled back to the Union lines.

Grant made two attempts to capture Vicksburg by direct attack. On May 19, 1863, General Ransom's brigade was ordered to charge. Civil War historian J. T. Headley reported: "The army moved gallantly to the assault, under a desolating fire, but the works were too strong to be carried." Colonel Humphrey of the 95th Illinois was wounded in the foot but remained in command. Pinned down by enemy fire, the regiment was ordered to withdraw under cover of darkness, having seven killed and fifty-four wounded in the battle. They had been constantly marching and fighting for twenty days.

After resting the troops and replenishing supplies for two days, Grant ordered another attack on May 22nd. The entire army was set in motion at 10:00 A.M., advancing like a mighty wave toward the Confederate earthworks. "Then commenced one of the wildest scenes of war," Headley reported.

> All along the frowning fortifications, there streamed an incessant sheet of fire, bursting through the thick smoke, on the brave, uncovered ranks below, that still pressed dauntlessly forward, heedless of the destruction that wasted them. . . . For two fearful hours, they struggled desperately to reach this blazing vortex, and quench its deadly fires, but struggled in vain . . . [and] the bleeding army was at length compelled to fall back, and abandon the struggle.

The bitter fight increased the total casualties of the 95th Illinois, for the two attacks, to twenty-five killed, 124 wounded, and ten missing. Fatigue and diseases attributed to the tropical climate decimated the ranks even more during the campaign.

Unable to overrun the Vicksburg defenses, Grant began the siege that lasted until July 4th, when the Confederate garrison, reduced by disease and starvation, was forced to surrender. Today, the Vicksburg battlefield monument to Illinois soldiers who fought there includes over 36,000 names, among them that of "Albert Cashier."

During 1864, the regiment campaigned against the famous Confederate cavalry chief, Nathan Bedford Forrest, in northern Mis-

sissippi. At Brice's Cross Roads on June 10th, Forrest's cavalry clashed with a force of 8,000 Union cavalry and infantry. Hot and humid weather and hard marching had left the brigade near exhaustion, but the 95th Illinois came up as rapidly as possible to enter the thickest part of the fight. Though outnumbered, Forrest scored a tactical victory and the Union soldiers retreated toward Memphis. Several officers were killed in the battle, among them regimental commander Colonel Humphrey and Company G commander Captain Bush.

The regiment also participated in the battle of Nashville, Tennessee, in December, 1864 and the siege of Mobile, Alabama, in the spring of 1865. Mobile was taken on April 12, 1865, two days before President Abraham Lincoln's assassination at Ford's Theater in Washington, D.C. After three years of hard service, survivors of the 95th Illinois returned to Camp Butler and were mustered out. "Albert Cashier" and his fellow soldiers received a hero's welcome in Belvidere. Cashier had taken part in forty battles and skirmishes and was never wounded.

After the war, Cashier returned to a quiet civilian life, working as a farmhand and handyman in small towns in Illinois, settling finally in Saunemin. According to a local history of the Soldiers' Home, "he [Cashier] was well liked, kept himself clean and neat, marched in patriotic parades in complete Civil War uniform, chewed a little tobacco, and was considered an asset to the community." Interviewed in 1991, Ruth Morehart, who was born in 1904 and lived in Saunemin, recalled in her youth knowing "Albert Cashier":

"He used to take a stepladder around town and turn the street lights on," she said. "A few hours later he would go around and turn them off again." Albert was also the caretaker of Ruth's church, and even taught her as a child how to toll the church bells. On Memorial Day, "Albert would dress in [his] Civil War uniform and lead the parade. Sometimes after the parade, [he] would treat us children to ice cream or cookies." When Cashier was found to be a woman in 1913, Morehart was nine years old. "Let me tell you," she said, "it was a shock."

Cashier first applied for a Government pension on February 13, 1890. Unable to read or write, he made his "mark" with an X. Since he refused to take the necessary medical examination, however, the pension was not granted. A later application claiming a three-fourths disability was approved, apparently with the com-

plicity of the physicians and, in 1907, Cashier began receiving twelve dollars a month.

Although a few people at the Soldiers' Home knew her secret after the accident in 1911, the story did not leak out to the general public until 1913. Cashier gradually had become erratic and difficult to manage. Finally, on March 28, 1913, she was judged "insane" and consigned to the Watertown (now East Moline) State Hospital for the Insane, though the evidence for insanity seems meager. Commitment papers listed the symptoms as "no memory, noisy at times, poor sleeper, and feeble." The old soldier was fading away. Next day the Washington Sunday *Star* headlined the story:

POSED AS MAN 60 YEARS

"Albert" Cashier, Who Served in Civil War, Committed to Insane Asylum

The story recounted her birth in Ireland and voyage to America as a stowaway, and her military service when the war broke out. Her postwar experiences and declining years also were described, including her placement in the Soldiers' Home. When her sex was discovered, the story concluded, "she refused to tell her family history." Only later did her real name emerge.

A local follow-up story in May was picked up by other newspapers and reprinted widely. Overnight, without her knowing it, she had become a national celebrity. A Quincy *Whig* reporter, who visited her in her room at the infirmary of the Soldiers' Home, wrote:

> The little woman does not know that the story of her secret has now been chronicled in every newspaper over the country, and is still under the belief that Colonel Anderson and one or two attachés of the hospital, together with ex-Senator Lish, are the only ones who know that she is a woman. She chatted freely yesterday with the reporter but was elusive of answering pointed questions. . . . Before the story of the revelation of the sex of Cashier was carried by the *Whig*, inmates of the home did not know that the little old veteran was a woman. Some of them suspicioned that she was, and had heard rumors that a woman-man soldier was harbored some place at the home, but they did not know that it was Cashier. Since the story of

her extraordinary life appeared in print, many pictures of her have been taken and probably at the present time one-third of the veterans in the home have photographs which will be preserved by their children and grandchildren as souvenirs.

Once the news was out, old comrades in the 95th Regimental Association talked about her at conventions, showed photographs of her as "Albert," and shared personal stories about her exploits. They spoke highly of "Albert Cashier's" soldierly skills. Some came to her aid, or to lend moral support. To them "the issue of gender was utterly secondary," according to historian Rodney O. Davis. "The veterans were protective of their fellow soldier, but that protection was simply due to one fallen on hard times, on the basis of past association and past performance. . . . bonds were even closer among those who had fought and bled together as members of the same units."

Tributes to Cashier stressed his bravery and fortitude. Apparently he impressed everyone with his nerveless performance in combat situations and tirelessness on the march. "In handling a musket in battle," wrote author Gerhard P. Clausius:

> He was the equal of any in the company. . . . In spite of his lack of height and brawn, he was able to withstand. . .the problems of an infantryman as well as his comrades who were bigger and brawnier. If a husky comrade assisted Albert in handling a heavy assignment [one which required lifting or pushing], Albert would volunteer to help with his chores of washing clothes or replacing buttons; Albert seemed especially adept at those tasks so despised by the infantryman.

Former First Sergeant Charles W. Ives visited his old comrade "Al" at Watertown. "I left Cashier, the fearless boy of twenty-two at the end of the Vicksburg campaign," he said. "When I went to Watertown, I found [her] a frail woman of 70, broken, because on discovery, she was compelled to put on skirts. They told me she was as awkward as could be in them. One day she tripped and fell, hurting her hip. She never recovered." During one visit she told Ives, "Lots of boys enlisted under the wrong name. So did I. The country needed men, and I wanted excitement."

Ives recalled an incident when they had become separated from the rest of the company and were too outnumbered to advance. They crouched behind a barricade of fallen trees, and the enemy was hidden in front of them. "Al hopped on top of the log and called: 'Hey! You darn rebels, why don't you get up where we can

see you?' " Another time Cashier had climbed a tall tree to put back a Union flag that had been shot down by the enemy. "Al did all the regular duties," Ives recalled. "Not knowing that she was a girl, I assigned her to picket duty and to carry water just as all the men did."

The doctors and nurses at Watertown took special care of Hodgers. She died there on October 10, 1915 at age 71. The Saunemin post of the Grand Army of the Republic arranged for her burial with full military honors, wearing her Union uniform, and she was buried in a flag-draped casket. The inscription on her tombstone in Saunemin Cemetery reads: ALBERT D. J. CASHIER, CO. G, 95 ILL. INF.

At the time of her death, "Albert Cashier's" pension payments had built up to about five hundred dollars in savings, which amply covered funeral and burial costs, leaving almost three hundred dollars in her estate. Within two months after her death, members of an Irish family named Rooney, some resident in the United States, filed claims in county court to be heirs to the estate. In the papers they claimed to be nieces and nephews of Jennie Hodgers. Michael Rooney, in Dundalk, Ireland, maintained that Jennie Hodgers was his mother's half-sister. The claims apparently could not be validated, and in 1914 the estate was turned over to the county treasurer.

*　　*　　*

Another female campaigner was temporarily "exposed" late in 1862 in Tennessee. At the end of December, Union General William S. Rosecrans opposed Confederate General Braxton Bragg in the contest for Tennessee. The two armies clashed on December 31st at Stone's River, near Murfreesboro, in a bloody conflict that dragged on for three days. The result was essentially a stalemate, but Bragg retreated and Rosecrans, holding the field, declared it a Union victory. When the smoke cleared, the casualities were staggering. The Union army had 1,730 dead and 7,802 wounded (with another 3,717 missing). The Confederate army had 1,294 dead and 7,945 wounded (with 1,027 missing). These numbers are only about 10 percent less than the casualties at Antietam, which is called the "bloodiest single day in the Civil War."

At the conclusion of the battle, a severely wounded soldier by the name of "Frank Martin," with the 2nd East Tennessee Cavalry

Regiment (Union), was found to be a woman, and she was mustered out, notwithstanding her "entreating earnestly with tears in her eyes to be continued in service." Her real name apparently was Frances Hook. Frances was one of a number of female soldiers who, when their sex was detected (or they feared it would be), migrated from regiment to regiment.

After recuperating from her wound, Frances reenlisted in the 8th Michigan Infantry (known as the "Wandering Regiment") where she was serving in 1863. At Louisville, Kentucky, that spring, the 25th Michigan Infantry was serving provost and guard duty. One day a captain, accompanied by a young soldier of about 17, arrived in charge of some Confederate prisoners. The engaging youth attracted the attention of the post commander "by his intelligence and sprightly appearance." He was detailed for garrison duty with the 25th Michigan, and soon became popular and liked by all. His name was "Frank Martin."

Before long "the startling secret was disclosed, and whispering went thick and fast, the young soldier was a *lady*; the fact was reported and established by a soldier who was raised in the same town with her [Alleghany City, Pennsylvania] and knew her parents." Confronted by the truth, "Frank" refused to give her proper name and begged to be allowed to stay in service, saying that she had already served for ten months. She was allowed to continue on duty in the hospital. She said that she had been born in New Bristol, Connecticut, raised in Pennsylvania, and sent to a convent in Wheeling, West Virginia, at age twelve, where she remained until the outbreak of the war. She then left the convent and enlisted in the East Tennessee Cavalry.

The 25th Michigan regimental history records that, "Frank was quite small, a beautiful figure, auburn hair, large blue eyes beaming with brightness and intelligence; her complexion naturally very fair, though bronzed by exposure. She was exceedingly pretty and very amiable. She was very patriotic and determined to see the war out." When the 25th left Louisville to join General W. T. Sherman's forces in the Atlanta campaign the following spring, "Frank" remained behind. That was the last that members of the regiment knew or heard about her. She is also reported to have served in the 90th Illinois Infantry Regiment later in the war.

Another female combatant who was wounded at Stone's River was Mrs. Frances Louisa Clayton, who had enlisted in a Minnesota regiment as a private to be with her husband. While serving in

Tennessee under General William S. Rosecrans, the regiment was engaged at Stone's River. During a charge on the enemy, her husband was hit and killed instantly barely five paces in front of her in the front rank. "She charged over his body with the rear line, driving the rebels with the bayonet," according to a newspaper account, "but was soon struck with a ball in the hip, and conveyed to the hospital, where her sex was of course discovered." To add insult to injury, after she was discharged on January 2, 1863, while riding on a train between Nashville and Louisville it was attacked by guerillas, who robbed her of her money and papers.

According to the newspaper, "While in the army, the better to conceal her sex, she learned to drink, smoke, chew and swear with the best, or worst, of the soldiers. She stood guard, went on picket duty, in rain and storm, and fought on the field with the rest, and was considered a good fighting *man*." She was described as a very tall, masculine looking woman, bronzed by exposure to the weather.

One of the most perplexing cases of long-term service is that of Bridget Deavers (sometimes given as Deaver or Divers, among several variations). Her story so far has defied historical research, and it is not even certain what unit she served in, though she usually is linked with the 1st Michigan Cavalry Regiment. Deavers is sometimes described as a "laundress" or as a *vivandiere*, and sometimes as a "half-soldier heroine." Perhaps there was more than one "Bridget" (or "Biddy") and their stories have melded into one. Yet, the existence of at least one Bridget is reported in numerous contemporary sources as having been in the field during the 1864 – 1865 campaigns in Virginia.

A report by the Michigan Civil War Centennial Observance Commission from 1963, titled *Michigan Women in the Civil War* notes that Deavers was said to have gone to war with her husband "but there was no one of the same name in any Michigan regiment. Nor can any evidence of her residence in Michigan be found." Other references to her are included in an encyclopedia (as "Deaver"), in Mary Livermore's memoirs (as "Devens"), and in a book about the United States Sanitary Commission (as "Devan"). Despite this confusion, there is strong documentation of her existence and activities.

An apocryphal story has "Irish Biddy" at the Battle of Fair Oaks (Seven Pines) during McClellan's Peninsula Campaign, May 31– June 1, 1862. She appears on the scene in a critical moment, supporting her wounded husband ("who had a ball through his leg") and urging the 7th Massachusetts Infantry Regiment to charge the enemy and revenge him. Her urgings to "go in, boys, and bate the bloody spalpeens, and revinge me husband" supposedly had an electric effect, and the 7th joined the 10th Massachusetts and other troops in a successful charge on the enemy. The only trouble with this story is that the 1st Michigan Cavalry was not at the battle of Fair Oaks (though the 7th and 10th Massachusetts Regiments were).

The most detailed information about Deavers comes from the 1864–1865 campaigns in Virginia, in which the 1st Michigan Cavalry *was* active. Various diaries and letters from that period sketch an intriguing portrait of her. Mrs. Charlotte E. McKay, a prominent Civil War nurse who kept a detailed hospital diary, noted in her entry for March 28, 1865 at City Point, Virginia:

> Visited, in company with Miss Bridget Deavers, two large camps of dismounted cavalrymen lying along the James River. . . . Bridget—or as the men call her, Biddy—has probably seen more of hardship and danger than any other woman during the war. She has been with the cavalry all the time, going out with them on their cavalry raids—always ready to succor the wounded on the field—often getting men off who, but for her, would be left to die, and, fearless of shell or bullet, among the last to leave.
>
> Protected by officers and respected by privates, with her little sun-burnt face, she makes her home in the saddle or the shelter-tent; often, indeed, sleeping in the open air without a tent, and by her courage and devotion "winning golden opinions from all sorts or people." She is an Irish woman, has been in the country sixteen years, and is now twenty-six years of age.

McKay then recounts the following exchange of dialogue with Bridget:

> "Where is the nice little horse you had with you at the hospital last summer [1864], Bridget?"
> "Oh, Moseby captured that from me. He came in while I was asleep on the ground, and took my horse and orderly. I jumped up and ran away."

She and Bridget visited a camp containing men just returned from General Phil Sheridan's last raid in the Shenandoah Valley.

> We found them lying under their shelter-tents or sitting on the ground in front of them, boiling coffee over their camp-fires and

eating their rations of salt pork and hard tack. They looked tired and sunburnt, but were every moment expecting horses and a call to "boots and saddles."

After distributing socks, towels, and other clothing to the troopers and having a snack, they remounted their horses and rode along the river back to their camp.

Barely a week later, on April 7th, another noted nurse, Rebecca Usher, wrote a letter home to Maine about her encounter with Bridget near City Point:

A few days ago I saw Bridget, who came out with the First Michigan Cavalry, and has been with the regiment ever since. She had just come in with the body of a captain who was killed in a cavalry skirmish. She had the body lashed to her horse, and carried him fifteen miles, where she procured a coffin, and sent him home. [An attack by General Pickett on Grant's left flank at Five Forks, near Petersburg, was beaten back by General Phil Sheridan's forces on April 1st, incuding the Michigan Cavalry Brigade. In another week the war ended. An account of the battle is included in Sheridan's memoirs.] She says this is the hardest battle they have had, and the ground was covered with the wounded. She had not slept for 48 hours, having worked incessantly with the wounded. She is brave, heroic, and a perfect enthusiast in her work.

Usher told her family that Bridget had urged the nurses to go out in the field and take care of the wounded men.

"We would like to go," I said, "but they won't let us."
"Well, they can't hinder *me*," she replied. "[General Phil] Sheridan won't let them."

Frank Moore, in an early postwar book, describes Bridget Deavers thus:

Acting now as *vivandiere* or daughter of the regiment, now as nurse, hospital steward, ward master, and sometimes as surgeon, she was invaluable in each capacity. From her long experience with wounds and disease, her judgment came to be excellent, and her practical skill equal often to that of a physician. . . . Her whole soul was in the work of aiding and sustaining the soldier. No day was too stormy or too cold to check her in an errand of mercy. She overcame all obstacles, and battled successfully with all sorts of rebuffs and discouragements in the prosecution of her duties.

Since she knew everyone in "her brigade" (the Michigan Cavalry Brigade), Bridget frequently was called on to assist the Christian

Commission in answering letters inquiring about a particular soldier who might have been in the division to which she was attached. She had a remarkable memory for names and places. According to Moore,

> When the brigade was in active service she was with it in the field, and shared all its dangers. She was a fearless and skilful rider, and as brave as the bravest under fire. In actual battle she had two or three horses killed under her, and in the course of the war lost eight or ten in various ways.
>
> In the battle of Cedar Creek [Oct. 19, 1864] she found herself at one time cut off and surrounded by the enemy, but managed, by an adroit movement, to escape capture. . . . Her personal appearance is not prepossessing or attractive. Sleeping on the ground like a soldier, and enduring hardships like the rest, her face has become browned by exposure, and her figure grown athletic by constant exercise and life in the open air. But the heart that beats under her plain cassock is as full of womanly tenderness as that of any princess in purple velvet.
>
> Not even with the close of the war did her self-imposed duties end. She has become attached to the free and spirited life of the cavalry soldier, and preferring camp life, with its hardships and adventures, to the comfort and tameness of villages, she is now [1866] with the detachment that has crossed the great plains and the Rocky Mountains for Indian service on the distant western frontier.

In another chapter of his book, entitled "Women as Soldiers," Moore marvels at the hardiness of "Irish Biddy." He confirms the anecdote reported by Rebecca Usher in which Bridget rescued the corpse of a captain and shipped it home, adding that while en route with the body she met up with a small wagon train whose teamsters were on the verge of fleeing and abandoning their train to the enemy. She talked them out of it and rallied them to continue with their work. (A third confirmation of this anecdote is a statement by Mrs. Mary Morris Husband "who knew her [Bridget] well," reported by Dr. L. P. Brockett in 1867.)

"She sometimes went out with the men on picket," Moore continued, "and remained all night on watch. At times, when sickness or hard service had thinned the ranks of the regiment, she would take the place of a soldier, and go out on a scouting or a raiding expedition, doing the full duty of a soldier."

The sketchy information available suggests that after the war, Deavers did occupation duty with her regiment in Texas for a while. She may have gone west with the 1st Michigan Cavalry, by this time a consolidation of the four regiments of the Michigan Cavalry Brigade, which belatedly was mustered out, paid off, and disbanded at Salt Lake City, Utah, on March 10, 1866. A dispute had arisen between Michigan authorities and the War Department over "what was considered to be the unlawful and unjust detention in service of members of the Michigan Cavalry Brigade." This Federal vs. State's rights dispute was a harbinger of things to come.

After the state cavalry was disbanded, Bridget, having grown accustomed to camp life, reportedly joined a regular army cavalry regiment and served in the west during the Indian Wars of the late 1860s and 1870s. But here the trail grows cold. The already sparse record of her escapades fades out. In effect, she vanishes from history. Even the Michigan Centennial Commission was unable to shed any further light on her story. No record has been found to confirm her postwar history, or when and where she died and under what circumstances.

Given that Bridget apparently was illiterate, this could partially explain the lack of an enduring record. However, the fact that she was so well known by Sanitary Commission personnel and knowledgable commentators about the war leaves us with a mystery: Why *don't* we know what became of someone who attained such notoriety in the latter stages of the war, and whose exploits were widely reported by others at the scene of combat? Having spent about fourteen years in this country before the Civil War started, what state had she lived in, if not Michigan? Did she, perhaps, die anonymously on some remote western battlefield while fighting the Indians with the United States cavalry, and does she lie buried in an unmarked grave on the windswept plains because there was no one to retrieve her body and send it "home"?

3

Anna Etheridge, Daughter of the Regiment

Passing under fire, regardless of shot and shell, engaged in the work of staunching blood and binding up wounds . . . she never flinched and never was wounded. . . . She was held in the highest veneration and esteem by the soldiers.
—Official record of service of
Michigan Volunteers in the Civil War.

With bands playing and flags flying, the 2nd Michigan Volunteer Infantry Regiment marched off to war in June, 1861. They had trained for two weeks at Fort Wayne, Detroit, and were headed for the nation's capital to answer President Abraham Lincoln's call for 75,000 troops to "put down the insurrection." The first order of business was to secure Washington, D.C., then to mount an attack on the Confederate homeland.

A contemporary newspaper account, reporting their arrival in Washington, notes:

> The regiment is a fine-looking body, numbering ten hundred and twenty. Their uniforms are dark blue, like the 1st Michigan, and they are armed partially with new Minie guns [rifles] and partially with the Harper's Ferry musket of 1846. They are well equipped with clothing and equipage. Thirty women, who will serve as nurses and laundresses, accompany the regiment.

Three women of the 2nd Michigan would go on to earn Government pensions for their work during the Civil War, one as a regimental nurse, another as a daughter of the regiment, and the third—perhaps the most remarkable of all—a young woman who disguised herself as a man, engaging in spying missions behind enemy lines in addition to performing "routine" soldiering and combat duties. Several of the men attained high rank by war's end, and a number became prominent citizens after the war. Altogether, the regiment comprised an impressive cross-section of American citizen-soldiers.

The early experiences of the 2nd Michigan were described by Perry Mayo of Company C in letters home to his parents:

> JUNE 10, 1861—We left Detroit on Thursday afternoon [June 6] after marching through the city for about three hours. We were greeted with the utmost enthusiasm. The girls were stationed at the windows waving flags and firing revolvers to cheer the men on to the great duty they had to perform. . . . We were nearly fed to death on the road through Ohio with pies, cakes, lemonade, and compliments. Flowers were showered on us at every station.
>
> JUNE 20, 1861—We are now in camp [Camp Winfield Scott] about eight miles from the city of Washington, which place we left after staying two days to rest. . . . [The regiment had been reviewed at the White House by President Lincoln and the army commander-in-chief.] We have been building forts for the defense of the Capitol. They are now done and the men are shooting down an old stone factory on the other side of the Potomac to try their cannon. They have about twenty large guns and make the stones fly some. . . . I have been on several scouting excursions into Virginia. . . . We take prisoners nearly every night.

Volunteer regiments from Maine, Massachusetts, New York, Rhode Island, Pennsylvania, Ohio, Illinois, and elsewhere were converging rapidly on the capital city. Across the Potomac River, Confederate forces lurked not far away in northern Virginia, posing a constant threat. A lot of brief clashes and skirmishes would be fought before the first major battle at Bull Run (Manassas) on July 21, 1861.

On July 18th, Brigadier General Daniel Tyler's division was on a reconnaissance mission probing Confederate General P.T.G. Beauregard's forces near the Manassas railroad junction. A brief, sharp engagement ensued at Blackburn's Ford, the first significant combat experience for the 2nd Michigan (along with the 3rd Michigan) and for Anna Etheridge, daughter of the regiment.

"Gentle Annie," as she was called by the soldiers, was one of those *vivandieres* who had no intention of being a mere parade ground ornament, as many were. While other women with the regiment dropped out along the way, she persisted to the very end. Although she epitomized the soldiers' concept of an angel of mercy,

Annie actually functioned more like a modern combat "medic." She became famous for her courageous first-aid work among the wounded on the battlefield, where she frequently was under direct enemy fire.

Armed with a pair of pistols stuck in her belt (which she was never known to use in anger), she would remain just behind the lines attended by the surgeon's orderly who carried a medicine chest. In the heat of battle they often became separated. Many times when Annie saw a man fall wounded, she would dash forward into the hottest part of the battle, lift the wounded soldier onto her horse, and carry him safely to the rear where he could receive prompt care.

After wintering over in the vicinity of Washington, the Army of the Potomac—newly organized under General George B. McClellan—began the march on the Confederate capital of Richmond in the spring of 1862. McClellan's army, some 100,000 strong, was transported by steamers to Fort Monroe, on the tip of the Virginia Peninsula between the York and the James Rivers. From there it would begin an arduous campaign northwest up the peninsula toward Richmond. The 2nd Michigan, led by Colonel Orlando M. Poe, would participate in every battle of the Peninsula Campaign as part of the Third Brigade (General Berry), Third Division (General Kearny), Third Corps (General Heintzelman).

When all women were ordered out of camp by McClellan, Annie was forced to leave the regiment temporarily. Not being the type to sit idly by when there was important work to be done, she reported to work with the Hospital Transport Service, a civilian volunteer organization formed by the United States Sanitary Commission in anticipation of heavy casualties on the peninsula. The Service was allowed to take possession of any unused government transports docked at Alexandria, Virginia, a motley collection of vessels of many different sizes and configurations. They included the *Ocean Queen*, the *Elm City*, and the *Vanderbilt*.

Annie Etheridge was assigned to the *Knickerbocker*, superintended by Amy M. Bradley, formerly a regimental nurse for the 3rd and 5th Maine Infantry Regiments and by war's end a famous nurse. The wounded were brought to the dock by trains from the front lines twice a day, and loaded on board in every available space on the decks, packed so thickly that it was difficult to work among them. Annie and the others would wash the blood and grime off the men, give them water and food, and prep them for attention by the surgeons and male nurses. When the *Knickerbocker* was filled to capacity (about 450 men), it set sail for ports and hospitals in Washington, Philadelphia, or New York, returning again and again for more precious cargo.

Amy Bradley recorded in her journal for May 29, 1862, that when she took charge of the *Knickerbocker* she found it in a very filthy condition, and several state rooms were filled with soiled clothing. She hired washerwomen to clean clothes, persuaded the ship's crew and the attendants to scrub down the decks, and obtained cots from the quartermaster. In the same entry she notes:

> Mrs. Annie Etheridge, of the Third Michigan, reported for duty. How faithfully she labored! We divided a little saloon at the forward part of the boat, leaving six berths on one side, and six on the other, making two rooms, the one occupied by the surgeon and his staff, the other by us.

On Sunday, June 1st, the wounded began to arrive from the battle of Seven Pines (Fair Oaks) about 4:00 P.M. "I shall never forget my feelings," she confided to her journal,

> as those mutilated forms were brought in on stretchers. . . . For nearly an hour I could not control my feelings. [When the surgeon admonished her that she must 'prepare to assist these poor fellows'] I realized that tears must be choked back, and the heart only know its own suffering! *Action* was the watchword of the hour. . . . We received more than three hundred, some very badly wounded. One poor fellow, shot through the bowels, suffered the most excruciating torture, calling constantly for water: his thirst seemed insatiable. He died before morning.

Amy, Annie, and the others labored until past midnight feeding and comforting the wounded soldiers, and then were up again at sunrise to wash and dress their wounds and change their blood-stained uniforms for clean hospital clothing. Then three hundred soldiers had to be fed again and their special needs attended to, according to the severity of their wounds.

Though Annie was much younger than Amy, they hit it off well from the start, both being hard workers and similar in their basic selflessness and good moral character. They continued to work together throughout the Peninsula Campaign, also serving on the *Daniel Webster* and the *Louisiana*. Together, they made three trips on a truce ship to receive wounded Union soldiers who had been captured by the Confederates.

The conditions under which the women who served on hospital transports labored also were described by Eliza (Mrs. John) Harris, wife of an eminent Philadelphia physician. At the same time that Amy Bradley and Annie Etheridge were caring for the casualties from the battle of Seven Pines on the *Knickerbocker*, Mrs. Harris was on board the *Vanderbilt*. She described the scene after arrival of wounded soldiers from that battle:

> There were eight hundred on board. Passage-ways, state-rooms, floors from the dark and fetid hold to the hurricane deck, were all more than filled; some on mattresses, some on blankets, others on straw; some in the death-struggle, others nearing it, some already beyond human sympathy and help; some in their blood as they had been brought from the battlefield . . . and all hungry and thirsty, not having had anything to eat or drink, except hard crackers, for twenty-four hours.

Threading their way through the suffering soldiers, the nurses and attendants distributed bread, oranges, and pickles. "The gruel, into which we had put a goodly quantity of wine, was relished, you cannot know how much." After many hours of caring for the soliders aboard the ship, they returned to the Hygeia Hospital, stopping long enough to stew some dried fruit for supper. Afterwards, Mrs. Harris reported:

> I disrobed, and bathing with bay rum, was glad to lie down, every bone aching, and head and heart throbbing, unwilling to cease work where so much was to be done, and yet wholly unable to do more. There I lay, with the sick, wounded, and dying all around, and slept from sheer exhaustion, the last sounds falling upon my ear being groans from the operating room.

As the first sustained campaign of the war and first serious attempt to capture Richmond, the bitter fighting on the peninsula, including the famous Seven Days battles before Richmond late in June, was a baptism in blood. It resulted in tens of thousands of casualties in the two armies. Spring rains and marshy conditions, mud and swollen rivers, added thousands of cases of disabling malaria, dysentery, and typhoid fever.

No precedent existed in American history for the vast numbers of wounded and ill soldiers who required medical attention. Almost every diary entry or letter home written at this time mentions not only the mangled bodies resulting from devastating shot and shell, but also the mud and swamps and "Chickahominy fever": the various "miasmic" diseases attributed to poisonous air from the swamps and marshes.

A surgeon in Sixth Corps recorded these comments about the Peninsula Campaign:

> Everything combined to exhaust the energies of the men and produce fevers, diarrheas and scurvy. Day after day the men worked under a burning sun . . . or toiled standing to their waists in water. . . . Night after night they were called to arms, to resist some threatened attack of the enemy. Their clothing and tents were drenched with frequent rains, and they often slept in beds of mud.
>
> With the hot weather, the malaria became more and more deadly. The whole country was alternately overflowed and drained; and the swamps were reeking with the poisoned air. The hospitals became daily more crowded. The strongest were constantly falling. Diarrhea, typhoid fever, and other miasmatic maladies, became almost universal. . . . [They were] burning with fever, tormented with insatiable thirst, racked with pains, or wild with delirium; their parched lips, and teeth blackened with sordes [crusts due to disease and fever], the hot breath and sunken eyes, the sallow skin and trembling pulse, all telling of the violent workings of these diseases.

From the soldier's perspective, Perry Mayo of the 2nd Michigan wrote to his parents on June 2nd, just after the battle of White Oak Swamp, calling it:

> One of the bloodiest battles ever fought. Our regiment is very badly cut up. . . . After the battles we have fought and the sickness occasioned by the hardships of camp life, the [regiment] can not raise more than 300 men now, fit for duty. . . . I was at the depot where the wounded were sent off on the cars [headed for the hospital transport ships] and helped load three trains with wounded men. The piles of arms and legs around the operating stands was enough to sicken anyone not used to such sights.

Reeling from a series of defeats or standoffs in his effort to capture Richmond, McClellan managed an orderly withdrawal of the remnants of his huge army to the safety of Harrison's Landing. Here he dug in and asked for reinforcements to renew the assault on Richmond. But Washington authorities, rightly or wrongly, had lost faith in McClellan. After a period of tense negotiation and internal political debate, Lincoln decided to abandon for now the effort to take Richmond, and bring the Army of the Potomac back to the defense of Washington.

Through the long summer the friendship between Amy Bradley and Anna Etheridge had grown, nourished by their companionship and fellowship as well as their mutual devotion to the welfare of the sick and maimed Union soldiers. With great sadness Amy said good-bye to Annie, and watched as the faithful young woman disappeared on shore at Harrison's Landing to rejoin the 2nd Michigan and accompany them in the retreat. Separations and sad good-byes were a natural part of war.

The army was withdrawn to the vicinity of Washington in August, over bitter protests by McClellan who wanted to obtain reinforcements and continue the assault on Richmond. But Robert E. Lee as the new general who had taken over command of the defense of Richmond, had begun pushing the war north, threatening Washington. His tactics were successful in diverting the scene of combat away from the gates of Richmond and into the north.

The threat of Confederate forces again massed near Manassas, just west of Washington, led to the second battle of Bull Run, August 29–30th. Early on the first day, Annie was with the regiment on a portion of the battlefield where a rocky ledge provided shelter for the wounded. As the battle raged, she helped several soldiers to this place of refuge and dressed their wounds. While she was treating a soldier of the 7th New York Infantry Regiment, a cannonball "tore him to pieces under her very hands." Then, as the rebels threatened to overrun her position, she was forced to flee.

Later, while binding up the wounds of a soldier on another part of the battlefield, she heard a gruff voice and looked up to see General Phil Kearny, who said: "I'm glad to see you here helping these poor fellows, and when this is over, I will have you made a regimental sergeant." Unfortunately, Kearny was killed two days later at Chantilly and she never received the appointment.

By early 1863, Annie's exploits had been noted by a newspaper correspondent from the Bangor, Maine, *Whig and Courier*. His January 20th dispatch from Washington, D.C. was widely reprinted in other newspapers, including the Detroit *Advertiser and Tribune* on February 16th. A transcription of this article, in neat script, was found in the records of the 2nd Michigan in the Michigan State Archives. It said, in part:

> We learn through a Washington correspondent . . . of the exploits of a heroine, Miss Anna Etheridge, formerly of this city, and who is

well known to many of our readers. She is now with the Army of the Potomac, and her history deserves to be conspicuous, fully justifying as it does that "truth is stranger than fiction," while it furnished an example believed to be without a parallel in the history of her sex.

She was born in Detroit and was about 23 years of age. Her father was once a man of wealth, and her early youth was passed in the lap of luxury, with no wish ungratified, and no want uncared for. But misfortune came and swept away his property, and, broken in fortune and depressed in spirit, he removed to Minnesota, where he died, leaving Anna at the age of twelve years in comparative poverty and want. On the breaking out of the rebellion, she was visiting her friends in the city.

Colonel [Israel B.] Richardson was engaged in raising the 2nd Michigan volunteers, and she and nineteen other females volunteered to accompany the regiment as nurses. Every other has been returned home and been discharged, but she has accompanied the regiment through all its fortunes, and declares her determination to remain with it during its entire term of service. She has for her use a horse furnished with side saddle, saddle-bags, etc. At the commencement of the battle she fills her saddle bags with lint and bandages, mounts her horse, and gallops to the front, passes under fire, and regardless of shot and shell, engages in the work of staunching and binding up the wounds of our soldiers. In this manner she has passed through every battle in which the regiment has been engaged, commencing with the battle of Blackburn's Ford, preceeding the first battle of Bull Run, including the battles of the Peninsula and terminating with the battle of Fredericksburg.

General Berry [brigade commander] declares that she has been under as hot fire of the enemy as himself . . . on many occasions her dress has been pierced by bullets and fragments of shell, yet she has never flinched and never been wounded. . . . When not actively engaged on the battle field or in the hospital, she superintends the cooking at the headquarters of the brigade. When the brigade moves, she mounts her horse and marches with the ambulances and surgeons, administering to the wants of the sick and wounded, and at the bivouac she wraps herself in her blanket and sleeps upon the ground with all the hardihood of a true soldier.

Anna is of Dutch descent, about five feet three inches in height, fair complexion (now somewhat browned by exposure), brown hair, vigourous constitution, and decidedly good looking . . . she is held in the highest veneration and esteem by the soldiers as an Angel of Mercy. She is indeed the idol of the brigade, every man of which would submit to almost any sacrifice in her behalf.

Shortly after this article appeared, the 2nd Michigan was transferred west to Kentucky, away from the Army of the Potomac
temporarily. Preferring to stay in the Army of the Potomac, Annie
switched to the 3rd Michigan, serving with it at Chancellorsville
and Gettysburg (and later with the 5th Michigan after the 3rd Michigan's three year term expired in June, 1864).

At Chancellorsville on May 2–3, 1863, the reorganized Army
of the Potomac under "Fighting Joe" Hooker tried to dislodge
Lee's army. Instead, they were out-generaled and defeated in a
fierce two-day battle, but the South suffered a major casualty with
the fatal wounding of General Thomas ("Stonewall") Jackson. In
the heat of the action the Federal XI Corps had been broken up,
and Annie found herself in a moment of peril with a detachment
of 3rd Michigan sharpshooters who were detailed as skirmishers
on the front lines. Annie took the lead, but the colonel ordered her
to the rear, warning that an attack was imminent.

A contemporary historian reported what happened next:

> Very loth to fall back, she turned and rode along the front of a
> line of shallow trenches filled with our men; she called to them,
> "Boys, do your duty and whip the rebels." The men partially rose
> and cheered her. . . . This revealed their position to the rebels, who
> immediately fired a volley in the direction of the cheering.

Annie then rode to the rear, pulling up near an officer on a horse.
At that moment the officer was shot and fell to the ground dead,
his body brushing her as he fell. Another bullet "grazed her hand,
pierced her dress, the skirt of which she was holding, and slightly
wounded her horse." The frightened animal ran away wildly
through the woods with Annie hanging on for dear life, emerging
into the midst of soldiers of XI Corps where his course was checked
by the soldiers. When they recognized her, the soldiers cheered.

At another point during the battle Annie was as usual working
among the wounded, when she discovered a badly wounded artillery man who was not receiving any care. Artillery batteries were
not usually accompanied by surgeons, and the infantry surgeons
normally had their hands full caring for their own men. Annie
bound up his wounds and had him taken inside the hospital area.
About a year later, she received a letter that was found on the body
of a Lieutenant Strachan of her division, who had been killed in
action. It read:

Washington, D.C., JANUARY 14th, 1864.

Annie—Dearest Friend:

I am not long for this world, and I wish to thank you for your kindness 'ere I go.

You were the only one who was ever kind to me, since I entered the Army. At Chancellorsville, I was shot through the body, the ball entering my side, and coming out through the shoulder. I was also hit in the arm, and was carried to the hospital in the woods, where I lay for hours, and not a surgeon would touch me; when you came along and gave me water, and bound up my wounds. I do not know what regiment you belong to, and I don't know if this will ever reach you. There is only one man in your division that I know. I will try and send this to him; his name is Strachan, orderly sergeant in Sixty-third Pennsylvania volunteers.

But should you get this, please accept my heartfelt gratitude; and may God bless you, and protect you from all dangers; may you be eminently successful in your present pursuit. . . . I know nothing of your history, but I hope you always have, and always may be happy; and since I will be unable to see you in this world, I hope I may meet you in that better world, where there is no war. May God bless you, both now and forever, is the wish of your grateful friend.

George H. Hill
Cleveland, Ohio

Once, during the Spotsylvania Court House campaign (May 7–19, 1864), Annie confronted a group of retreating soldiers:

She expostulated with them, and at last shamed them into doing their duty, by offering to lead them back into the fight, which she did under a heavy fire from the enemy. She had done the same thing on other battlefields, not by flourishing a sword or rifle, for she carried neither; nor by waving a flag, for she was never color-bearer; but by inspiring the men to deeds of valor by her own example.

That June in the Virginia campaigns, Annie one day became separated from her regiment (by this time the 5th Michigan). She and the surgeon's orderly started out in search of the regiment. Before long they accidentally passed beyond the line of Union pickets, and a reconnoitering officer warned them to turn back at once because Confederate troops were approaching. Suddenly Confederate skirmishers appeared, the officer spurred his horse and galloped away. Annie and the orderly turned quickly to follow him back into the Union lines. Miraculously, the Confederates held their fire, apparently to avoid giving alarm, and Annie probably owed her life to this happenstance.

Some individuals in combat seem to be specially blessed, or lucky beyond chance, constantly exposed to danger and narrowly eluding the Grim Reaper. Even though others close around them may be violently killed, they are at worst barely scratched, as if they were surrounded by some magic protective shield. Such a one was Anna Etheridge of Detroit.

For her bravery and humane services, Annie Etheridge was awarded the Kearny Cross, a divisional decoration designed as a "cross of valor" for enlisted men. It was a fitting decoration, for it was named after the late General Phil Kearny who had wanted to honor Annie. The medal was presented to her by division commander, General David B. Birney.

Dr. L. P. Brockett, a prominent historian and writer of the Civil War era, summed it up: "General Birney never performed an act more heartily approved by his entire command, than when in the presence of his troops, he presented her with the Kearny cross."

During the summer of 1864, General Ulysses S. Grant ordered all women to leave the camps and lines. Although the officers of III Corps united in a petition to the commander in chief, asking him to make an exception in Annie's case, it was denied. For the second time, she was forced to leave the regiment and went into hospital service at City Point, Virginia. From there, she sent gifts of precious commodities such as onions and potatoes to her adopted soldiers in the 5th Michigan Regiment.

City Point served as the nerve center and focal point of Union operations for the final year of the war. Grant established his personal headquarters there on June 15, 1864. A new wharf was built to handle river traffic, and a large new hospital was built to care for 6,000 patients. Other nurses flocked to City Point to be where the action was, among them the famous Quaker nurse Cornelia Hancock, who condemned the Civil War carnage as "a hellish way to settle a dispute."

Miss Hancock's letters home included rich descriptions of hospital life, and of the wounded and suffering soldiers. She knew Annie Etheridge, and made several references to Annie in her letters written between June, 1864 and April, 1865, among them the following comments:

"White House [Landing], JUNE 15, 1864. My Dear Mother. . . . I met with Anna Etheridge, who has been in the army for three years.

She looks as sunburned as any soldiers. She has never left the field till part of the men went home on Veteran leave, when she accompanied them as far as Washington. She returned in the transports to her Regt., the third Michigan infantry." (This is a reference to the veterans of the 3rd Michigan being mustered out after completion of their three-year term, after which the remaining members were merged into the 5th Michigan regiment.)

City Point, JULY 7, 1864. My Dear Sarah [her niece]. . . . I went, day before yesterday, out 6 miles with Anna Etheridge to see some sick in the 1st Michigan cavalry. I rode on horse back up hills and down dale over ditches, &c. I shall soon be all right on horse back and it is very convenient here as ambulances are difficult to obtain and horses very plenty.

SEPT. 12TH, 1864 [from City Point]. My Dear Mother. . . . This is Monday morning. It is splendid here. Last night Anna Etheridge staid all night with me. She is of newspaper renown and is deserving I guess. Has staid with the third Michigan Regt. for more than three years.

MARCH 3RD, 1865 [from City Point]. My Dear Sister. . . . Annie Etheridge is now ordered from the front to stay at the hospt. and is very bare of clothes. She wants thee to buy her a skirt exactly like mine and two pairs of stockings like my old brown ones. . . . I thought of sending Anne's money in this letter, but thought it might get lost. Dr. will give it to thee.

By mid-June of 1864, the remnant of the 3rd Michigan had been permanently consolidated with the 5th Michigan, when veterans of the 3rd were mustered out as their term expired. Before that they fought together in May in the Wilderness, Spotsylvania Court House (where Annie had urged retreating soldiers back into action), and Cold Harbor. Afterwards, the 5th was engaged in the Petersburg Campaign, and in 1865 participated in the capture of Petersburg on April 3rd, and on the firing line at Appomattox Court House on April 9th when Lee surrendered to Grant.

At the conclusion of the war, the 5th Michigan returned to Detroit and was paid off and disbanded on July 17, 1865. Sergeant Daniel G. Crotty, regimental color-bearer, described the emotional scene in his memoirs: "Noble Annie is with us to the last, and her brave womanly spirit breaks down, and scalding tears trickle down her beautiful bronze face as each of the boys and comrades bid her goodbye."

The ultimate tribute to Annie was articulated by author Frank Moore:

Were our Government to order a gold medal to be given to the woman who has most distinguished herself by heroic courage on the field, and by the most patient and effective service in military hospitals, there can be little doubt that the united voices of the soldiers and of all the army nurses would assign the honor to Anna Etheridge, of Michigan. . . . Few soldiers were in the war longer, or served with so slight intermissions, or had so little need of rest.

4

"Franklin Thompson's" Secret Service

He was a whole-souled, enthusiastic youngster, frank and fearless.
—DAMON STEWART, Co. F, 2nd Michigan Infantry.

As volunteer regiments arrived from the North and West in June of 1861, Washington, D.C., bustled with activity. The soldiers were set to work building fortifications and roads for the defense of the city. They set up new camps, pitched tents, were drilled, fired weapons, stood guard, and did picket duty. Members of the 2nd Michigan—among them "Franklin Thompson," a private in Company F—busied themselves with these routine army duties.

After performing the daily chores of army life, "Franklin" (or "Frank," as he was more commonly called) worked as a male nurse in the brigade hospital. He believed that he had a "gift of nursing" learned from his mother, including a special ability to soothe delirious patients. During that first summer in Washington, "Frank" worked closely with William Shakespeare of Company K, Orderly Sergeant Frederick Schneider of Company A, and Albert E. Cowles (from a Lansing regiment) who was in charge of supplies for the hospital. (Later on, these companions of early hospital days would attain high rank and important positions, and would come to "Frank's" aid in a time of need after the war.)

What none of "Frank's" hospital coworkers or friends from Flint realized at the time, nor for almost twenty-five years thereafter, was that "Frank" was a woman!

In a narrative first published in 1864, before the war had ended, Sarah Emma Edmonds ("Frank's" real name) described her adventures during the first three years of the war. The book, *Nurse and Spy*, was written as if the author were a *female* nurse and spy who sometimes used a male disguise. She was not yet ready to reveal the truth, and took pains to disguise her identity as a "male" soldier in the 2nd Michigan. That would come later.

At the 1st battle of Bull Run, Emma (as "Frank") was first introduced to warfare by the sight of mangled bodies stacked in heaps. She was on hospital duty at a stone church between the Manassas battlefield and Centreville, Virginia. Hard at work caring for the stream of wounded soldiers, she did not realize at first that the Union army had retreated toward Washington in near panic, and she was forced to flee on foot, hiding in the brush from pursuing Confederates.

"The streets [of Centreville] were full of cavalry," she wrote,

> But not near enough to discover me as the night was exceedingly dark and the rain came down in torrents. One glance was sufficient to convince me that I could not escape by either street. The only way was to climb a fence and go across lots, which I immediately did, and came out on the Fairfax road about a mile from the village, and then started out for Washington on the 'double-quick.' I did not reach Alexandria until noon the next day—almost exhausted, and my shoes literally worn off my feet.

The Union defeat at Manassas sent shock waves through the North and resulted in chaos and confusion in Washington, since overconfident authorities had predicted a quick and decisive victory. General George B. McClellan was appointed commander in chief of the demoralized army, and spent the next eight months drilling and training the volunteers into some semblance of a fighting force. All through the winter of 1861–1862, the reorganization and training continued.

By the spring of 1862, the Army of the Potomac was taking shape. Expectations were high. Many felt that it was time to march on Richmond and put an end to the rebellion.

On March 4, 1862, Colonel Orlando M. Poe, commanding the 2nd Michigan, issued orders appointing "Frank Thompson" regimental mail carrier. Postal duties permitted Emma to be in and out of camp constantly, a perfect cover for her "secret service" spying missions behind enemy lines, and away from prying eyes, when soldiers in camp during comparative leisure time might have seen through her disguise. Constantly on the go, she often slept on the ground beside the roadway or in the woods rather than in camp. And while in camp, her hospital duties during periods of combat usually kept her busy through the night, catching a few hours sleep here and there.

About this time, "Frank" was recommended for secret service by his friend Chaplain B. (whose identity still remains a mystery), and was summoned to Washington to be interviewed by Generals George B. McClellan, Samuel P. Heintzelman, and Thomas F. Meagher. In *Nurse and Spy*, she describes being questioned vigorously about her motives and political views, and being given a phrenological examination as part of the tests! Apparently she passed the tests, and later reported back personally to senior generals after each spying mission, according to her memoirs.

When McClellan's huge—but green and untested—army moved out of the Washington area in the spring of 1862 under heavy political pressure to take action, it departed on steamships down the Potomac River and through Chesapeake Bay to Fort Monroe, on the tip of the Virginia peninsula between the York and James Rivers (at the present site of Hampton, Virginia). From there, it would advance northwest up the peninsula toward Richmond. The battle cry was "On to Richmond!"

The first obstacle in the way was General John Magruder's force of about 10,000–15,000 Confederate soldiers in a line across the peninsula. Magruder cleverly maneuvered his forces to make them seem much larger than they were. As part of his deception he employed "Quaker guns" (logs painted to look like cannons). McClellan's intelligence chief, Allan Pinkerton, was also feeding him wildly inaccurate estimates of Confederate strength. These circumstances combined to fool McClellan and help persuade him to set Yorktown under siege rather than to attack with his much larger army.

At this critical time Emma was sent on her first "secret service" mission. Her assignment was to penetrate the lines of Yorktown, and to determine the ordinance and layout of defenses. Taking on a disguise within a disguise, "Frank" had her head shaved, acquired a wig of curly hair and typical clothing of black slaves, and colored her head, face, neck, and arms black.

After trying out her disguise on the wife of Chaplain B. (who she said failed to recognize "Frank"), Emma—using the name "Ned"—departed that night on foot, carrying only a few hard crackers and a loaded revolver. By midnight she had penetrated the Confederate picket line, passing within a short distance of a picket who failed to see her, and then laid down on the ground and rested until morning.

"The night was chilly and the ground cold and damp," she reported in *Nurse and Spy*, "and I passed the weary hours in fear and trembling. The first object which met my view in the morning was a party of negroes carrying out hot coffee and provisions to the rebel pickets . . . I immediately made their acquaintance, and was rewarded for my promptness by receiving a cup of coffee and a piece of corn bread, which helped very much to chase away the lingering chills of the preceding night." After that, "Ned" proceeded into Yorktown without arousing any suspicions.

Emma was immediately pressed into service building fortifications, along with about one hundred other negroes. "I was soon furnished with a pick axe, shovel, and a monstrous wheelbarrow, and I commenced forthwith to imitate my companions in bondage." By the end of the day "Ned's" hands and fingers were raw and blistered from the hard labor. In the evening she was allowed to wander around within the fortifications, and made extensive notes on the numbers and types of cannon, as well as a rough sketch of the outer works, which she then concealed in her shoe.

Next day, to avoid further shoveling because of her raw hands, "Ned" exchanged jobs with a young man who was assigned to carry water to the troops. "I had only to supply one brigade with water, which did not require much exertion, for the day was cool and the well not far distant; consequently I had an opportunity of lounging a little among the soldiers, and of hearing important subjects discussed. In that way I learned the number of reinforcements which had arrived from different places, and also had the pleasure of seeing General [Robert E.] Lee, who arrived while I was there."

Armed with important information, Emma sought an opportunity to escape back into Union lines. When "Ned" was sent to carry food and drink to the outer Confederate pickets, that chance came. Some of the pickets were black and some white, so "Ned" fraternized with the blacks. When one of the pickets was shot and killed, "Ned" was pressed into temporary duty to guard that post. He was handed a rifle and sternly warned to use it if he saw anyone approaching, and if he fell asleep on duty, he was told that he would be shot like a dog. The night was very dark, and it began to rain.

> I was all alone now, but how long before the officer might return with some one to fill my place I did not know, and I thought the best thing I could do was to make good use of the present moment. After ascertaining as well as possible the position of the picket on each side of me, each of whom I found to be enjoying the shelter of the nearest tree, I deliberately and noiselessly stepped into the dark-

ness, and was soon gliding swiftly through the forest toward the "land of the free," with my splendid rifle grasped tightly lest I should lose the prize.

After the Confederates were forced to abandon Yorktown, McClellan's army stalked them toward Richmond. On May 5, 1862, General Joe Hooker began an attack near Williamsburg, and the 2nd Michigan was rushed forward as reinforcements. Emma was in the ranks as they marched eight miles through a drenching rain.

After the long, exhausting march, only sixty members of the regiment were able to go into battle. Rushed into the hottest part of the fight, they sustained twelve casualties, among them Captain William McCreery and "Frank Thompson's" friend Damon Stewart, both wounded and taken from the field. While Emma was aiding Stewart, Captain William Morse fell, hit by a musket ball below the knee. She now rushed to help Morse, one of her earliest friends in Flint, Michigan.

Emma and several other soldiers of Company F lifted Morse onto a stretcher and carried him to an ambulance. When the ambulance broke down, they carried their wounded captain for five miles on a litter, to Williamsburg landing. Early next morning, suffering intense pain, Morse was put aboard the hospital transport *Commodore* with a boat full of wounded headed for Fort Monroe and points north. Morse was taken to a hospital in Brooklyn, New York, and Stewart was sent home to Flint to recuperate from a serious wound in the hand.

In ferocious fighting, the tide was turned at Williamsburg when General Phil Kearny arrived with fresh troops, to the wild cheering of the army. Although casualties were high, the Confederates were chased from the field.

Continuing her dual role as soldier and nurse, Emma then pitched in to help at the field hospital, working all night on May 6th along with the doctors and sanitary workers. A torrent of rain poured down on the battlefield, which was eerily illuminated as soldiers carrying torches waded through thick mud searching for the wounded and trying to identify and bury the dead.

"The dead having been buried and the wounded removed to the churches and college buildings in Williamsburg, the fatigued troops sought repose," Emma wrote:

> Upon visiting the wounded rebels I saw several whom I had met in Yorktown, among them the sergeant of the picket post who had

given me a friendly shake and told me if I slept on my post he would shoot me like a dog. He was pretty badly wounded, and did not seem to remember me.

Emma may have momentarily forgotten that she was no longer disguised as "Ned," but as a white Union soldier whom the Confederate sergeant would not recognize in any case.

Later in May as McClellan's army slowly worked its way up the peninsula, Emma went behind enemy lines on her second mission.

Having had this in view before leaving Williamsburg, I procured the dress and outfit of an Irish female peddler, following the army, selling cakes, pies, etc., together with a considerable amount of brogue, and a set of Irish phrases, which did much toward characterizing me as one of the "rale ould stock of bog-trotters."

Emma's mother was an Irish immigrant in New Brunswick, and she also had been exposed to other Irish immigrants in her childhood.

With her new disguise packed in her cake and pie basket, Emma forded the Chickahominy River on horseback, dismounted, and let the horse swim back across the river where a soldier awaited his return. (Describing this incident in *Nurse and Spy*, she gives the name of her horse as "Frank!").

It was now evening; I did not know the precise distance to the enemy's picket line, but thought it best to avoid the roads, and consequently I must spend the night in the swamp, as the only safe retreat. It required some little time to don my new disguise, and feel at home in the clothes.

Accordingly, she planned to take her time in preparing, and then present herself at the picket line next day as a fugitive fleeing from the Yankees.

Emma then discovered that in crossing the river with the basket strapped to her back, the entire contents had been drenched. She bundled up in a wet quilt from the hospital, trying to ward off the chill night air as best she could.

"That night I was attacked by severe chills," she reported,

Chills beyond description, or even conception, except by those who have experienced the freezing sensation of a genuine ague chill. During the latter part of the night the other extreme presented itself, and it seemed as if I should roast alive, and not a single drop of water to cool my parched tongue. . . . My mind began to wander, and I became quite delirious. There seemed to be the horrors of a thousand deaths concentrated around me; I was tortured by fiends of every conceivable shape and magnitude. . . . Morning at last came, and I was aroused from the horrible night-mare which had paralyzed my senses through the night, by the roar of cannon and the screaming of shell through the forest.

Emma lay there helplessly, all alone and unable to move, thinking back over the chain of circumstances that had brought her to this lonely and desperate state of affairs. The cannonading proved to be the result of a reconnaissance and ceased in a few hours. But her fever and chills continued for two days and two nights.

At the end of that time I was an object of pity. With no medicine, no food, and consequently little strength; I was nearly in a state of starvation. My pies and cakes were spoiled in the basket . . . and now I had no means of procuring more. But something must be done; I could not bear the thought of thus starving to death in that inglorious manner; better die upon the scaffold at Richmond, or be shot by the rebel pickets; anything but this.

Rallying her strength, Emma arranged her disguise and emerged from concealment in the swamp. About nine o'clock in the morning of the third day after crossing the river she started out for the enemy lines. As a result of her illness, her disguise was all the more convincing: "A more broken-hearted, forlorn-looking 'Bridget' never left 'ould Ireland' than I appeared to be that morning."

After traveling all day, she found herself deeper in the swamp than when she had started, totally lost. It was a dark, gloomy day with no sun to help in determining directions. But at five o'clock she heard "the sweetest and most soul-inspiring music that ever greeted my ear," the booming of cannons that told her which direction to go in. Before long she found her way out of the swamp.

In the distance Emma could see a small white house, so she trudged wearily toward it, weak and famished. Inside lying helplessly on an old straw mattress was a sick rebel soldier. Assuming the Irish brogue, she asked how he came to be left alone. Speaking in a low whisper, the soldier said he had been ill with typhoid fever and had fallen by the wayside from his company, taking shelter in the abandoned house. He was starving, and mentioned that the former owner had left behind some flour and corn meal.

"Bridget" quickly went to work kindling a fire and cooking a large hoecake. Searching around, she managed to find some tea that the departing family had overlooked, packed away in a small basket. "My cake being cooked, and tea made, I fed the poor famished rebel as tenderly as if he had been my brother, and he seemed as grateful for my kindness, and thanked me with as much politeness, as if I had been Mrs. Jeff Davis [wife of the president of the Confederacy]." After slaking her own appetite, she took a closer look at the ill man and found him "pleasing and intelligent looking," deciding that she wouldn't mind caring for him until he got well if she didn't have other, more important, work to attend to.

"It is strange," she wrote in *Nurse and Spy,*

> How sickness and disease disarm our antipathy and remove our prejudices. There lay before me an enemy to the Government for which I was daily and willingly exposing my life and suffering unspeakable privation. . . . and yet, as I looked upon him in his helpless condition, I did not feel the least resentment, or entertain an unkind thought toward him personally, but looked upon him only as an unfortunate, suffering man, whose sad condition called forth the best feelings of my nature, and I longed to restore him to health and strength; not considering that the very health and strength which I wished to secure for him would be employed against the cause which I had espoused.

Thus Emma's loving instincts and "gift of nursing" learned in childhood came in conflict with her political views, and also tested her strong Christian beliefs. What transpired next is very revealing about Emma's personality and psychology.

> I had a great desire to know more of this man who had so strangely called forth my sympathies, and finding that he had grown stronger since he had partaken of some nourishment, I entered into conversation with him.

She found that he was a conscientious Confederate soldier, but not a typical Yankee-hater, full of venom against the North. She gently questioned him about what right he felt the rebels had to take up arms against the United States Government.

> At length I asked him if he professed to be a Soldier of the Cross; he replied [affirmatively] with emotion and enthusiasm. . . . My next and last question on the subject was—"Can you, as a disciple of Christ, conscientiously and consistently uphold the institution of slavery?

The Confederate soldier made no reply, but Emma—perhaps reading into his expression what she would like to believe—interpreted the nonresponse as a silent admission that he could not defend his beliefs.

"In this earnest conversation," she continued,

> I had unconsciously forgotten much of my Hibernian accent, and I thought that the sick man began to suspect that I was not what my appearance indicated. It alarmed me for a moment, but I soon recovered my composure after stepping forward and examining his pulse, for he was sinking fast, and the little strength which he seemed to have a short time before was nearly exhausted. After studying my countenance a few moments he asked me to pray with him. I did not dare to refuse the dying man's request, nor did I dare to approach my Maker in an assumed tone of voice; so I knelt beside him, and in my own natural voice breathed a brief and earnest prayer for the departing soldier.
>
> When I rose from my knees he grasped my hand eagerly and said: "Please tell me who you are. I cannot, if I would, betray you, for I shall very soon be standing before that God whom you have just addressed." I could not tell him the truth and I would not tell him a falsehood, so I evaded a direct reply, but promised that when he became stronger I would tell him my history. He smiled languidly and closed his eyes, as much as to say that he understood me.

It was growing late and she was not far from the Confederate lines, but in her debilitated condition Emma was content to remain overnight with the dying soldier. Frying a piece of salt pork, she made a light by immersing a cotton rag in the fat. Then she prepared some cornmeal gruel for the soldier and settled in for the night beside him. As she examined his pulse and wiped his perspiring forehead, his eyes thanked her for her acts of kindness.

> He felt in his heart that I did not sympathize with him as a rebel, but that I was willing to do all that a sister could do for him in this hour of trial. This seemed to call forth more gratitude than if I had been heart and hand with the South. He looked up suddenly and saw me weeping—for I could not restrain my tears—he seemed then to understand that he was really dying.

The soldier told Emma his name was Allen Hall, and gave her the name of his regiment. He asked her to take the gold watch from his pocket and deliver it to a Major McKee of General Richard Ewell's staff in Confederate camp toward Richmond, and to tell him that he (Hall) had died peacefully. Taking a ring from his finger, he gave it to her and thanked her for her ministrations. A little later he died. Emma found herself alone with a dead man, past midnight on a dark, gloomy night. The silence was profound.

I felt it good thus to be drawn away from the tumult of war, and there, in the presence of the angel of death, hold communion with my own heart and drink deep from the well of holy meditation. I thought there were happy spirits hovering round the lifeless form [of] the bright spirit whose companionship had made some southern home bright and joyous.

At peace with herself, Emma lay down near the corpse and slept soundly until 6:00 A.M., when she awoke much refreshed.

Allen Hall's gold watch, she realized, guaranteed her entree to Confederate headquarters. A further search of the house turned up some items useful for perfecting her disguise: mustard, pepper, an old pair of green spectacles, some ochre (coloring), and a bottle of red ink. Emma made a strong mustard plaster and applied it to one side of her face until it blistered, put on a patch of black court plaster, painted a red line around her eyes, and tinged her pale complexion a deeper color with the ochre. Then she packed her baskets with household items appropriate for a refugee to be carrying, in anticipation of being searched before being allowed into the Confederate lines.

Burying her pistol and some other articles that she thought might arouse suspicion, she headed directly for the Confederate picket line, safe in the knowledge that the gold watch and a message for Major McKee would ensure her passage. After hiking about five miles toward Richmond she saw a sentinel in the distance, and sat down to rest and prepare herself for the encounter.

"While thus waiting to have my courage reinforced, I took from my basket the black pepper and sprinkled a little of it on my pocket handkerchief, which I applied to my eyes." After checking her disguise and tearful visage in a small pocket mirror, she displayed a flag of truce and the picket signalled her to advance. He proved to be a smiling Englishman, apparently amused by the spectacle she presented. As he casually questioned her, she occasionally applied the peppery handkerchief to her eyes, inducing tears to run down her face. The good-natured guard let her pass, with the warning that she had better not linger in camp as a Yankee attack was imminent. He also pointed out some masked batteries to her.

Going directly to headquarters, Emma inquired for Major McKee, but was told that he would not be there before evening as he had gone out to set a trap for the Yankees. Emma made up her mind at once that she must find out as much as possible before night, and get back to Union lines before the impending battle.

Finding some Negro women who were cooking a meal, she asked for something to eat and was fed some boiled beef and crude bread.

About 5:00 P.M. Major McKee arrived. "Bridget" lost no time in presenting herself, announcing the death of his friend, and delivering the watch along with a package of Allen Hall's possessions. This time she didn't need the peppery handkerchief; the memory of the past night's events brought tears to her eyes naturally.

> The Major, rough and stern as he was, sat there with his face between his hands and sobbed like a child. Soon he rose to his feet, surveyed me from head to foot, and said, "You are a faithful woman, and you shall be rewarded."

When she agreed to lead McKee's men to the house to recover Hall's body, he offered her a ten dollar Federal bill, but she declined to take the money. This seemed to puzzle him, and Emma quickly realized that he must consider it strange for a woman in her apparent circumstances to refuse money. Fearful that she might have given herself away, Emma quickly burst into a fit of weeping and exclaimed passionately in brogue that her conscience would not allow her to accept money for delivering this sad message. Major McKee seemed satisfied, and went to round up a detachment of men.

When he returned with the men, "Bridget" asked for a horse on the excuse that she had been sick for several days, had little sleep, and felt too weak to walk all the way to the house. Major McKee readily complied, immediately ordering a horse to be saddled for her.

Emma felt guilty:

> I really felt mean, and for the first time since I had acted in the capacity of a spy, I despised myself for the very act which I was about to perform. I must betray the confidence which that man reposed in me. He was too generous to harbor a suspicion against me, and thus furnished me the very means of betraying him. (Long after the war, when Emma's story was known to the public, she did not like to talk about her "secret service" escapades.)

As they started out on their mission, however, Major McKee eased her conscience by instructing his men to bring back "Captain" Hall's body "if you have to walk through Yankee blood to the knees." Until then, Emma had not realized that Hall was an officer. His uniform bore no emblems of rank.

Emma rode at the head of the detachment of twenty-four men

under a sergeant and a corporal, acting as guide, not knowing whether they would encounter Union troops and be fired upon. The five miles were passed in silence, and without incident. As they neared the house, the sun had gone down and the shadows were deepening. They stopped to reconnoiter, and seeing no sign of the enemy regretted that they had not brought an ambulance.

"I did not regret it," she later wrote, "for the present arrangement suited me exactly."

Nearing the house, the sergeant ordered the corporal and a squad of men to go inside and bring out the body while he stationed the remaining men to guard all approaches. Then he asked "Bridget" to ride down the road a little way, and if she should see any sign of the Yankees to ride back as fast as possible.

> I assented, and joyfully complied with the first part of his request. . . . I turned and rode slowly down the road, but not "seeing or hearing anything of the Yankees," I thought it best to keep on in that direction until I did. I was like the Zouave [colorfully uniformed soldier] after the battle of Bull Run, who said he was ordered to retreat, but not being ordered to halt at any particular place, he preferred to keep on until he reached New York.

After getting out of sight of the Confederate detachment, Emma spurred her horse and galloped back to the Chickahominy River, crossed it, and made her report to a Federal general. "I had no desire to have that little escort captured," she confided in *Nurse and Spy* "and consequently said nothing about it in my report; so the sergeant, with his men, were permitted to return to the rebel camp unmolested, bearing with them the remains of their beloved captain."

Spring floods swelling the Chickahominy River influenced the course of battle at the end of May, 1862. In his history of the Army of the Potomac, William Swinton explains how the Union army came to be divided on either side of the river, with III Corps (including General Kearny and the 2nd Michigan) and IV Corps on the south side and the rest of the army on the north side. Bridges across the river became critical to the safety of the army.

Swinton describes the Chickahominy's course from northwest of Richmond around to the east and south, where it empties into the James River. "In itself," he reports,

> this river does not form any considerable barrier to the advance of an army; but with its accessories it constitutes one of the most for-

midable military obstacles imaginable. The stream flows through a belt of heavily timbered swamp . . . sometimes in a single channel, more frequently divided into several, and when but a foot or two above its summer level, overspreads the whole swamp. The bottom-lands between the swamp and the highlands, in width from three-quarters of a mile to a mile and a quarter, are little elevated at their margin above the swamp, so that a rise of the stream by a few feet, overflows large areas of these bottoms.

In such treacherous terrain were several key battles fought on the peninsula, among them the battle of Seven Pines (or Fair Oaks) on May 31st and June 1st. General Joseph Johnston already had resolved to strike a blow at the divided Union army when nature intervened. "During the night of the 30th," Swinton relates, "there came a storm of unwonted violence" that changed Johnston's plans. The storm, however, presented the opportunity for an even greater victory, when the downpour swelled the river and swamped the two bridges that had been constructed for the passage of the Union army.

Emma in *Nurse and Spy* describes the scene as follows:

A most fearful storm swept over the Peninsula, accompanied with terrible exhibitions of lightning and explosions of thunder. The water came down all night and all day in perfect floods . . . turning the narrow stream into a broad river, converting the swamps into lakes, and carrying away one bridge and rendering the other unsafe.

During the battle of Seven Pines, "Frank Thompson" was acting orderly for General Philip Kearny, whose regular orderly was ill. She rode around the battlefield with the general, carrying various dispatches at his orders. The Confederate forces attacked vigorously and were threatening to drive the beleagured Union forces back into the river. General Kearny, suddenly reigning in his horse, took an envelope out of his pocket and hastily scribbled on it a note in pencil, urgently requesting reinforcements. This he handed to his orderly with instructions to deliver it to "General G." (McClellan?). The orderly galloped off to the river, barely managing to ford it, and delivered the message. "Frank" found "General G." making his way toward the shakey, half-awash grapevine bridge.

Emma's narrative continues:

Engineers were at once set to work to strengthen the crazy structure, which was swaying to and fro with the rushing tide. The eager, excited troops dashed into the water waist-deep, and getting upon the floating planks went pouring over in massive columns. I preferred to swim my horse back again rather than risk myself upon such a bridge, for I looked every moment to see it give way and engulf the whole division in the turbid waters of the swollen creek. However, all reached the other side in safety, and started along the flooded road on the double quick. This was cheering news to carry back to General K.

Plunging back into the river, she returned to the battlefield and reported to General Kearny that reinforcements were on the way. Kearny immediately shouted out the news and passed the word along the exhausted line of soldiers. "Swinging his hat in the air he perfectly electrified the whole line as far as his voice could reach . . . until that almost exhausted line was reanimated and inspired with new hope."

Shortly thereafter, "General H." (Gen. Oliver O. Howard, who later was awarded the Medal of Honor for bravery during the battle) was badly wounded in the arm, a short distance away from Emma. Obtaining Kearny's permission, she rode to Howard's assistance and started to treat his wound. As she reached into her saddlebags to get some bandages, her captured "rebel" horse suddenly bit her and "almost tore the flesh from the bone [then] turned his heels in an instant and kicked with both feet, sending me about a rod." Her side and arm were badly bruised. Other than life-long problems with malaria, this proved to be the most severe and lasting injury Emma ever suffered in the army.

General Johnston was also wounded that day, and the next day General Robert E. Lee was installed in command of the Confederate forces, which proved to be one of the most profound results of the battle. McClellan now had to face Lee the rest of the way.

Emma returned to the battlefield next day in time to see General George B. McClellan ride along the front, receiving the cheers of the army. The cheers "told as plainly as words could express that their beloved commander was with them, amid that desperate struggle for victory. . . . It was enough to make angels weep, to look down upon that field of carnage."

The regimental history and official records note that the 2nd Michigan was "conspicuously marked for bravery" at Seven Pines/ Fair Oaks. A contemporary newspaper account cites the important role played by Kearny's division:

Meantime, Heintzelman had sent forward Kearny to recover Casey's lost ground, and a desperate fight was going on at the extreme left. The enemy had been successfully held in front of Couch's old entrenched camp, until Kearny's division arrived, when he staid the torrent of battle. One after another his gallant regiments pushed forward, and pressed back the fiery rebels with more daring than their own. Here the 55th New York won new laurels, and Poe's 2nd Michigan was bathed in blood. Five hundred of them charged across the open field against ten times their number, and stopped them in mid-career, losing seventeen brave fellows in that one desperate essay.

Each side had approximately 42,000 troops engaged; Federal casualties were 5,031 and Confederate 6,134. Three members of "Frank Thompson's" Company F, 2nd Michigan, were killed in action: Daniel J. Ensign, Sheldon B. Kelley, and Delion McConnell.

Shortly after the battle, Emma obtained leave for a week to recuperate from the lame side and arm delivered by her horse, and to regain her general health. But she was back on duty for the Seven Days battles before Richmond late in June, while McClellan was changing his base from the York River to the James River, in the process performing a well-executed "strategic retreat."

During the battle of Gaines' Mill on June 27th, "Frank" was sent around to field hospitals to warn them of the army's retreat, and to advise them to take care of themselves as best they could. At one hospital she reports meeting a male nurse who refused to leave the helpless patients under his care, and finally was captured when the hospital was overrun by Confederate forces.

"By making inquiry afterwards I found out that his name was J. Robbins of the Second Michigan Regiment," she wrote, "and after he had undergone the hardships of imprisonment and had been exchanged, I had the honor of meeting and congratulating him. I felt that it was a greater honor than to converse with many of our major generals."

(Jerome Robbins of Company I, 2nd Michigan, *was* taken prisoner at Savage's Station on June 29th as described, and Emma was very fond of him. However, she had already known him for about eight months before he was captured. The probable reason why she disguised this fact in *Nurse and Spy* will be explained later.)

Having given up her horse to some officers just recovering from fever at one of the hospitals, Emma struck out on foot to find her way to the James River. Spotting some livestock at a deserted farmhouse, she "appropriated" a pony and set out down the road. By this time she was caught between Federal and Confederate skirmishers.

> Turning off from the main road, I struck out into the woods and rode as fast as possible. The woods were open and clear so that I could see a long way ahead. On I went until I came near a thicket so dense that I could not see anything beyond its border. Not desiring to go any place which looked suspicious, I turned to go round it, when my ear caught the click, click of a dozen rifles, and a shower of Minie balls came round me as thick as hailstones, but not one of them pierced even my clothing.
>
> I soon came to an open field and saw in the distance a large number of soldiers. One glance convinced me that they were Federals, for they wore United States uniform. Bounding over the field in an instant I had come within a hundred yards of them before I noticed that they were prisoners, guarded by a band of rebels. The first thing that caused me to discover this fact was one of the prisoners waving his hand for me to go in another direction, upon seeing which one of the rebel guards sprang forward and struck the prisoner with the butt of his musket.
>
> This little demonstration revealed to me at once my position, and turning I fled in the direction indicated by the prisoner, when another volley followed me which proved as harmless as the first. I began now to think that I was about as safe inside the rebel lines as anywhere, for their bullets seemed quite harmless so far as I was personally concerned.

Emma was reminded of her mother during her childhood telling a Scottish clergyman that she (Emma) would probably meet with a violent death, for she was always in some dangerous mischief, such as riding the wildest colt on the farm, firing off her father's shotgun, and climbing to the highest point of buildings. The clergyman had advised her mother not to worry, as "a wean that's born to be hung 'ill ne'er be droon'd."

"Or be shot either," Emma thought. But the fates might also be reserving her to hang from a scaffold in Richmond as a northern spy.

Riding for her life between enemy and friendly lines, Emma saw

> a perfect blaze both of musketry and artillery. Nothing but the power of the Almighty could have shielded me from such a storm of shot and shell, and brought me through unscathed. It seems to me now that it was almost as much of a miracle as that of the three

Hebrew children coming forth from the fiery furnace without even the smell of fire upon them. (Like Anna Etheridge, Sarah Emma Edmonds seemed to have a magic protective "shield." She attributed it to God.)

Through the Seven Days, General Lee—never relinquishing the initiative—tried to destroy McClellan's army. The armies clashed at Oak Grove (June 25th); Mechanicsville or Beaver Creek Dam (June 26th); Gaines' Mill (June 27th); Golding's Farm (June 28th); Allen's Farm or Savage's Station (June 29th); White Oak Swamp/ Frayser's Farm (June 30th); and the final battle at Malvern Hill (July 1st).

Many eyewitnesses gave dramatic descriptions of the spectacular finale to the Seven Days, the battle at Malvern Hill. The prominence along the James River southeast of Richmond was strongly defended by the retreating Army of the Potomac.

Emma wrote in *Nurse and Spy:*

> The battle of Malvern Hill presented, by far, the most sublime spectacle I ever witnessed. . . . The elevated position which the army occupied, the concentration of such an immense force in so small a compass, such a quantity of artillery on those hills all in operation at the same time, the reflection of the flashes of fire from hundreds of guns upon the dense cloud of smoke which hung suspended in the heavens . . . the vivid flashes of lightning, the terrific peals of thunder mingled with the continuous blaze of musketry, sudden explosions of shell and the deafening roar of cannon, combined to make a scene which was *awfully grand.* My soul was filled with the sublimity and grandeur of the scene, notwithstanding the ghastly wounds and piteous groans of the mangled, helpless ones around me. Thus it continued from seven to nine in the evening, the most thrilling picture which the imagination can conceive.

The well-entrenched Federal troops, in tiers up the hillside, easily repulsed the Confederate regiments that repeatedly stormed across the open space in an attempt to charge the batteries that were cutting them to pieces. McClellan had placed his army well, and secured a safe withdrawal to Harrison's landing next day.

Lee's effort to crush McClellan during the Seven Days resulted in appalling casualties, with the Confederates having more than twice as many killed and wounded. (Union: 1,734 killed, 8,062 wounded; total 9,796. Confederacy: 3,286 killed, 15,909 wounded; total 19,195.)

The Peninsula Campaign ended with a bang on July 1st, but its whimper continued for another month, as McClellan pleaded for reinforcements to continue the assault on Richmond. Once the Confederate capital was saved from immediate threat, Lee reorganized his army into two corps under Generals Thomas "Stonewall" Jackson and James Longstreet. He determined to carry the war to the North.

After a lot of political maneuvering, McClellan was ordered to withdraw to Aquia Creek and then join up with Major General John Pope, newly appointed commander of the Army of Virginia, to fight on another front. The first attempt by the Army of the Potomac to take Richmond had ended, and the stage was set for climactic clashes with Lee's Army of Northern Virginia as it pushed north to threaten Washington, D.C.

The Mystery of "Franklin Thompson"

A mystery appears to be connected with him [Franklin Thompson] which is impossible for me to fathom.
—JEROME ROBBINS, November, 1861 diary entry.

After the 2nd Michigan Regiment returned to Washington, by steamer from Yorktown to Alexandria, Virginia, "Frank Thompson" was active as postmaster, carrying mail and dispatches back and forth between Washington and the regiment in the Virginia countryside. The regiment had arrived about noon on August 28th, and proceeded to Centreville. Lieutenant Colonel Louis Dillman was now temporarily in command, since Colonel Orlando Poe had been promoted to brigade commander. The regiment crossed Bull Run, moved to the front, and was engaged through the next day in the 2nd Battle of Bull Run (Manassas).

About this time, Emma (as "Frank") was assigned by General Samuel P. Heintzelman to perform another spying mission behind Confederate lines. In Washington she procured the disguise of a female contraband (escaped Negro slave), and passed through enemy lines in the company of a small group of blacks who preferred to be with their friends in captivity. Several of the group, Emma among them, were taken to Confederate headquarters to cook rations for the soldiers.

Emma noted that the officers at headquarters generally talked in low tones, but occasionally became excited and blurted out information, apparently forgetting the Negro cooks or not considering them a threat. "When I had been there a few hours," she wrote, "I had obtained the very information which I had been sent for. I had heard the plan of the morrow discussed, the number of troops at several important points, and the number expected to arrive during the night; and this, too, from the lips of the commanding general and his staff."

On the other hand, security on the front line was so strong that she did not dare to try to return that night, instead waiting anxiously for dawn. Early next morning, while assisting with breakfast, she removed a coat from a camp stool which was in the way, and a number of papers fell from the pocket. Seizing the opportunity, she concealed the papers and hurriedly prepared for an escape for fear the documents would be missed. When breakfast was announced, she abruptly departed.

Heading toward the picket line nearest the Federal position, she came to an old house and quickly hid in the cellar. Soon a battle broke out and shot and shell began to shake the house in which she had taken refuge, until it began tumbling down around her. But she was unharmed and held her ground. Finally, the Confederates were compelled to fall back and take a new position. When the firing ceased, she found herself safely within the Federal lines.

Going immediately to headquarters, Emma reported what she had heard and turned over the papers. These proved to be orders intended for corps commanders to ensure concerted action in their plan to capture Washington.

During General Pope's northern Virginia campaign, Emma visited Confederate headquarters three times in the space of ten days, each time coming away unsuspected and unmolested and bearing valuable information. While the battle of 2nd Bull Run was in progress, she was part of the time in Confederate headquarters and then back within Federal lines, having made her escape while the battle raged.

The last of her visits to Confederate headquarters was made the night before the battle of Chantilly (which she reports, apparently phonetically, as "Chentilla."). On September 1st the regiment and brigade broke camp at Centreville, marching toward Fairfax Court House. About three miles out, at 4:00 P.M., they met Confederate troops at Chantilly. "A severe and bloody engagement took place," as reported in the regimental history, "continuing until dark, which put an end to the contest."

Early in the battle a thunderstorm broke, with driving sheets of rain and a torrential downpour turning the fields to mud. In the gathering darkness at the end of the day, the famous one-armed general, Phil Kearny, accidentally rode into enemy lines. When he realized his error he wheeled his horse around and tried to escape, but was shot from the saddle and killed.

Kearny had arrived on the field late, and perceiving that the right flank was in danger, he was furiously trying to position the 21st Massachusetts on the right. However, they had earlier been in a fight in the woods during the thunderstorm, and their powder charges were soaked. Two companies with serviceable weapons finally were deployed to the right, but stopped in a corn field as they neared the lines of a Georgia regiment which they had clashed with earlier. Kearny, not believing the enemy was that near, took their hesitation to be cowardice, and angrily spurred off into the enemy lines.

As luck would have it, Emma was a witness to his death and wrote of it in *Nurse and Spy*:

> I was within a few rods of [Kearny] when he fell, and was in the act of returning to the Union camp under cover of the extreme darkness of that never-to-be-forgotten night. I saw him ride up to the line, but supposed him to be a rebel officer until the pickets fired at him, and even then I thought they had fired at me, until I saw him fall from his horse, and heard their exclamations of joy when they discovered who he was; for the one-armed general was known throughout both armies for his bravery and brilliant career.
>
> When I learned who was their victim, I regretted that it had not been me instead of him. . . . I lost no time in making good my escape, while the attention of the pickets were [sic] drawn in another direction. When I came to our lines, I found it almost as difficult to get through as I had found it on the other side. The night was so dark I could not make any sign by which the pickets could recognize me, and I was in the depths of the forest, where the rustling of the leaves and the crackling of dry branches under my feet betrayed my footsteps as I went along.

Finally she crawled close to the line and managed to convince the pickets to let her through.

> Coming within the lines, I saw a group of men kneeling on the ground digging a grave with their bayonets, with the least possible noise; for the picket lines were within half musket shot of each other. One of their comrades had been killed, and they were thus preparing this last resting-place. . . . [amidst] the vivid flashes of lurid flame which the lightning cast upon the sad scene, lighting up for a moment the surrounding forest, and then dying away, leaving the darkness more intolerable.

During the 2nd Bull Run campaign, while carrying mail and messages back and forth between camp and Washington, Emma received a serious leg injury when her horse fell while trying to jump a ditch. She also had apparent internal injuries and reported suffering from "frequent hemmorhaging from the lungs." She concealed the seriousness of her injuries for fear of being discovered. During this critical period, her comrades Robert Bostwick, Richard Halsted, and Sam Houlton took care of her, bringing medicines and food to her tent.

While the 2nd Michigan remained in the defense of Washington, Emma was sent to Antietam with a detachment of doctors and nurses, and was present during the battle on September 17, 1862. Afterwards, while attending to the wounded, she came across a dying soldier who caught her eye:

In passing among the wounded after they had been carried from the field, my attention was attracted by the pale, sweet face of a youthful soldier who was severely wounded in the neck. The wound still bled profusely, and the boy was growing faint from loss of blood. I stooped down and asked him if there was anything he would like to have done for him. The soldier turned a pair of beautiful, clear, intelligent eyes upon me for a moment in an earnest gaze, and then, as if satisfied with the scrutiny, said faintly: "Yes, yes; there is something to be done, and that quickly, for I am dying."

Something in the tone and voice made me look more closely at the face of the speaker, and that look satisfied me that my suspicion was well founded. I went to one of the surgeons in attendance, and requested him to come and see my patient. He did so, and after a moment's examination of the wound told me that nothing could be done whatever to save him. He then left me, and I administered a little brandy and water to strengthen the wounded boy, for he evidently wished to tell me something that was on his mind before he died. The little trembling hand beckoned me closer, and I knelt down beside him and bent my head until it touched the golden locks on the pale brow before me; I listened with breathless attention to catch every sound which fell from those dying lips, the substance of which was as follows.

"I can trust you, and will tell you a secret. I am not what I seem, but am a female. I enlisted from the purest motives, and have remained undiscovered and unsuspected. I have neither father, mother nor sister. My only brother was killed today. I closed his eyes about an hour before I was wounded. I shall soon be with him. I am a Christian, and have maintained the Christian character ever since I entered the army. . . . I wish you to bury me with your own hands, that none may know after my death that I am other than my appearance indicates."

I assured her that she might place implicit confidence in me, and that I would do as she had desired me. . . . I remained with her until she died, which was about an hour. Then making a grave for her under the shadow of a mulberry tree near the battle-field, apart from all others. . . . I carried her remains to that lonely spot and gave her a soldier's burial, without coffin or shroud, only a blanket for a winding-sheet. There she sleeps in that beautiful forest where the soft southern breezes sigh mournfully through the foliage, and the little birds sing sweetly above her grave.

Sarah Emma Edmonds was a romantic, and capable of poetic expression that belied her humble origins. This story might be only an expression of what she hoped would happen in the event that she were mortally wounded on the battlefield; that some sympathetic soul would hear her story and preserve her secret.

On November 17, 1862, the 2nd Michigan Regiment—now transferred to 1st Brigade (commanded by Poe), Burns's Division, 9th Corps—marched from Warrenton Junction toward Fredericksburg, Virginia, arriving on the 19th. On November 29th the regiment was placed on duty supporting a battery in front of Fredericksburg. On the first day of the Battle of Fredericksburg, December 12th, the regiment crossed the Rappahannock River and was held in reserve, but was shelled by the enemy, sustaining two casualties.

Emma reports in *Nurse and Spy* that on November 7, 1862 (Major General Ambrose Burnside having been appointed Commander of the Army of the Potomac), General McClellan gave his farewell address to the army. The new commander marched the army immediately to Falmouth, opposite Fredericksburg. "Of the incidents of that march I know nothing, for I went to Washington, and from thence to Aquia Creek by water [steamer]," she wrote. From there she rode on horseback to Falmouth, where she found the army encamped in the mud along the banks of the Rappahannock. At this point the river was very narrow, and she often saw pickets on both sides throwing stones across it for amusement.

"All the mud and bad roads on the Peninsula," she wrote

Could not bear the least comparison with that of Falmouth and along the Rappahannock. It was now December and the weather was extremely cold, yet the constant rains kept the roads in the most terrible state imaginable. On riding along the brink of the river we

could see distinctly the rebel batteries frowning on the heights beyond the city of Fredericksburg, and the rebel sentinels walking their
rounds within talking distance of our own pickets.

She watched the soldiers trying to construct pontoon bridges
across the river, while Confederate sharpshooters kept them under
constant fire. Finally, several companies of men, led by soldiers of
the 7th Michigan, rowed across the river to silence the sharpshooters. Thereafter, on December 12th, the Union army crossed the
river and assaulted the Confederate line.

Although Emma reports in *Nurse and Spy* being appointed as an
aide to "General H." (Heintzelman?) during the battle, historical
records show that she actually served as a battlefield courier for
now-Brigadier General Orlando M. Poe. (For whatever reasons,
she occasionally substituted different initials for real people, as she
apparently did with "General G." on the peninsula.)

Accurately reporting what happened at Fredericksburg, she de-
cried the folly of

> charging again and again upon those terrible stone walls and for-
> tifications, after being repulsed every time with more than half their
> number lying on the ground. . . . But when it was proved to a dem-
> onstration that it was morally impossible to take and retain those
> heights, in consequence of the natural advantage of position which
> the rebels occupied . . . whose fault was it that the attempt was made
> time after time, until the field was literally piled with dead and ran
> red with blood?

The same question has been asked by historians and military
analysts many times since her 1864 account.

Emma's story continued:

> During the progress of that battle I saw many strange sights—
> although I had been in many a fierce battle before. I never saw till
> then, a man deliberately shoot himself, with his own pistol, in order
> to save the rebels the satisfaction of doing so, as it would seem.
>
> As one brigade was ordered into line of battle, I saw an officer take
> out his pistol and shoot himself through the side—not mortally, I
> am sorry to say, but just sufficient to unfit him for duty; so he was
> carried to the rear—he protesting that it was done by accident.
>
> Of the wounded of this battle I can say but little, for my time was
> fully occupied in the responsible duties which I had volunteered to
> perform; and so constantly was I employed, that I was not out of
> the saddle but once in twelve hours.

The magnitude of the Union defeat at Fredericksburg soon became clear. General Ambrose Burnside pulled the army back across the Rappahannock, where they camped in the cold and mud for several weeks, defeated and demoralized. Finally, on January 20, 1863, the order came to move out. However, the mud quickly thwarted Burnside's plans and the army remained literally bogged down through the harsh winter.

On January 26th, Lincoln replaced Burnside, appointing Joseph Hooker as commander of the Army of the Potomac. Burnside, resuming command of the 9th Corps, was sent west where elements of the corps, including the 2nd Michigan, garrisoned Kentucky. The 2nd Michigan went on to serve with distinction in Mississippi and Tennessee, before returning to the Army of the Potomac for the final campaigns in Virginia in 1864–1865.

But Kentucky was to be Emma's last battlefield, the scene of her final military and spying adventures. "On the arrival of the troops at Louisville," she reported,

> they were sent in detachments to different places—some to Bardstown, some to Lebanon, and others to guard different portions of the railroad. The third day after my arrival I went out with a reconnoitering expedition, under command of General M. It was entirely composed of cavalry. We rode thirty-six miles that afternoon—the roads were splendid.

Striking out through the woods, the party emerged into a clearing and came upon a small force of Confederate cavalry. After a sharp skirmish, they captured five prisoners. That evening they celebrated by having a good dinner at a hotel in Louisville.

Next day, dressed in one of the prisoner's clothes (not a uniform but generally butternut color), Emma set out by railroad to Lebanon and passed beyond through the enemy lines. She pretended to be buying up butter and eggs at the farm houses for the rebel army. At one point she came upon a wedding party of a recruiting officer, Captain Logan:

> I was questioned pretty sharply by the handsome captain in regard to the nature of my business in that locality, but finding me an innocent, straightforward Kentuckian, he came to the conclusion that I was all right. But he also arrived at the conclusion that I was old enough to be in the army.

Captain Logan put her under guard and impressed her into Confederate service in a unit just being organized.

I did not despair, but trusted in Providence and my own ingenuity to escape from this dilemma. . . . I was glad to find that it was a company of cavalry that was being organized, for if I could once get on a good horse there would be some hope of my escape.

At daylight the next morning, the company started off, the captain complimenting Emma (what male name she used is not stated) for her horsemanship. After about half an hour they encountered a Federal reconnoitering party, cavalry in advance and infantry in the rear, and were ordered to advance in line. "The company advanced," she wrote, "but my horse suddenly became unmanagable, and it required a second or two to bring him right again; and before I could overtake the company and get in line the contending parties had met in a hand to hand fight."

In the confusion, Emma found herself on the Federal side of the line where the officer recognized her and signed for her to fall in beside him. This brought her face to face with Captain Logan, whom she shot with her pistol, wounding him seriously but not mortally. As a result, several of the rebels dashed toward her, aiming saber strokes at her head. But the Federal cavalrymen intervened and drove the attackers back. The Federal infantry now deployed and poured in volleys of fire that decimated the Confederate force whose survivors turned and fled.

"I escaped without receiving a scratch," she wrote,

> but my horse was badly cut across the neck with a saber. . . . We returned to camp with our prisoners and the wounded, and I rejoiced at having once more escaped from the Confederate lines.
>
> I was highly commended by the commanding general for my coolness throughout the whole affair, and was told kindly and candidly that I would not be permitted to go out again in that vicinity, in the capacity of a spy, as I would most assuredly meet with some of those who had seen me desert their ranks, and I would consequently be hung up to the nearest tree.

Being prohibited from missions outside the lines, Emma was appointed as a detective inside the lines to try to identify spies in their midst who were known to be daily giving information to the enemy. Dressing in civilian clothes, "Frank" mingled with the citizens of Louisville, striking up acquaintances among them. One, who bitterly denounced the Yankees, was a merchant. She asked him for a job as clerk in his store. In due course she was asked to go out to the nearest camp to sell various small articles to the soldiers. Being an experienced salesperson, she was very successful at this, which pleased her employer and helped her to gain his confidence.

After about two weeks, she succeeded in gaining a clue to three rebel spies then within the Federal lines. She then expressed to the merchant a desire to enter the Confederate service, asking his advice on how she could get through the Yankee lines for that purpose. After long discussion and planning, the merchant arranged for her to go through the lines next night with one of the rebel spies who had successfully passed himself off as a good Union man.

> That afternoon I was sent out again to dispose of some goods to the soldiers, and while I was gone took the favorable opportunity of informing the Provost Marshal of my intended escape the following night together with my brother spy.

Back at the store she was introduced to the spy. As prearranged, the Provost Marshal came into the store and was slipped a message informing him of their intended departure time and route.

> The night came, and we started about nine o'clock. As we walked along toward the rebel lines the spy seemed to think that I was a true patriot in the rebel cause, for he entertained me with a long conversation concerning his exploits in the secret service; and of the other two [spies] who were still in camp he said one of them was a sutler, and the other sold photographs of our generals.
>
> We were pursuing our way in the darkness, talking in a low, confidential tone, when suddenly a number of cavalry dashed upon us and took us both prisoners. As soon as we were captured we were searched, and documents found on my companion which condemned him as a spy. . . . The next thing to be done was to find the other two spies. The sutler was found and put under arrest, and his goods confiscated, but the dealer in photographs had made his escape.
>
> I never dared go back to Louisville again, for I had ample reason to believe that my life would pay the penalty if I did.

In mid-April of 1863, Emma was in a hospital at Lebanon, Kentucky, suffering from a serious bout with malarial fever. Her secret world was on the verge of falling apart, and, fearing disclosure, she applied for leave. The leave was denied. Apparently in a state of near desperation, she applied her spying skills one last time, slipping through the lines in disguise and vanishing into the night.

The regimental history from contemporary records reports the desertion of "Frank Thompson" at Lebanon, Kentucky, in April 1863, "but where [he] went remains a mystery." (The exact date is unclear, but the evidence of a diary indicates April 17th or shortly before that.)

The mystery of "Frank Thompson" would not be cleared up until a quarter of a century later. In an interview after the war, when the mystery had been solved, Captain William B. Morse said: "Franklin [Thompson] was known by every man in the regiment and her desertion was the topic of every campfire. The beardless boy was a universal favorite, and much anxiety was expressed for her safety." (Note the confusion of pronouns.)

"Frank's" face was a familiar sight throughout the brigade, as soldiers watched for him to bring the mail from home. To all appearances, this faithful soldier and companion had suddenly deserted under mysterious circumstances, for reasons unknown. But the regiment's long stretch of combat continued, and they were too preoccupied to dwell on the mystery for long.

Swept along by events, the 2nd Michigan went on to lasting glory. Sarah Emma Edmonds, after regaining her health, embarked on a new career away from the Army of the Potomac.

6

Sarah Emma Edmonds: Childhood and Youth

[Because of her father's repressive behavior] . . . she looked upon man as the "implacable foe" of women. . . . Emma had decided at an early age that she had no desire to share her life with a man and submit herself physically and mentally to a husband.

—SYLVIA DANNETT in *She Rode With the Generals,*
biography of Sarah Emma Edmonds.

Sarah Emma Evelyn Edmonson was born in December, 1841 in New Brunswick, Canada, the youngest of six children born to Isaac Edmonson (of Scotch-Irish ancestry) and his wife, Elizabeth ("Betsy") Leeper (an Irishwoman). The couple had emigrated from the British Isles in the early 19th century. The family name later was changed to Edmondson (with another "d"), then shortened to Edmonds (probably by Sarah Emma herself). Sarah Emma had four sisters and a brother.

The children attended an Anglican parish school, where Sarah Emma received a good basic education in "the three R's" which laid the foundation for her writing ability later in life.

Isaac and the family eked out a living as farmers, with the sisters—dressed in boys' clothes—pressed into service as farmhands since their only brother was sickly. They cultivated vegetable gardens, milked the cows, looked after the horses and other livestock, and chopped wood. Disappointed by his lack of strapping sons, the father was a hard taskmaster. Trying to please him, Sarah Emma set out to show that she could "outwork, outshoot, and outride any boy he had ever known."

Always seeking her stern father's approval, Sarah Emma learned to swim, hunt, fish, paddle a canoe, and row a boat. Spending many hours hunting in the woods she became an expert shot, and learned such other survival skills as how to build a fire even in the rain. These skills would stand her in good stead as a soldier. The "tomboy" life and outdoor activities made her wiry, lithe, and hard-muscled.

At the same time, Sarah Emma was devoted to her mother and learned gentler skills from her, including home remedies for aches and pains and other nursing techniques. Late in life she referred to her mother fondly while recounting her childhood experiences during an interview.

> I think I was born into this world with some dormant antagonism toward man. I hope I have outgrown it measurably, but my infant soul was impressed with a sense of my mother's wrongs before I ever saw the light. . . . In our family the women were not sheltered but enslaved; hence I naturally grew up to think of man as the implacable foe of my sex. (From her detailed newspaper interviews reported in the Lansing *State Republican*, June 19–26, 1900.)

Sarah Emma yearned for freedom and independence, but those were largely male prerogatives in the latter half of the 19th century. "I greatly preferred the privilege of earning my own bread and butter," she later said. "When I was 13 years-old, one of those peculiar little incidents occurred which seems like God's own finger pointing out the way to a struggling soul."

Late one evening a weary old peddler made his way to the Edmondson household and Betsy, typically, invited him in for supper and lodging for the night. "She never let an opportunity escape of doing a kindness to a stranger, or, in fact, to any of God's creatures who were weak or weary," Sarah Emma said.

Next morning the peddler, grateful for the kindnesses he had been shown, presented Sarah Emma with a book entitled *Fanny Campbell, the Female Pirate Captain, A Tale of the Revolution.* "There were four sisters of us, and I was the youngest—a mere child. Why should that man have selected me as the recipient of such a gift?" That day Sarah Emma and one of her sisters were sent out into the field to plant potatoes in a new patch far away from the house. They packed a lunch, and took the book along. The potato planting suffered somewhat as she began reading the book.

"That was the most wonderful day in all my life," she later said.

Surely I must have been inspired! I felt as if an angel had touched me with a live coal from off the altar. All the latent energy of my nature was aroused, and each exploit of the heroine thrilled me to my finger tips. I went home that night with the problem of my life solved. I felt equal to the emergency. I was emancipated, and could never be a slave again.

When I read where "Fanny" cut off her brown curls and donned the blue jacket, and stepped into the freedom and glorious independence of masculinity, I threw up my old straw hat and shouted, as I have since heard McClellan's soldiers do, when he rode past the troops on a march—only one small throat could not make quite so much noise.

The only thing that bothered Sarah Emma about Fanny Campbell's story was that the heroine had adopted her male disguise in order to rescue an imprisoned lover.

I pitied her that she was only a poor love-sick girl, after all, like so many I had known, and I regretted that she had no higher ambition than running after a man. Perhaps later on in life I had more charity and gave her a credit mark for rescuing anybody—even a lover. From that time forth I never ceased planning my escape, although it was years before I accomplished it.

At some point in the mid-1850s Sarah Emma's father decided to marry her off to an old farmer in the neighborhood, and she obediently became engaged. But, "while the preparations were going on for the wedding, one starless night I most unceremoniously left for parts unknown." According to her biographers, the "escape" was orchestrated by her mother who arranged for an old friend, an Irish lady named Annie Moffitt who had a millinery shop in Salisbury, to take Sarah Emma in as an apprentice. There she learned her Irish brogue.

Some time in 1858 (when she would have been 16 or 17 years-old), Sarah Emma and a friend were operating a millinery business of their own in Moncton, when her mother wrote to warn her that her father had somehow discovered where she was. Fearing the loss of her freedom and independence, she made a fateful decision. She had to get away. Cutting her curly hair and donning male clothing, she adopted the identity of "Franklin Thompson," moving to St. John, New Brunswick, and began living in male disguise.

How would "Franklin Thompson" make a living and be self-supporting? Sarah Emma had noticed ads by publishing houses in the United States looking for a salesman to sell Bibles and other religious books in New Brunswick. During 1859 she experimented with canvassing and became a salesman covering rural areas of New Brunswick, avoiding Fredericton and Moncton. Tentatively, she tried out her male disguise, and found to her surprise that she was readily accepted as a male.

Long after the war she said in an interview:

> I soon became a famous bookseller. The publishing company told me that they had employed agents for 30 years, and they never had employed one that could outsell me. I made money, dressed well, owned and drove a fine horse and buggy—silver mounted harness and all the paraphernalia of a nice turnout; took my lady friends out riding occasionally and had a nice time generally. (Lansing *State Republican*, June 19, 1900.)

After about a year away from home (1859?) Sarah Emma got a touch of homesickness and decided to risk a trip home in disguise, knowing that her mother would take in a stranger. She introduced herself as "Frank Thompson," and was received kindly and invited to stay for dinner. While one of her sisters prepared dinner, her mother regaled her with a brief history of her lost daughter: "I sat there and listened and talked for an hour to the mother that bore me, and she never knew that I was her child. Was that not a complete disguise?"

Her father was not home, but her brother Thomas came in from his farm chores and was introduced to "Mr. Thompson" without recognizing his sister. She told him she was interested in buying a good saddle horse, and they went out to look at the horses.

> My pets in the barnyard knew me better than my human friends and came crowding around me. Under pretense of examining the horses' mouths, I put my arm around their necks and hugged their dear old heads, and they rubbed their noses against me in recognition. The sheep, too, knew me, and flocked around, licking my hands and nibbling at my clothing and refused to be driven away. The loving remembrance of those dear, dumb creatures made me cry, and I turned aside to hide my tears.

Sarah Emma decided not to buy any of the horses and they returned to the house for dinner. They sat down to eat, but to her

> It was the hardest dinner to swallow of any I ever ate; finally I stopped trying to eat and sat with folded arms looking at them. My mother, looking up through a mist of tears, asked my sister, "Fanny, [Emma's sister, Francis, married to James Saunders, owner of the

neighboring farm] don't you think this young man looks like your poor sister?" That was the straw that broke the camel's back. I burst into tears and went and knelt beside her and said, "Mother, dear, don't you know me?" But she declared it was simply impossible for her to believe that I was her daughter.

"No, you are not my child," my mother exclaimed. "My daughter had a mole on her left cheek, but there is none here."

"Mother," I said, "get your glasses and you will see the scar. I had the mole removed for fear I might be detected by it."

But not waiting for her mother to react, she ran to the other room and brought the glasses from the shelf where she knew her mother kept them and placed them on her face just as she used to do.

Then she saw that the mole had really been removed and became convinced. She cried and laughed both at once and I caught her up in my strong arms as if she were a baby, and carried her around the room and held her and kissed her until she forgave me for running away.

I never saw anybody look so completely outdone as my brother when I told him who I was. He didn't say a word for some time; then said, "Well, I thought it was mighty strange that the livestock made such a _____ fuss about the fellow."

Later that afternoon she bade her family good-bye and returned to her "self-imposed duties," hiking about nineteen miles to her destination across the fields and through the woods.

Soon after the visit home, a "strange catastrophe" (not fully explained) befell her. "I lost every dollar that I owned and all my books except a Bible, my sample, and my valise," she said. Sarah Emma was not indecisive; when the time seemed ripe or when the fates turned against her, she made up her mind to strike out on a new course. Typically, she took quick action. "I sold the Bible for $5, and with that in my pocket I started for the United States, in mid-winter snow, three feet deep in New Brunswick." Except for a few miles of rides that she managed to obtain, she hiked the entire distance to Hartford, Connecticut, approximately 450 miles!

Oh! I could tell you a tale of suffering and hardships and weariness endured on that journey that no experience of mine in the army ever equaled. I reached Hartford in a most forlorn condition. A stranger in a strange country—a fit subject for a hospital—without money and without friends.

But Sarah Emma lived by her wits and was endlessly resourceful.

I went to a hotel just as if I had plenty of money, and rested several days before presenting myself to the publishers. My feet were badly frostbitten and my boots literally worn out, and my last suit of clothes rather the worse for wear, and my linen—well, it is hardly worth speaking of. But I had a good watch and chain, which I pawned for sum sufficient to enable me to make a more respectable appearance.

All this was by way of preparation to introduce herself to the proprietors of Hurlburt and Company publishers, seeking gainful employment, having proved her salesmanship in the Canadian provinces.

She then introduced herself under her male alias "and almost in the same breath I asked them if they had any use for a boy who had neither money nor friends, but who was hard to beat on selling books." They replied that "we will be both money and friends to you" if he could sell books. "I told them they would have to take me on trial, as I had no security to give them." A Mr. Scranton of the firm replied, "We'll take your face for it."

Mr. Hurlburt, who later published her book *Nurse and Spy*, took "Frank Thompson" home with him and introduced him to his family as "a boy who was hard to beat on selling books."

I dined there that day, and after dinner was invited to go with them in their carriage for a drive around the city. The kindness I received that day was worth a thousand dollars to me. I have never forgotten it and hope they have never had reason to regret it.

The next day she was employed as their agent and given an expense account to sell their books in Nova Scotia.

"Oh, how manly I felt; and what pride I took in proving to them that their confidence in me was not misplaced," she later recalled.

I went to Nova Scotia in February and returned in November of the same year, and in that time I cleared $900. I stopped at first-class houses, lived well, dressed well, and gave away more money to benevolent societies, etc., than in all the rest of my life, and came near marrying a pretty little girl who was bound that I should not leave Nova Scotia without her.

After her successes in Nova Scotia, Sarah Edmonds made the fateful decision in 1860 to follow Horace Greeley's advice to "go west and grow up with the country."

"But," she said, "before I had time to grow up much the war broke out and I became a soldier."

In Michigan she lived for a while with Mr. & Mrs. Charles Pratt on a farm in Rose Township, Oakland County, between Detroit and Flint. There she made friends with an Elder Berry, a school teacher and Baptist minister—one of several ministers or strongly religious persons with whom she apparently had close rapport throughout her life.

Later she lived in the home of the Reverend T. J. Joslin, pastor of the Flint Methodist Church. In Flint she became friends with William R. Morse, a member of the Flint Union Greys, a volunteer militia company that had been organized in 1857.

With war impending, the Michigan legislature passed and Governor Austin Blair approved on March 16, 1861, an act "to accept and muster into the military service of the state" two regiments of militia consisting of ten companies each, which could be transferred to Federal service in case of war. But the legislature failed to provide funds to supply equipment and pay the soldiers.

On April 12th, Confederate shore batteries at Charleston, South Carolina, opened fire on Fort Sumter. The news reached the people of Michigan next day, and patriotic meetings were held all over the state, the aroused citizens pledging united support for the Federal government. On April 15th, President Abraham Lincoln issued a proclamation formally declaring that an "insurrection" existed, asking the loyal states to furnish 75,000 troops. Since the Michigan treasury did not have the money to clothe and equip a regiment, citizens raised the needed funds through private contributions to an "emergency war loan."

Whether caught up in the martial spirit of her adopted country or for more complex motives, Sarah Emma Edmonds enlisted in the Flint Union Greys on April 17, 1861, under the name Franklin Thompson. She described her feelings at this time in an interview after the war:

> [I] was present when the first troops bade farewell to home and friends and marched to their place of rendezvous at Detroit, Michigan. It was while witnessing the anguish of that first parting that I became convinced that I, too, had a duty to perform in the sacred cause of Truth and Freedom.
>
> I spent days and nights of anxious thought in deciding in what capacity I should try to serve the Union cause; and during all my deliberations this fact was borne in upon me, viz: That I could best serve the interests of the Union cause in male attire—could better perform the necessary duties for sick and wounded men, and with

less embarrassment to them and to myself as a man than as a woman.

I had no other motive in enlisting than love to God, and love for suffering humanity. I felt called to go and do what I could for the defense of the right—if I could not fight I could take the place of someone who could and thus add one more soldier to the ranks. . . . I went with no other ambition than to nurse the sick and care for the wounded. I had inherited from my mother a rare gift of nursing, and when not too weary or exhausted, there was a magnetic power in my hands to soothe the delirium.

This last sentence would appear to be a reference to the "laying on of hands" of a spiritual "healer," the only such reference I have seen in the entire literature about her.

On April 18th, "Franklin Thompson" was among those who attended "a large and extremely enthusiastic public meeting held at the court-house in Flint. A circular letter of the War Committee, in Detroit, was read and acted on, and the meeting adopted a series of intensely patriotic resolutions. . . ." The practical effect of the meeting for Sarah Emma Edmonds was that members of the Flint Union Greys voted to become a volunteer company for Federal service. The Greys met on April 23rd to elect officers: Captain, William R. Morse; 1st Lieutenant, William Turver; 2nd Lieutenant, James Farrand.

The first volunteer infantry regiment to be organized in Michigan—with companies from Detroit, Jackson, Coldwater, Manchester, Ann Arbor, Burr Oak, Ypsilanti, Marshall, and Adrian—was officially formed on April 24th under command of Colonel Orlando B. Willcox of Detoit. It was a three-months regiment, but on June 28th was authorized to reorganize as a three-year regiment, including members from all parts of southern Michigan.

The next day (April 25th) formation of the 2nd Michigan Infantry was completed, with companies from Detroit, Hudson, Battle Creek, Adrian, Niles, Flint, Constantine, East Saginaw, and Kalamazoo. Originally, it was to be another three-month regiment. Instead, on orders from the War Department, it became the first three-year regiment from Michigan and was the first full-term regiment to reach the nation's capital from the western states.

The night before their departure to join the 2nd Michigan Infantry Regiment, the Greys paraded through the streets of Flint and were addressed in the presence of a throng of spectators by Colonel W. M. Fenton (later commander of the 8th Michigan) who had helped organize the Flint company. At the request of Captain

Morse, he exhorted the officers and men on the importance of the duties they were about to undertake, what was expected of them, and how they would comport themselves (including "strict cleanliness, and temperance in both meat and drink").

Next the company took the following oath:

"I do solemnly swear, in the presence of Almighty God, that I will support the constitution of the United States, and maintain it and my country's flag, if necessary, with my life; that I will obey the commands of my superior officers while in service, and will defend and protect my comrades in battle to the best of my physical ability."

It was a "solemn and impressive" occasion, and was closed by a benediction from the Reverend Mr. Joslin, "Frank Thompson's" Methodist pastor friend. Each member of the company was presented a copy of the New Testament inscribed by the Flint Methodist Episcopal Church. Franklin Ellis's *History of Genesee County* states:

This presentation was made while the Greys stood in line, with open ranks, at the corner of Saginaw and Kearsley Streets. A number of ladies of Flint passed along the line, and pinned upon the breast of each soldier a tri-colored rosette, bearing the words, *"The Union and the Constitution!"* and nearly every one of the spectators wore the red, white, and blue upon some part of their dress. A presentation of revolvers to the commissioned officers of the company was made by the Honorable E. H. Thomson.

On May 25, 1861, the 2nd Michigan was officially mustered into service at Fort Wayne, Detroit, commanded by Colonel Israel B. Richardson, with the Greys designated as Company F. After a brief training period, the regiment left for the nation's capital on June 6th, arriving in Washington, D.C. on June 10th, where they were reviewed by President Lincoln at the White House before going into camp.

7

Emma E. Seelye, Army Nurse

Franklin [Thompson] was known by every man in the regiment and her desertion was the topic of every campfire. The beardless boy was a universal favorite, and much anxiety was expressed for her safety.
—WILLIAM R. MORSE, Captain of 2nd Michigan Regiment, to a newspaper reporter after the war.

Suffering from a serious bout with malaria and afraid of being exposed as a woman if placed in hospital, Sarah Emma Edmonds deserted from Lebanon, Kentucky, in April, 1863. With her usual resourcefulness, she eluded the pickets and slipped away undetected into the dark, somehow making her way to Oberlin, Ohio. There, still in army uniform, she rented a room in a boardinghouse where she spent some time recuperating and deciding on her next course of action. She was ill, exhausted, and in emotional turmoil.

After recuperating for about four weeks at Oberlin, she went to Pittsburgh, Pennsylvania, acquired new clothing, "and resumed my own proper dress, and have never worn any disguises since, except when sitting for pictures." She then returned to the same boardinghouse in Oberlin and was not recognized as "Frank."

During this period, as the war continued, she wrote the book *Nurse and Spy*, and took the manuscript to her old friends at Hurlburt and Williams Co., in Hartford, Connecticut. They published the first edition in 1864. Her book was an instant best seller, reportedly selling more than 175,000 copies. *Nurse and Spy* was dedicated "To the sick and wounded soldiers of the Army of the Potomac." True to her word, Sarah Emma Edmonds instructed the publisher to contribute most of the proceeds to the Sanitary Commission, the Christian Commission, and various soldier aid societies. In a postwar interview, she also pointed out that the book "furnished remunerative employment to many disabled soldiers and war widows in selling it by subscription."

In order to conceal her identity as "Franklin Thompson," Emma partially fictionalized her adventures, and presented them as if experienced by a female nurse, though occasionally in male disguise for reasons that are not always made clear. Her service in the 2nd Michigan is not explicitly mentioned in the book, though she refers to several members of the regiment by name and leaves a trail of clues throughout. Her disingenuousness misled a number of historians and commentators into considering her story to be mostly fiction, and others into accepting as fact some anecdotes that probably are fictitious.

Asked long after the war whether her book was authentic, she replied: "Not strictly so. Still, most of the experiences there recorded were either my own or came under my own observation. I would like, however, to write differently of that portion of my life." She was working on a sequel to *Nurse and Spy* which promised to clear up the question of what was factual and what fictional. Unfortunately, the sequel was never published and the manuscript apparently has been lost.

Still totally dedicated to the Union cause, Emma returned to hospital duty as a female nurse under the auspices of the Christian Commission at Harpers Ferry, serving in hospitals of the Army of the Cumberland until the close of the war. At Harper's Ferry she met Linus H. Seelye, a widower from New Brunswick, Canada, who was working as a carpenter.

After the war ended, she made a visit home to New Brunswick in 1866 and stayed until the fall of that year, probably visiting her sister and brother, Frances and Thomas, but both of her parents had died. One can only imagine her trying to put her life back together, wondering what to do next. She returned to Ohio to study at Oberlin College, but "found it too monotonous, after so much excitement."

Linus H. Seelye, who apparently had followed her to Oberlin, proposed marriage to her early in 1867, and they were married on April 27, 1867 in Cleveland, Ohio. As a carpenter, Linus was able to find work most anywhere, and they moved frequently, as if restlessly looking for new horizons. In subsequent years they traveled to Michigan, Illinois, Missouri, Louisiana, Alabama, Kansas, and Texas.

First they moved to Charlevoix, Michigan, in 1869 where their first child, Linus, Jr., was born on April 14, then soon afterwards moved to Evanston, Illinois. Their second son, Homer, was born June 21, 1871, but died within twenty-four hours. Linus, Jr., lived not quite three years.

Having returned to Oberlin to seek medical care for Linus, Jr., they decided to stay there after his death, and there Emma gave birth to Alice Louise on August 12, 1874. She lived only six years. Meanwhile, Linus and Emma adopted two boys, George Frederick (born in 1872) and Charles Finney (born in 1874), whom they raised with loving care. As of 1900, Charles was serving in the U.S. Army, stationed with his regiment in the Philippine Islands, and George was married and living in LaPorte, Texas.

On March 4, 1865, the U.S. Congress had established the Bureau of Relief of Freedmen and Refugees (popularly known as the Freedmen's Bureau) to oversee the welfare of former slaves. The highly regarded Major General Oliver O. Howard was appointed commissioner. Idealistic northerners, including Linus and Sarah Seelye (she had begun using the name Sarah since her marriage), volunteered to help freedmen find jobs and to help educate them so they could join mainstream society.

In 1875 Linus and Sarah were recruited to take charge of a Negro orphans' home in Lateche, St. Mary's Parish, Louisiana. There they labored for three years helping to raise and educate black orphans, until Sarah fell ill with malaria and "congestive chills."

In her definitive biography, Sylvia Dannett (who does not hesitate to report what she considers Sarah Emma's bad traits) says, simply and eloquently:

> A good part of [her] life, aside from her daring and adventurous exploits in the Union army, was devoted to helping other people, both before and after her marriage. . . . Perhaps this great selflessness is what makes Emma Seelye appear so much more admirable than many of her contemporaries.

Unlike many other female soldiers and spies who took to the lecture circuit to make money, she did not attempt to capitalize on her war experiences and instead was totally engaged in helping to relieve human suffering and pain. Surely her mother was an important role model for her in this respect. As also shines through *Nurse and Spy*, her Christian sentiments were real and important to her.

Far from bragging about her spying exploits, she felt somewhat ashamed of them and preferred not to talk about the subject. In a sworn statement to Congress, which was considering a bill to grant her a pension in the 1880s, she said:

> I make no statement of any secret services. In my mind there is almost as much odium attached to the word "spy" as there is to the word "deserter." There is so much *mean* deception necessarily practiced by a spy that I much prefer [that] every one should believe that I never was beyond the enemy's lines rather than fasten upon me by oath a thing that I despise so much. It may do in war time, but it is not pleasant to think upon in time of peace.

Taken ill in Mobile, Alabama, she and the family left the damp climate of their home in New Orleans seeking a healthier environment. They settled for a time in the small town of California, Missouri, first staying in a hotel where she lay ill for weeks with fever. The children also had measles, but all recovered eventually. Alice Louise died there later on December 25, 1880.

After about two years, Sarah and Linus moved on to Fort Scott, Kansas, where they settled and actually took roots for the first time. There they lived for about twelve years, as well-known and respected members of the community. They prospered in Fort Scott, accumulating considerable property, and Sarah planned to build a soldiers' home for the old soldiers who were living in county poorhouses.

Correspondents in Fort Scott later told Colonel Frederick Schneider, who wrote a series of articles about "Franklin Thompson," that the Seelyes "had the respect and esteem of all who knew them, to an eminent degree. That Mr. Seelye, who is a carpenter and builder, was a finished and skilled mechanic and very industrious. That Mrs. Seelye was noted as a great Christian worker and a very liberal contributor to many charities and a magazine writer of some note."

During their long periods of struggle before these successful years, friends had urged Sarah to apply for a soldier's pension and bounty, but she had resisted. Perhaps feeling some shame, or being worried about being a technical deserter, gave her pause. Now, with her health failing and her dream of building a soldier's home stymied by lack of money, she began taking steps to obtain a pension.

First she had to establish her identity and then clear her name of the charge of desertion. She would need affidavits from her old comrades. For all they knew, "Frank Thompson" had disappeared off the face of the earth more than twenty years ago from their camp in Kentucky. They had often wondered what had become of the popular young lad.

*   *   *

There was also another side of the story known to only a few. During Emma's two years in the army, at least one person knew and others suspected that "Frank Thompson" was a woman.

In later life, she maintained that fear of being found out, along with general exhaustion, were the reasons for her desertion. But historical research has turned up evidence that her secret world may have been crumbling at the same time. The evidence of two diaries indicate that Emma may have had a romantic (if not sexual) relationship with either of two soldiers, but in any case, one of them knew her true sex as early as October, 1861. Rumors to the same effect, it appears, probably contributed to her decision to desert in April, 1863.

Jerome Robbins, mentioned by Emma in *Nurse and Spy* as a male nurse who had been captured during the Virginia Peninsula Campaign when his hospital was overrun by Confederate soldiers, had enlisted in Company I of the 2nd Michigan at the beginning of the war. Before the war ended he was commissioned Assistant Surgeon, and he became a doctor after the war.

Robbins's wartime diary surfaced in 1963, acquired by the Michigan Historical Collections, University of Michigan. The first mention of "Frank Thompson" in the diary is on October 30, 1861, when Robbins had talked with "Frank" at the army hospital at Camp Scott, Washington, D.C. He remarked that he had had a pleasant conversation with "Thompson" about religion, adding:

> One of the few cherished friends made while at Camp Scott. He is an assistant in the Hosp. and one I think well calculated to win open the hearts of those about him. A mystery seems to be connected with him hard to unravel.

They continued on hospital duty together, and Robbins made many references to taking walks, attending prayer meetings, and conversing with "Thompson." On November 11, 1861, he wrote in his diary:

> I have which as I receive as a blessing, the society of a friend so pleasant as Frank I hail with joy. Though foolish as it may seem a

mystery appears to be connected with him which it is impossible for me to fathom. Yet these may be false surmises. Would that I might be free from them for not for worlds would I wrong a friend who so sincerely appreciates confiding friendship.

A few weeks later Robbins had solved the mystery. His entry for November 16, 1861 (the pages of which in his diary he had sealed closed) said: "Though never frankly asserted by her, it will be understood that my friend Frank is a female, which accounts for the singularity of the use of pronouns." Before this passage, Robbins had switched from using the pronoun "him" and had started referring to "Frank" as "her."

Betty Fladeland, who first reported the finding of the diary and its references to "Frank Thompson," added that the entries contain evidence that "Frank" had fallen in love with Jerome Robbins and was jealous of rivals for his affection. Then they had a falling out.

After being taken prisoner by the Confederates in 1862, Robbins was paroled in a camp until December. He and "Frank" corresponded during that period in what appeared to be a cordial relationship. Robbins's diary through 1862 and into 1863 confirms that "Frank" had a warm friendship with Lieutenant James Reid of the 79th New York regiment, assistant adjutant general at brigade headquarters.

In his entries for April 17 and 18, 1863, Robbins recorded the news that "Thompson" had deserted, and on April 20 that Lieutenant Reid had resigned and left the army. (Previously it had been believed that Emma deserted sometime between April 19 and April 23. The regimental history says April, 1863 without giving a specific date, and notes that "Thompson" was "ascertained afterward and about the time he left the regiment to have been a female, and a good looking one at that.")

In his entry for April 20, Robbins says:

> Frank has deserted for which I do not blame him. His was a strange history. He prepared me for his departure in part. Yet I did not think it would be so premature. (Note the return to use of the masculine pronoun.)

Robbins goes on to express bitterness about "Frank's" alleged "ingratitude and utter disregard for the finer sensibilities of others." He refers to some unspecified betrayal and "petty baseness" involving "Frank" and Lieutenant Reid, suggesting that there was a triangle of sorts involving the three of them.

The diary of William Boston of the 20th Michigan, also in the Michigan Historical Collections, includes the following entry for April 22, 1863:

> We are having quite a time at the expense of our brigade postmaster. He turns out to be a girl, and has deserted when his lover, Inspector Read [sic] and General Poe resigned. She went by the name Frank Crandall [sic] and was a pretty girl. She came out with Co. F of the Second Michigan Regiment and has been with them ever since.

(Boston's diary entry is misleading about General Poe, who had departed some time before. In March, 1863 Poe's appointment to brigadier general was not confirmed by the Senate, and his rank reverted from colonel to captain of engineers. Later that month he transferred to the Department of the Ohio, and was not at brigade headquarters when Emma deserted. He continued service as an engineer and was brevetted brigadier general at the end of the war.)

Thus, at least a few people suspected in 1863 not only that "Frank" was a woman, but also that something was amiss at brigade headquarters. Sylvia Dannett speculates that Emma may have had an affair with either Reid, or earlier with Colonel Orlando Poe. Still, she acknowledges that we may never know the truth.

Was the departure of "Frank" and Lieutenant Reid within days of each other only a coincidence? Betty Fladeland concludes that Robbins diary "substantiates the conclusion that Edmonds deserted . . . because she was in love with Reid and did not want to be separated from him." She also presents evidence indicating that scarcely a month after Emma's desertion, she was corresponding with both Jerome Robbins (their off and on friendship was "on" again, and continued for some time) *and* with James Reid!

On May 10, 1863, Fladeland reports, Emma wrote Jerome Robbins a letter from Washington, D.C. indicating that she had also received a letter from Reid. He had told her of having a long conversation with Robbins about her, and she was curious to know "the import of it." Emma also told Robbins, "he [Reid] says he wants me to come and visit his wife who is very anxious to see me."

This letter raises many interesting questions. First, Emma supposedly was in Oberlin, Ohio, with a brief side trip to Pittsburgh, at this time. However, she may have made another unreported side trip to Washington, D.C. More interestingly, as Fladeland notes, "if Reid and Sarah Emma Edmonds had been lovers, it would appear to be a bit unusual for him to be telling his wife about her and inviting her to their home." More likely her friendship with Reid was purely platonic, though she may have used Reid to make Robbins jealous.

The preponderance of evidence suggests that Emma's real love interest was Robbins, and that she had become upset when the love was not reciprocated. Robbins already had a serious girlfriend at home whom he intended to marry. He seemed to like "Frank" very much as a good Christian friend, but that was all. Their correspondence continued for several years, and when Robbins notified her of his marriage, she sent congratulations, adding:

> I do not love you less because you love another, but rather more, for your nobleness of character displayed in your love for her—may God make her worthy of so good a husband.

Here, ironically, was the type of "lovesick girl" that Emma in her youth had pitied.

Most curious of all, in Emma's letter to Robbins, is the information that she was in touch with Reid. Was there, after all, some significance in the timing of their departures from camp? Was he in on her secret while still in camp, or only afterwards? Who initiated the correspondence between them? If he did, how did he know where to find her? Perhaps she had written to him confessing the truth, which he may or may not have previously suspected. However, as a deserter she would be taking a serious risk by revealing where she could be found.

Even if there was some sort of "love triangle" in camp, it could have been an essentially innocent one involving warm, Christian friendship among gentle people who found comfort in each others presence. Considering all we know about Sarah Emma Edmonds, a puppy love in context of Christian fellowship seems to be a reasonable interpretation. She was barely over twenty years old at this time, and just beginning to change her negative opinions about men in general.

Although it is possible, even in the narrow confines of camp, that a sexually awakening Emma had an affair with Reid if not with Robbins, there is no strong evidence of that. Unless missing papers of James Reid come to light some day, we will probably never know for certain.

In any case, it is not an overridingly important point. Sylvia Dannett's suspicions and speculations about "Frank Thompson's" possible sexual liaisons probably are unfair to the memory of Sarah Emma Edmonds, who in almost all respects lived an exemplary— if unusual—life. Whatever sexual interaction she *may* have had with a fellow soldier is a trivial issue.

*   *   *

Returning to Flint, Michigan in 1882, Sarah paid a surprise visit to her former close friend and comrade in arms, Damon Stewart, now a prosperous merchant. Stewart had served with her in the 2nd Michigan during the early part of the war, before being wounded in action on the Virginia Peninsula in May, 1862. Their dramatic encounter after a hiatus of twenty years was described by Colonel Frederick Schneider in one of a series of newspaper articles at the turn of the century, quoting the very surprised Stewart.

While seated at his desk at his place of business one day, Stewart saw a woman wearing a veil enter the store and heard her ask for him. She was referred to him, and they looked directly at each other. The dialogue went approximately as follows:

"Are you Mr. Damon Stewart?"
"Yes."
"Can you give me the present address of Franklin Thompson?"

She had raised her veil while talking, and the mention of his former friend's name brought back memories of the early war years. Momentarily forgetting that so many years had passed, he asked,

"Are you Frank Thompson's mother?"
"No, I am not his mother," she replied.
"His sister, perhaps?"

Just then they heard footsteps approaching, and she took a pencil from his hand and wrote on a card:

"Be quiet! I am Frank Thompson."

Stewart was totally taken aback, and had to sit down, later telling a reporter: "If I was nonplussed, the woman before me was not. She was as tranquil and self-possessed as ever my little friend Frank had been."

Damon Stewart searched his memory, and quickly invited Sarah home, introduced her to his wife, and invited her to be a houseguest for as long as she wished to stay. Then he sent a letter to a friend who was a newspaper correspondent in East Saginaw (whose initials were given as A.M.G.):

> While doing service in the Union army during the years of 1861 and 1862, I had a companion, chum, campfellow. I thought it was a man! I hope to die if it was not a woman! She's up at our house now. Come out!

A.M.G. responded quickly and, fortunately for posterity, conducted the very illuminating interview that was first published in the Detroit *Post and Tribune* on May 26, 1883, and reprinted in other newspapers at least twice in later years. Since a substantial portion of the story was personally written by Sarah Emma Edmonds, answering questions about her youth contained in a follow-up letter from A.M.G., it is a crucial source of information about her early years and her motivations.

Sarah had not expected that her entire letter would be quoted in the story verbatim, but she wrote so well that the reporter incorporated it intact as if it were oral commentary. She first learned about it when another soldier who had served with "Frank Thompson" in hospital work at Washington, D.C., read the story. Albert E. Cowles, now a judge, wrote her a letter and enclosed the clipping. They continued to correspond, and Cowles's sympathetic support also was helpful in paving the way for her reconciliation with the survivors of the 2nd Michigan.

Still a feisty feminist, she justified her request for a pension in letters to Judge Cowles by suggesting that Uncle Sam ought to be willing to pension a female soldier who had given faithful, hard service "when he has pensioned so many male effeminates who never smelt powder on a battlefield." She explained to him the circumstances of her leaving the army.

> From my standpoint, I never for a moment considered myself a deserter. I simply left because I could hold out no longer, and to remain and become a helpless patient in a hospital was sure discovery, which to me was far worse than death.

Describing her continued hospital service and many contributions to soldiers' aid for the rest of the war, she concluded: "Now, my dear brother soldiers, I will leave it to you to decide whether I deserted the Union cause or not."

The sudden reappearance of "Frank Thompson" as a mature woman twenty years later was a sensation, and the news spread rapidly. Sarah Emma continued to write many letters to former officers, soldiers, and congressmen in her campaign for a pension. Cowles, meanwhile, relayed to her an invitation from Colonel Schneider, the last commander of the 2nd Michigan, to attend the regimental reunion in 1883. She was very touched by the invitation, but declined on the grounds of poor health, asking that her letter of gratitude be read at the reunion. As it happened, the letter did not arrive in time, but the veterans were delighted that the mystery of "Frank Thompson's" disappearance had been cleared up.

Afterwards, her old comrades rallied to her support. Affidavits were obtained to testify to her identity as "Franklin Thompson" and to her arduous and faithful service. The 2nd Michigan veterans also began laying the groundwork for her to attend the 1884 reunion, held in Flint, Michigan in October, even raising the funds to cover the costs of her transportation.

Early in 1884, an unusual private reunion took place. William R. Morse, former captain of Company F, who had been wounded at Williamsburg and assisted off the field by "Franklin Thompson," had read *Nurse and Spy* and suspected that the author was "Franklin Thompson." Later the word had spread that "Franklin Thompson" had reemerged as Mrs. Seelye. While visiting in Fort Scott, Kansas, Morse heard the name and decided to check for himself:

> I called at the house; a little girl met me at the door. I told her to tell her mother that a gentleman wished to see her, but did not send in my name. I was shown into a neat but plain little parlor. In a few minutes the lady made her appearance and recognized me. I spent a very pleasant hour in talking over old times and in listening to the story of her life.

House Report No. 820 to accompany bill H.R. 5334 was introduced in the House Military Affairs Committee by Congressman Byron Cutcheon of Michigan on March 18, 1884, recommending passage of the bill "to remove the charge of desertion from the record of Franklin Thompson, alias S.E.E. Seelye." Congressman Cutcheon had served in the 20th Michigan regiment, attaining the rank of lieutenant colonel, and had gone on to higher command.

House Report No. 849, same day, to accompany bill H.R. 5335 was introduced in the House Invalid Pensions Committee by Congressman E. B. Winans of Michigan (a former governor), recommending passage of the bill "granting a pension to Mrs. Sarah E.E. Seelye, alias Franklin Thompson."

Despite the impressive testimonials for Sarah Emma Edmonds

these reports contained, it would take a few more years to cut through bureaucratic red tape.

House Report No. 820, on H.R. 5334, not only contains a concise and interesting summary of her career, but also includes affidavits from which the following excerpts are taken:

> You ask if S.E.E. Edmunds [sic] and Frank Thompson are one and the same. I answer yes. You, Mrs. Seelye, have done everything in your power for the sick and wounded soldiers and for the Union cause. You deserve a pension from the Government. (A.M. Hulbert [sic], publisher of *Nurse and Spy*.)

(Also, a letter from Hulbert [sic] is printed in House Report No. 849. In it he certifies that "Frank Thompson" and Sarah Edmonds are one and the same person, and that many hundreds of dollars of profit from the book were distributed for the aid of sick and wounded soldiers at her request.)

Former member of Company F, 2nd Michigan Regiment, Sumner Howard, at this time a U.S. District Attorney in Utah swore on March 22, 1882 that "Frank Thompson" served faithfully as a private soldier and nurse:

> More than one member of the company can attest [to] the care, kindness, and self-sacrificing devotion of "Frank" to the sick soldiers of the regiment. . . . Frank's "manly bearing," soldierly qualities, kindness, and devotion to the sick deserve to be recognized in a liberal and substantial manner.

Stewart's testimony was thus:

> S. Emma E. Seelye is the identical person who enlisted under the name of Franklin Thompson. . . . and performed cheerfully and fully and at all times any duty which was assigned her . . . and was always ready for duty. (Damon Stewart, former Corporal in Company F, 2nd Michigan, and later Captain of Company K, 23rd Michigan.)

An especially touching affidavit was submitted by William R. Morse, original Captain of Company F:

> S. Emma E. Seelye, by her uniform faithfulness, bravery, and efficiency, and by her pure morals and Christian character, won the respect, admiration, and confidence of both officers and men in said company and regiment. I make this statement from personal knowledge, having known that Franklin Thompson remained with the regiment and performed these services . . . and I do know that S. Emma Seelye is the identical Franklin Thompson as aforesaid.

Another key testimonial came from a truly remarkable person in his own right (notwithstanding his familiar name), one William Shakespeare, of whom Sarah Emma herself jokingly said that she was surprised by his military skill as opposed to his literary achievements.

Shakespeare enlisted in Company K of the 2nd Michigan in May, 1861 as a corporal. He was severely wounded through both legs, including fractures of both thigh bones (supposed to be mortal wounds) on July 11, 1863 at Jackson, Mississippi, and was given a disability discharge on June 1, 1864 at Cincinnati, Ohio. Defying all odds he survived, later to become a brigadier general and after the war quartermaster general of Michigan in 1883–1884.

Shakespeare testified that he "was well acquainted with Frank Thompson of Company F . . . and that he knew Frank Thompson was a strong, healthy, and robust soldier, ever willing and ready for duty."

Private James H. Brown and two colonels of the 2nd Michigan also jointly signed a statement attesting that "S. E. Edmonds, alias Frank Thompson," had

> served faithfully as a good and loyal soldier for nearly two years and until her health became greatly impaired by reason of such arduous service. . . . In view of her many ministrations of tenderness and mercy, thousands of soldiers who were the recipients of her timely attention and nursing must remember her with the most filial regard.

They recommended granting a pension "for the remainder of her life and any other favors which in your wisdom and generosity you deem just and politic."

"Frank Thompson" obviously had earned lasting respect from male soldiers of all ranks with whom "he" had come in contact, and despite the shock of learning that "Frank" was a woman, they joined forces to testify in favor of removing the charge of desertion and granting her a pension. One person whose testimony, significantly, did not appear was Jerome Robbins. All the favorable testimony came from people who, apparently, knew and liked "Frank Thompson" and had no idea at the time that "he" was a woman.

The government pension bill finally was passed on July 5, 1884, and signed into law by President Chester A. Arthur, even before consideration of the desertion charge. Then, two years later, on July 3, 1886, the charge of desertion against "Franklin Thompson" (née Sarah Emma Edmonds) finally was removed when the bill passed and was signed into law by President Grover Cleveland on July 7th.

Sarah wrote a letter of gratitude to Congressman Byron Cutcheon, who replied from Washington, D.C., July 16, 1886:

> Your very kind and appreciative note of the 12th is received. I am very glad to have been of service to you, for though you don't remember Major Cutcheon of the Twentieth, I remember Frank Thompson, an orderly, very well. I saw you almost every day at Fredericksburg and repeatedly during the battle of Fredericksburg.

However, Sarah Emma's victory proved to be a hollow one. It was not until 1889 that her back pay and bounty actually came through, and then the amount was severely disappointing—just over $100, bounty and all. Disillusioned, she had to give up her cherished notion of establishing a veteran's home and face up to the reality that her dreams were not to be realized.

Then, financial misfortune befell the Seelyes during the commercial "panic" of 1893 and they lost their home and nearly all of their belongings. They moved to LaPorte, Texas, at their son's urging and managed to make a comfortable living from then on.

In April, 1897 Sarah Emma was accepted into membership in the Grand Army of the Republic (GAR) at the Houston, Texas, post, the only woman ever to receive this honor. A story about her induction that appeared in the Detroit *Journal* on May 19, 1898 said:

> Every now and then a woman has appeared who claimed membership in the Grand Army of the Republic and proceeded to work the old boys or the community for transportation, cash or board, but they have always proved to be frauds . . . [her] discharge was found to be regular in all respects. There was no excuse for refusing her request, so she was duly received . . . she is highly respected by all classes.

After briefly recounting her story, the reporter concluded: "There was not even a shadow of humbug about the soldiership of Frank Thompson, the woman veteran just made a member of the Grand Army."

Recurring attacks of malaria weakened Sarah Emma, and she died on September 5, 1898. During her latter years, she was a very respected figure, highly regarded by all who had known her, and beloved by her family. She was buried in the LaPorte cemetery, the funeral conducted by a delegation from Houston GAR Post

No. 9. In 1901, the coffin was exhumed, and in a special Memorial Day ceremony, reburied in a GAR plot at Washington Cemetery in Houston.

Sarah Emma Evelyn Edmonds Seelye had always been proudest of her service as a nurse. The inscription on her gravestone reads simply:

EMMA E. SEELY(E)
ARMY NURSE

Confederate Officers and Gentlewomen

*A beautiful, dashing lady, in the uniform of a [Confederate]
Captain, passed on the Northern train towards Richmond yes-
terday afternoon.*
—Lynchburg *Virginian*, October 6, 1864.

After the battle of Chickamauga, Tennessee, on September 19–20,
1863, a captured Union soldier was returned through the lines with
the following note: "As the Confederates do not use women in
war, this woman, wounded in battle, is returned to you." The
Confederate commander who penned this note would be surprised—more probably astonished—to learn how wrong he was.

In 1876, General Jubal Early was outraged by Loreta Janeta
Velazquez's claims to have served in the Confederate Army. Although he did raise some serious questions about portions of her
memoirs, the bottom line was that she did not fit his preconceptions
about the flower of southern womanhood, who in his estimation
would not have done the things she claimed to have done. Indeed,
he refused to believe that she could be a southern woman and
insisted that she must be from the North.

In the South, at the outset of the war, even the notion of women
serving as military nurses in battlefield areas was frowned upon,
and though some Confederate units had *vivandieres* or the equiv-
alent, the numbers appear to have been fewer and the role somewhat different. In some instances "mother figures" (typically the
wife of a soldier) served on or near the battlefield, sharing the
dangers and tending to the wounded. These were the closest par-
allels in the South to the young women like Anna Etheridge and
Bridget Deavers who served openly as women, and whose battlefield exploits were widely admired. In the South they tended to be

"mothers of the regiment," and their presence seems to have been justified in terms of "motherly" care of the soldiers. In the North the young women provided "sisterly" care to the soldiers and were romanticized as inspirational "angels" of the battlefield, setting an example of bravery and encouraging the men on to greater exploits.

Despite what the Confederate commander at Chickamauga thought, however, women did find their way into the ranks of the Confederate Army. Aside from Velazquez, one of the more remarkable stories is that of Mrs. Amy Clarke who served in General Braxton Bragg's Army of the Tennessee. The oft-repeated legend has her enlisting with her husband, continuing in service after he is killed at Shiloh (April 6–7, 1862), her later being wounded and captured, her sex discovered, and her release back into Confederate lines in a dress that Union officials insisted she wear. This core story has appeared in a number of sources.

Some important clues that may eventually help to uncover her whole story were found by Professor Stuart Sprague of Morehead State University, Kentucky. The Cairo City *Gazette* of December 25, 1862 reports that one "Anna Clark" (almost certainly Amy Clarke, since it mentions her husband's death at Shiloh, her capture and release in a dress) was a prisoner of war about to be exchanged. She had been serving as a private soldier in the 11th Tennessee Infantry using the name "Richard Anderson," was born in Iuka, Tennessee, and her husband's name was Walter. She was said to be "well informed upon politics, literature, and other general topics."

Less than a week later, Clarke was seen in Jackson, Mississippi, having been exchanged, and was on her way back to Bragg's command. Repeating the core story about Shiloh, the *Jackson Mississippian* of December 30, 1862 added that she had personally buried her husband on that battlefield. She had then continued fighting in the ranks until "twice wounded—once in the ankle, and then in the breast."

Evidence that she in fact did return to Bragg's command is contained in an August, 1863 letter home by Robert Hodges, Jr., a Texas cavalry soldier. Hodges told his father of an unexpected encounter with a female lieutenant at Turner's Station, Tennessee. Outside of camp shortly before August 7th, he found a crowd of people and asked what was going on:

> One of the soldiers directed my attention to a youth apparently about seventeen years of age well dressed with a lieutenant's badge

on his collar. I remarked that I saw nothing strange. He then told me that the young man was not a man but a female.

(This was one of several mentions of Clarke that lends credence to the basic story.) Hodges told his father that he had heard of the brave deeds of the female soldier, and repeated the basic story of her husband's death at Shiloh, her later being wounded and captured. (According to him "she was twice wounded in the ankle and then in the breast" before being released wearing a dress.)

How she came to be an officer, serving (apparently) openly as a woman, is not clear. It also seems odd that someone so famous would abruptly vanish from the pages of history, but the 1863 encounter in Tennessee was the last record that could be found. No information was found about whether she survived the war, or about her later life, and death. Possibly a more complete story will emerge in time.

*   *   *

Lucy Matilda Thompson, on the other hand, we know lived a long and full life even though badly wounded while serving as a soldier. She lived to be 112 years old! Born on November 21, 1812 in Bladensboro, North Carolina, her father was part Indian (Waccamau tribe). At 17 years-old, Lucy was tall and masculine in appearance, weighing 165 pounds. She learned to ride and hunt, and became an expert shot with a rifle. In 1861, at the age of 49, she married Bryant Gauss. When her husband enlisted in the Confederate army, she was not content to sit at home. "She cut her thick hair very close, remodeled Bryant's suit to fit herself, oiled her squirrel musket and went off to enlist," according to a summary of her life by John Mull, curator of the National Women's Military Museum.

Lucy's disguise was successful, and she joined her husband as a member of the "Bladen Light Infantry," which became Company D of the 18th North Carolina Infantry. Whether the company officers knew her true identity is not known. "If they did," Mull said, "they kept it to themselves. After all, what mattered most was that she was an expert shot. In addition, she sang well in a husky voice which helped keep up the spirits of the troops on the long, rainy marches between the battles." According to the story, she was wounded severely at 1st Bull Run by a piece of shrapnel that tore her scalp open. (Regimental records do not show that the 18th North Carolina was at 1st Bull Run, but it *was* at 2nd Bull Run where it had twelve casualties, and that probably is where it happened.)

Bryant Gauss was wounded three times early in the war, and was killed in action during the Seven Days battles near Richmond in May–June of 1862. About the same time, Lucy was again wounded in the head by shrapnel from a shell, this time more serious than before. During a sixty-day stay in the hospital a silver plate was placed in her skull to protect her brain. During this hospital stay her sex apparently was discovered. When she was released, she obtained a permanent furlough and took her husband's body home for a proper burial. Thus ended her combat career, with little or no publicity.

At age 51 in January of 1864, Lucy gave birth to her first child, a girl. She stayed at home in North Carolina for the rest of the war. Shortly after the war she moved to Savannah, Georgia, where she met and married Union veteran Joseph Patrick Henry Kenney (born in 1806 and therefore about 60 years-old). They settled in Savannah where Joe was a street cleaner, and had six children, including a set of twins born when Lucy was 55 years old. She gave birth to her last child at age 68!

Her husband, Joe, died in 1913 at the age of 107, possibly without knowing that his wife had fought on the opposite side during the Civil War. Only in 1914, when she told her pastor about her military record, did the story of her Civil War combat service begin to emerge. At this time she became something of a celebrity, frequently giving out interviews about her wartime experiences. During an interview on her 109th birthday she expressed opposition to women's suffrage.

Lucy died on June 22, 1925 (having survived through, and at least indirectly experienced World War I) at the age of 112 years. She is buried at Meeks Cemetery near Nicholls, Georgia.

*　　*　　*

The careers of some female soldiers were very short. Quite a few were unable to conceal their sex more than a few days or weeks in training camp, before they were discovered and sent home. Some were there in the first place only to be with their husbands or lovers and, unlike Amy Clarke or Frances Day, did not care to carry on alone. Such a case was Sarah Malinda Blaylock of Watauga County, North Carolina.

In 1856, at age 16 or 17, Sarah married William McKesson ("Keith") Blaylock. Keith, a Unionist, refused to enlist in the Confederate army in 1861 when the war broke out, but faced with conscription in the spring of 1862, he elected to enlist before being drafted, fully intending to desert at the first opportunity. Sarah cut her hair short and, wearing loose fitting clothes, enlisted in the 26th North Carolina on March 20th as "Sam" Blaylock, along with her husband and a neighbor boy, James D. Moore.

"Sam" was five feet, four inches tall, and weighed about 130 pounds. She performed all the soldierly duties along with the other members of Company F, and was adept at drilling and the manual of arms. She tented and ate with Keith, and no one saw through her disguise. Finding no opportunity to desert, Keith took matters in his own hands and rubbed poison sumac all over his body. The puzzled surgeons, seeing him covered with skin eruptions, considered him unfit for service and gave him a medical discharge on April 20, 1862. "Sam" immediately revealed her disguise to the colonel, and that startled man discharged her on the same day.

The 26th North Carolina fought on the Virginia Peninsula that summer in the Seven Days battles before Richmond, and then fought in Lee's Army of Northern Virginia from Gettysburg to Cold Harbor. More than 80 percent of the regiment was disabled at Gettysburg of the 843 engaged, and the regiment had nearly 100 casualties at Bristoe (October 9–22, 1863). At the surrender on April 9, 1865, only ten officers and 120 men survived. There is no telling how Keith and Sarah may have fared had they elected to stay with the regiment, but the odds would have been heavily against their surviving unscathed.

Keith and Sarah went on to experience a life of violence despite leaving the army. They returned to their home at Grandfather Mountain in the northwest corner of North Carolina, where he treated his skin eruptions with brine baths. However, his Confederate neighbors pressed him about why he did not return to service. Again he was threatened with conscription, so he and Sarah fled into the wilderness on top of the mountain, but zealous neighbors pursued them and Keith was shot in the arm. As a result they continued on across the mountains into east Tennessee. Keith became a Unionist partisan, leading raids into North Carolina and helping escaped prisoners and other North Carolina Unionists to escape into Tennessee, with Sarah participating in some of these escapades.

When the Moore family let it be known that they intended to kill Keith Blaylock, he and Sarah led a raiding party into North Carolina and attacked the Moore home. The patriarch, Carroll Moore, was wounded in the fight, but the Blaylock party had to retreat when Sarah was shot in the shoulder. In another exchange of gunfire later on, Keith shot one of the Moore boys in the heel, but in turn had one of his eyes shot out. The partisan raids were continued throughout the war.

After the war the passions eventually cooled, and Keith and Sarah lived out their lives in what is now Avery County. Sarah died in 1903 of natural causes. Keith died violently in 1913 at age 77 in a railroad-handcar accident.

Whether it was true or not, women who disguised themselves as men to be soldiers were popularly considered to have "loose morals," unless—like Sarah Malinda Blaylock—they served with their husbands. In the fall of 1864, two soldiers in General Jubal Early's command in the Shenandoah Valley were arrested. Although they had been known for two years as "Tom Parker" and "Bob Martin," their real names were Mary and Molly Bell. The captain had identified them as "common camp followers" who, he said, had been demoralizing his men. No specific charges were reported. General Early sent them to prison at Castle Thunder in Richmond where they spent three weeks before being sent home to Pulaski County, still dressed in their uniforms.

Francis Butler Simkins and James Welch Patton provide a rich source of anecdotes about female soldiers, spies, scouts, and nurses in their 1936 book *The Women of the Confederacy*. They described numerous acts of heroism and unselfishness by southern women, including women who braved Federal fire on the battlefield. One of these was Allie McPeak,

> an humble Georgian upon whose farm the Battle of Jonesboro was fought [August 31–September 1, 1864]. Exposing herself during the battle to the fire of both armies, she moved about fearlessly relieving both friend and foe. General Schofield, the Federal commander, touched by her heroism, sent her provisions and caused his adjutant to write her a letter of thanks.

A notable female scout was Nancy Hart, a mountain woman from western Virginia who led Jackson's cavalry in surprise attacks on Federal outposts. Because of her success in these adventures, Federal officials put a price on her head. In July, 1862, she was finally caught at Summerville by Colonel Starr of the 9th West Virginia Regiment. She escaped by shooting her guard and fleeing on Starr's horse. A few days later she led a force of two hundred Confederates into Summerville, and they captured Starr and some of his men.

A group of women in LaGrange, Georgia (Troup County), known as the Nancy Harts (named after a Georgia Revolutionary War heroine, not the Virginia woman) may have been the only female militia unit formed during the Civil War. With all the men away at war, Mrs. J. Brown Morgan (wife of a major in the 6th Georgia Infantry) and Mrs. Peter Heard (wife of a minister) organized a company of women soldiers to defend the town. The company originally had about forty members. Mrs. Morgan was elected captain and Mrs. Heard first lieutenant. No complete roster exists for the company, but "their numbers and martial air were sufficient to encourage spectators to gather and watch their frequent parades through the streets of LaGrange." *(Randall Allen, TCHS Newsletter)*.

The Nancy Harts met regularly on Saturdays for drill and target practice. Instead of uniforms, they wore "ruffled skirts and flower-trimmed hats." After several weeks "they became expert marksmen, indifferent to the snap of a cap, the flash of powder or the kick of a gun." After target practice

> it was their custom to parade the streets of LaGrange for the purpose of inspiring their friends with confidence and striking terror to the hearts of the would-be evil doers. Thus they patrolled the streets for four years. Their reputation as markswomen became widespread. (LaGrange, Georgia, *Daily News*, January 19, 1937.)

LaGrange became a hospital town late in 1863, and members of the Nancy Harts also helped care for wounded soldiers. Their contributions, therefore, included policelike security services, inspiration to the townspeople, and hospital work.

According to legend, the Nancy Harts also faced down a troop of Union cavalry in a post-surrender incident on April 17, 1865, resisting the entrance into LaGrange of elements of General William Tecumseh Sherman's army. The apocryphal story (though it is supported by quotes from First Corporal Pullen of the Nancy Harts) says that a Yankee cavalry force under (the coincidentally named) Colonel Oscar H. LaGrange of the 1st Wisconsin Cavalry approached the town from the west. The Nancy Harts—allegedly "drawn up in line, their guns to their shoulders"—were ordered to go to their homes, but refused to do so and stood fast.

The diplomatic Union cavalry colonel made peace with the women, and then fraternized with them over tea. In admiration of their courage, Colonel LaGrange spared the houses of the town, and this was viewed as a successful "mission" for the Nancy Harts without a shot being fired. "Thus it was that the girl soldiers accomplished the object of their existence. They did not fire volleys nor execute military maneuvers at this critical period, but they used methods equally effective: they stood between their homes and destruction." (LaGrange, Georgia, *Daily News*, January 19, 1937.)

Additionally, the legend had Colonel LaGrange later marrying 2nd Corporal Sally Bull of the Nancy Harts, but this is disputed.

Partial Roster of the Nancy Harts
(Reconstructed from material in Troup County Archives)
Mrs. J. Brown Morgan, Captain
Mrs. Peter B. Heard, 1st Lieutenant
Alice ("Aley") Smith, 2nd Lieutenant
Andelia Bull, 3rd Lieutenant
Augusta Hill, 1st Sergeant
Pack Beall, 2nd Sergeant (Later Mrs. Charles Ridley)
Lelia (or Leila) Pullen, 1st Corporal
(Later Mrs. James Allen Morris)
Sally Bull, 2nd Corporal
Mrs. John T. Gay, 3rd Corporal
M. E. Colquitt
Mrs. Frank Frost
Ella Key

Other fragmentary accounts of female Confederate officers are included in Chapter 12. Ironically, southern culture at the outset of the war was against women having anything to do with warfare in the field, but by war's end a number of women apparently had served as officers. While there are many references to female non-coms in the North, there are none for the South. As with most other aspects of the Civil War, information about women at war is more readily available for the Union than it is for the Confederacy.

As suggested by the death at Gettysburg of a Confederate female soldier serving with her husband and other reports (see Chapter 12), it is very likely that the presence of women in the Confederate army has been seriously underreported.

Famous Union Nurses, engraving (A. D. Worthington & Company, 1887).
Clockwise from top left: Mrs. Jane C. Hoge; Mrs. Mary "Mother"
Bickerdyke; Mrs. Cordelia Harvey; and Miss Mary J. Safford.

Kady Brownwell, 1st Rhode Island Infantry, in army costume. (Engraving by G. E. Perine from *Women of the War*, 1866).

Belle Reynolds. (Engraving from *Women of the War*).

Marie Tebe, 114th Pennsylvania Infantry. (Photograph by Robert P. Swiatek, from *Music on the March*, 1862–1865, 1892).

Union Generals. Seated: Windfield Scott Hancock. Standing (l. to r.): Francis G. Barlow (whose wife served at front as nurse), David B. Birney (who awarded Kearny Cross to Anna Etheridge and Marie Tebe), and John Gibbon.

"Albert Cashier" in 1864 and 1913, dual photo. (Courtesy Illinois State Historical Society.)

"Albert Cashier " (r.) with friend in 95th Illinois
Infantry. (Courtesy Spencer H. Watterson.)

Bridget Deavers in romantic engraving by J. J. Cade. (Photograph by
Robert P. Swiatek from *My Story of the War*, by Mary Livermore,
1887.)

Israel B. Richardson, first colonel of
2nd Michigan. Killed Antietam.
(Photo courtesy of Marvel Ireland
from *Michigan Volunteers in the Civil
War*, circa 1915.)

Engraving of Annie Etheridge in battle. (From
Woman's Work in the Civil War, 1887.)

Photograph of Anna Etheridge later in life, wearing military medals. (Courtesy of the State Archives of Michigan.)

Photograph of Sarah Emma Edmonds as "Franklin Thompson." (Courtesy of State Archives of Michigan.)

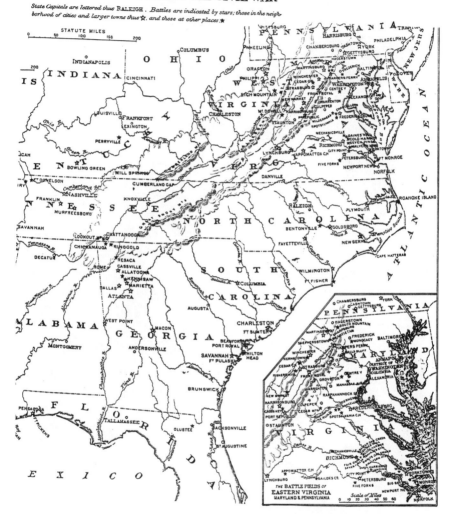

Virginia Peninsula and other battlefields. (Adapted from *Century War Book*, 1894.)

MAKING HOE-CAKE FOR A SICK REBEL.—Page 153.

Emma as "Bridget" caring for rebel soldier. (Engraving by Abbie Crane, from *Nurse and Spy*, *1865*.)

Emma as "Ned" at Yorktown. (Engraving by Abbie Crane from *Nurse and Spy*.)

DISGUISED AS A CONTRABAND.—Page 113.

ACTING ORDERLY.—Page 178.

← enlarge?

"Frank Thompson," on horse at left, as orderly at Battle of Seven Pines. (Engraving from *Nurse and Spy*.)

General Phil Kearny, inspirational leader at Seven Pines.

Colonel Orlando M. Poe, 2nd Michigan Infantry. (Photo courtesy of Marvel Ireland from *Michigan Volunteers in the Civil War*, circa 1915.)

Sergeant William Shakespeare, 2nd Michigan
Infantry. (Photo courtesy of Marvel Ireland from
Michigan Volunteers in the Civil War.)

AN INTERESTING PATIENT.—Page 271.

"Frank Thompson" comforts dying female soldier at Antietam.
(Engraving from *Nurse and Spy*.)

Officers of 2nd Michigan during training at Ft. Wayne, Detroit, 1861. (Courtesy of Burton Historical Collection, Detroit Public Library.)

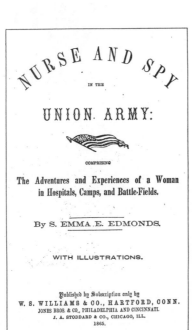

Title page of *Nurse and Spy*, 1865.

Sarah E. E. Seelye, postwar photograph. (Courtesy of State Archives of Michigan.)

Damon Stewart after the war. (Photo courtesy of Marvel Ireland from *History of Genesee County*.)

William B. McCreery vouched for "Frank Thompson." (Photo courtesy of Marvel Ireland from *History of Genesee County*.)

Frederick Schneider, last colonel of 2nd Michigan Infantry, author of several articles written in 1900 about Sarah Edmonds in Lansing newspaper. (Courtesy of State Archives of Michigan.)

Sarah Malinda "Sam" Blaylock holding small photograph of her husband. (Courtesy Southern Historical Collection, University of North Carolina, Chapel Hill.)

Lieutenant "Harry T. Buford," C.S.A. (Engraving from the *The Woman in Battle*, 1876; photograph by Robert P. Swiatek.)

Death of Colonel Edward Baker, Federal commander at Ball's Bluff, Virginia. (Engraving from *The Great Rebellion*, 1866; photograph by Robert P. Swiatek.)

Velasquez interrogated by General Benjamin Butler, military governor of New Orleans. (Engraving from *The Woman in Battle*.)

WOUNDED BY A SHELL.

Lt. "Buford," at right, wounded at Shiloh battlefield. (Engraving from
The Woman in Battle.)

MADAM VELASQUEZ IN FEMALE ATTIRE.

Engraving of Loreta Janeta
Velasquez (from *The Woman
in Battle*) compared to photo
of Kentucky mystery woman
who served as Confederate
spy, which shows striking resemblance.

YOUNG CONFEDERATE WIDOW WHO WAS A MESSENGER FOR THE
ST. ALBAN'S RAIDERS IN GETTING THE PROPER PAPERS
FROM THE CONFEDERATE GOVERNMENT

Frances L. Clalin, said to have served in a Missouri militia or Maine cavalry unit, but no confirmation has been found. (Photos courtesy of the Trustees of the Boston Public Library.)

In cavalry uniform.

In 19th-century female attire.

Harriet Tubman led military raids for the Union.

"Lieutenant Harry T. Buford," C.S.A.

To be a Second Joan of Arc [proved to be] a mere girlish
fancy, which my very first experiences as a soldier dissipated
forever.
—Memoirs of LORETA JANETA VELAZQUEZ.

On a hot summer day in Washington, D.C., July 20, 1861, the
Federal hierarchy had decided that it was time to take decisive
action. A Confederate force under Brigadier General P.G.T.
Beauregard was in position near the vital Manassas railroad junction, a scant twenty-five miles west and south of the city. A Federal
army commanded by Brigadier General Irvin McDowell was sent
to drive them away, and destroy them if possible. A crowd of
picnickers and onlookers, including some government officials,
tagged along expecting to see a glorious spectacle.

The battle of First Bull Run (or Manassas) on the next day was
the first large-scale clash of armies during the Civil War. For many
regiments on both sides, it was their first exposure to all-out combat. Many of them approached it with enthusiasm, under the common self-delusion that they would quickly dispose of the enemy;
it would be a short and glorious war. A number of regiments on
the field had been enlisted optimistically for only three months'
service. For the most part, the green troops were led by ill-trained
and inexperienced officers.

On the Confederate side, eager for battle, was a young "independent" lieutenant, Harry T. Buford, not formally attached to a
specific unit. Unbeknownst to fellow officers, "Lieutenant Buford" was a woman in male disguise, complete with artificial beard
and mustache. Her real name was Loreta Janeta Velazquez. Born
in Cuba from a wealthy family, she was raised in New Orleans,

Louisiana, by an aunt. She was able to pay for all her own supplies and equipment, and sought combat assignments or commissions from battlefield commanders on an opportunistic basis.

Traveling with Velazquez, and apparently unaware of her female identity, was a black servant, Bob. They had participated in the skirmish at Blackburn's Ford on July 18th and helped to bury the dead. When a company commander was killed, "Lieutenant Buford" had been placed in temporary command. Now "Buford" was eager to distinguish herself by leading the company in battle before being replaced by a more senior officer. All Velazquez wanted was "an opportunity to make a first-rate display of my fighting qualities."

On July 20th, Confederate reinforcements arrived on the field near Manassas Junction, including Barnard E. Bee with the 4th Alabama and 2nd Mississippi Regiments and a few companies of the 11th Mississippi. For part of that day, "Lieutenant Buford" served as a courier for General Barnard Bee, and that night fell into a deep and dreamless sleep. She later recalled:

> I had fancied that sleep would be impossible to me under such circumstances; but a very little experience as a soldier was sufficient for me to be able to fall into a soldier's way of doing things, and I soon learned to take my rest as naturally and composedly upon the bare ground as if on the most downy couch, and not even the excitements and anxieties incident to an impending battle could prevent my tired eyes from closing after a long and fatiguing day passed under a broiling July sun.

Next morning the battle commenced. From the Confederate perspective, clouds of dust rising from tramping boots signalled the approach of the enemy.

Velazquez later reported in her memoirs:

> The morning was a beautiful one, although it gave the promise of a sweltering day; and the scene presented to my eyes, as I surveyed the field, was one of marvelous beauty and grandeur. I cannot pretend to express in words what I felt, as I found myself one among thousands of combatants, who were about to engage in a deadly and desperate struggle.
>
> The supreme moment of my life had arrived, and all the glorious aspirations of my romantic girlhood were on the point of realization. I was elated beyond measure, although cool-headed enough. . . . Fear was a word I did not know the meaning of; and as I noted the ashy faces, and the trembling limbs of some of the men about me, I

almost wished that I could feel a little fear, if only for the sake of sympathizing with the poor devils. I do not say this for brag, for I despise braggarts as much as I do cowards.

Loreta Janeta Velazquez's childhood fantasy was coming true. As a young girl she had eagerly read books about kings and princes and soldiers. "The story of the siege of Orleans, in particular, I remember, thrilled my young heart, fired my imagination, and sent my blood bounding through my veins with excitement," she would later recall. "Joan of Arc became my heroine, and I longed for an opportunity to become another such as she. I built air-castles without number, and in my day-dreams I was fond of imagining myself as the hero of the most stupendous adventures. I wished that I was a man . . . and could discover new worlds, or explore unknown regions of the earth."

The battle broke on the hilly terrain near the creek called Bull Run; the rolling hills sometimes concealed maneuvering soldiers until they were practically on top of each other. Complicating matters further, at this early stage of the war, some Federal soldiers had gray uniforms and some Confederate soldiers were garbed in blue. The resulting hesitations and doubts in identification of friends and foes often proved fatal. The skirmishers appearing suddenly over a rise, the choking dust and smoke, the close range cannon fire, led to widespread confusion and disorder.

Reverberations of artillery could be heard all the way to Alexandria, and even in Washington, as clouds of smoke rose out of the woods. The dust and heat quickly became stifling. At first the thin Confederate ranks had difficulty holding back the large Federal columns. The left of Beauregard's line was severely pressured, and everything seemed to be going for the Union forces through a series of attacks and counterattacks during the morning. By late morning the Federal commanders thought they had won, but their celebration proved to be premature.

Through late morning and into afternoon, fresh forces continued to arrive on the battlefield, and were hastily rushed into position by the opposing commanders. Beauregard continued to shift reinforcements to the beleaguered left of the line, among them Jubal Early and M. L. Bonham, and gradually the Confederate forces converged on Henry Hill. The battle for Henry Hill began in earnest about 2:00 P.M., continuing for about two hours.

In mid-afternoon, two of Bonham's regiments arrived on the left of the Confederate line to reinforce the 6th North Carolina regiment which had been valiantly defending the exposed left. Sometime between 4:00 and 4:30 P.M. the right of McDowell's Federal battle line began crumbling, and with timely help from Jubal Early's troops, the Confederate left broke through and sent the Federal army fleeing in full retreat.

"Lieutenant Buford," with Bee's command at the focal point of the final crucial battle, had watched as the panorama unfolded:

> Ere the morning was far advanced, the sharp rattling of the musketry, the roar of the artillery, and the yelling of the soldiers, developed into an incessant tumult; while along the entire line, for miles, arose clouds of yellow dust and blue smoke, as the desperateness of the conflict increased, and the men on either side became excited with the work they had in hand.

"Buford" was chagrined when Bee, finding his soldiers surrounded on three sides and the 4th Alabama in danger of being overrun, ordered a retreat.

> I was wrought up to such a pitch of excitement, while the fight was going on, that I had no comprehension whatever of the value of the movements being made by the different commanders. I only saw the enemy before me, and was inspired by an eager desire to conquer him . . . so, when by the general's command, we were compelled to fall back, I was overcome with rage and indignation, and felt all the shame and mortification of a personal defeat.

But the wisdom of Bee's move soon became apparent. "This movement on the part of Bee," Velazquez wrote,

> afforded me an opportunity to cool off a little, and to observe the ebb and flow of the tide of battle more critically. . . . From this point, therefore, the battle became more interesting than ever, and while none the less exciting, simply as a personal adventure—for my spirit rose and sank as victory or defeat seemed likely to rest upon our banners—I was more under the dominion of my reason, and less of my passions, than I had been when the fight commenced.

As the battle reached a peak, she said, it was a spectacle that "was grand beyond description," bringing to mind scenes of the Sahara Desert, with a broiling sun and roiling clouds of dust mingled with smoke, and dry, choking air. The smoke rose in huge columns, marking the most hotly contested points on the field. "It was a sight never to be forgotten," wrote Velazquez. "One of those magnificent spectacles that cannot be imagined, and that no description, no matter how eloquent, can do justice to . . . a sublime, living drama."

(The following spring, as McClellan's army retreated at the conclusion of the Virginia Peninsula Campaign, having failed to take Richmond, the final battle at Malvern Hill, with its panoramic artillery barrage and hail of musketry, light flashes and smoke clouds, would similarly cause Sarah Emma Edmonds to wax rapturous about the grand spectacle she observed.)

"The fiercer the conflict grew the more my courage rose," said Velazquez. "The example of my commanders, the desire to avenge my slaughtered comrades, the salvation of the cause which I had espoused, all inspired me to do my utmost; and no man on the field that day fought with more energy or determination than the woman who figured as Lieutenant Harry T. Buford."

At midday a courier rode up with a message for General Joseph Johnston that a heavy force of Federals had arrived on the field. "Fortunately, however, the advancing troops were those of [Confederate] Kirby Smith," she reported, "and consisted of about two thousand infantry and Beekman's artillery. The arrival of this force decided the fate of the battle, and the Federals fled, defeated, from the field." (Actually, though Smith's arrival close to noon was very beneficial, it was Jubal Early's timely appearance in late afternoon that helped carry the day.)

By the end of the day Velazquez was satisfied that her performance under fire deserved recognition:

> After the battle, I appealed to General [Thomas "Stonewall"] Jackson for the promotion which I considered that I had fully earned, and he gave me a recommendation to General Bragg for a recruiting commission. This I did not care about, for I thought that I did not need his permission or his aid to do recruiting duty, and determined to wait and see if something better would not offer.

The Confederate victory at 1st Bull Run elated the South and shocked the North. The battle "only quickened my ardor to participate in another affair of a similar kind . . . there is a positive enjoyment in the deadly perils of the occasion that nothing can equal" she concluded.

For several months the opposing armies jockeyed for position in northern Virginia, the Confederate forces lurking just across the Potomac River menacing Washington, D.C. Finally, one of those accidental battles developed that have happened throughout history, when elements of opposing armies stumble onto each other and fate takes over. What started out as a "demonstration" by a brigade commanded by Colonel Edward D. Baker, across the Potomac toward Leesburg, Virginia, where Brigadier General Nathan G. Evans had a small Confederate force, quickly evolved into a sharp, bitter fight on October 21, 1861.

On October 10th, "Lieutenant Buford" had gone to General Evans's headquarters seeking an assignment, but there were no vacancies. On October 21st, she tagged along with the 8th Virginia Infantry into battle.

The Union force had climbed a narrow pathway up Balls Bluff, a 70-foot precipice on the Virginia side of the Potomac, about twenty-five miles up the river northwest of Washington. However, not expecting anything more than a scouting mission, they committed a fundamental mistake by failing to arrange for vessels to recross the river or for an alternate escape route in case they needed to retreat. This proved to be a fatal error.

The scene that greeted "Lieutenant Buford" atop the bluff was:

> a tolerably open piece of ground, cut up somewhat by ridges and hollows, and surrounded by a thick growth of woods. This timber for a while concealed the combatants from each other, and it was impossible for us to tell what force we were contending with. The woods seemed to be alive with combatants, and it was thought that the enemy was strongly fortified. . . . The enemy certainly fought exceedingly well, especially considering the precariousness of their position, although, of course, we did not know at the time the attack was made that our foes were in such a desperate predicament.

Shortly after the Confederate attack began, "Lieutenant Buford" took charge of a company that had lost all of its officers and endeavoured to "set them an example." After the battle, the 1st lieutenant of the company reappeared and relieved her, claiming that he had been taken prisoner but had managed to escape. She had serious doubts about his story, and assumed that he had run for cover when the firing started.

As dusk approached, the Union forces found themselves hemmed in on three sides and finally broke, scrambling and tumbling back down the bluff, discarding their equipment as they fled. Struggling soldiers quickly swamped the one or two boats on hand and, floundering in the swift current, dozens were drowned. The Confederate soldiers, shrieking and yelling, stood atop the bluff raining lead down into the frantic Yankees, like shooting fish in a barrel. It was bloody murder, and for the first time Velazquez had doubts about the "glory" or "nobility" of war:

> This horrible spectacle made me shudder. . . . I was willing to fight them to death's door in the open field, and to ask no favors, taking the same chances for life as they had; but I had no heart for their ruthless slaughter. All the woman in me revolted at the fiendish delight which some of our soldiers displayed at the sight of the terrible agony endured by those who had, but a short time before, been contesting the field with them so valiantly.

Her impulse was to try to stop the carnage, even at the expense of betraying her secret, but she restrained herself. "Such scenes as these," she noted, "are inseparable from warfare, and they must be endured by those who adopt a soldier's career." But the experience soured her on war. "[It] had the effect of satisfying my appetite for fighting for a time; and after it was over, I was by no means as anxious for another battle, as I had been after the victory at Bull Run."

The sight of the enemy stampeding like buffalo into the river, and hundreds being shot down, had made her "sick with horror."

> As the cold shivers ran through me, and my heart stood still in my bosom, I shut my eyes for a moment, wishing that it was all over, but only to open them again to gaze on a spectacle that had a terrible fascination for me, in spite of its horrors.

Still, she fired her revolver at a Union officer as he was jumping in the river, and saw him spring into the air and fall. "[I] then turned my head away, shuddering at what I had done, although I believed that it was only my duty." As she watched the boats overloaded with the wounded and dying sink into the river, she "turned away, sick at heart, unable to endure the sight of it."

In the aftermath, Velazquez reassessed her career and decided it was time to make a change. Disillusioned, and bored with the routine of camp life, she began to think of other ways to contribute to the Confederate cause. Battles were exhilarating, but they were few and far between, and sometimes disturbing in their inhumanity.

"To be a second Joan of Arc," she decided,

> was a mere girlish fancy, which my very first experiences as a soldier dissipated forever . . . convincing me that a woman like myself, who had a talent for assuming disguises . . . was possessed of courage, resolution, and energy, backed up by a ready wit, a plausible

address, and attractive manners, had it in her power to perform many services of the most vital importance, which it would be impossible for a man to even attempt.

Thus began her career as a spy. Leaving Bob with others, she resumed female garb, lying to a Negro woman to obtain some women's clothes from her:

> I really felt sorry at deceiving her, but quieted my conscience with the thought that lying was as necessary as fighting in warfare, and that the prospects were that I would be compelled to do much more fibbing than this before the errand upon which I was about starting would be achieved.

Her free-lance experimentation with spying proved to be short-lived. Crossing into Maryland, she made her way into Washington, D.C. There she mingled in society and claimed to have met Lincoln and other Federal officials. She found it disconcertingly easy to pry information from Union officers and officials, and yearned for an official appointment in the Confederate detective corps to show what she could do.

After about two weeks of trying out her wings, Velazquez concluded that she had the abilities to be a good spy and detective who could obtain valuable information for the cause. Satisfied with this, she made her way back to Leesburg and retrieved her uniform from the Negro woman who had concealed it for her. She would look for a detective commission down the road, but for now she was drawn back into uniform.

Resuming male disguise, Velazquez rejoined Bob and set out for Columbus, Tennessee, determined to seek an assignment from General Leonidas Polk. Sadder and wiser, and more realistic about the true nature of war, she now understood that it would be a long and difficult affair:

> It became apparent . . . that a single battle was not going to finish the war, and that if the South was to achieve its independence, it must go through a long and bloody conflict. My visit to Washington more than confirmed the opinion I had formed, that the Federals were in command of enormous resources in comparison with ours, and that they were settling down to a deadly determination to bring all their resources to bear for the purposes of fighting the thing out to the bitter end.

General Polk assigned her to the detective corps, as a military conductor on railroad cars on the Nashville Railroad. Armed with powers of arrest, her duties included examination of passes and furlough papers. "Lieutenant Buford" found the female passengers all too eager to flirt with the jaunty young officer:

> I was a personage of considerable importance, not only to the officers and soldiers who were going back and forth, but to the ladies, who courted me with remarkable assiduity, with a view of inducing me to grant them favors. The women folk tormented me a good deal more than the men did, for the average masculine [sic] had a wholesome dread of the rigors of military discipline, and was consequently manageable, while my own sex relied on accomplishing, by means of their fascinations, what was impossible to the men.

The women, she said, would make all kinds of excuses and tell all kinds of improbable stories to persuade "Lieutenant Buford" to pass them:

> Occasionally some of my would-be charmers, finding it impossible to make any impression on me, would abuse me roundly for refusing to grant their request. This, of course, did not have any other effect than to afford me much amusement; but it enabled me to understand why my predecessor seemed so well pleased at being relieved, although I have doubts as to whether he was as strict in enforcing the regulations as myself.

On one occasion a would-be passenger who "Buford" would not let travel without the proper papers trumped up a false charge against the lieutenant in retaliation. To check on the situation, General Polk himself boarded the train and tried to persuade "Lieutenant Buford" to let him travel without proper travel papers. "Buford" stood "his" ground, until Polk—laughing—produced legitimate leave papers. He later apologized, but "Buford" was upset by his lack of trust and his surveillance of her: "I told him very plainly . . . that I did not like that sort of thing, and that I proposed to tender my resignation shortly."

Her stint as a military conductor had lasted barely three weeks. After an interlude of partying, during which she played up to the ladies to enhance her masculine image, she returned to the field and was involved in the battle of Fort Donelson, Tennessee, during February 13–16, 1862.

Velazquez had arrived at Fort Donelson the day before the battle and sized up the situation. She was struck by the contrast with 1st Bull Run, which had been fought in open country during hot summer weather, and she had a premonition of defeat:

It was a very different thing, from defending a series of earthworks from a combined attack, by land and by water, in the dead of winter. . . . The whole proceeding seemed unseasonable, and this peculiar feeling, combined with a singular sense of discomfort and constraint at being shut in fortifications from which there was next to no escape, except by driving off the enemy, or surrendering to him, had a powerful effect in dampening my ardor.

She and Bob pitched in to work on the entrenchments, hoping for the best. Velazquez noted in her memoirs that Bob proved to be a "much better man than I was" when it came to shoveling dirt:

There are some things which men can do better than women, and digging intrenchments [sic] in the frozen ground is one of them . . . nature had evidently intended me for a warrior rather than for a dirt-digger.

Volunteering for picket duty, "Lieutenant Buford" had problems adjusting to the wintry climate. When the weather abruptly turned intensely cold, she began to doubt her qualifications for this kind of service: "I confess that, as the sleet stung my face, and the biting winds cut me to the bones, I wished myself well out of it, and longed for the siege to be over in some shape, even if relief came only through defeat."

Her only consolation was that there were "thousands of brave men around, who were suffering from these wintry blasts as much as I."

Fort Donelson, on the Cumberland River, blocked Federal forces from controlling Kentucky and western Tennessee. An up-and-coming general named U. S. Grant advanced his army of about 15,000 into position to attack the fort. The initial assaults by several Illinois regiments were repulsed, with heavy casualties. In charge of defending the fort were Brigadier General John B. Floyd, Major General Gideon L. Pillow, and Brigadier General Simon B. Buckner.

The Illinois troops dug in within rifle range of the fort, without tents or other supplies. "At dark," according to an early history of the war,

a cold, heavy rain began to fall, which soon turned into sleet and snow, accompanied by fierce gusts of wintry wind. It was a night of great hardship and suffering. . . . For twelve long hours the men lay in the cold, pelting storm.

The plan was for the army to beseige the fort, while Flag Officer Andrew H. Foote's gunboats poured shells into it from the river and forced the garrison to surrender. Foote's flotilla steamed upriver on February 14th, but were met by deadly fire from the high ground above the river. Two of the gunboats were disabled, and Foote was wounded in the foot and forced to withdraw. It became evident that if the fort were to be taken, it would have to be by the ground forces.

Meanwhile, the Confederate commanders deliberated and decided that their only chance was to fight their way out by breaking through the Union lines upriver and escaping to open country toward Nashville. A force under General Pillow succeeded in breaking through the Union lines, not only leaving an open road for the garrison to make its escape, but also threatening to sweep the entire field. But Grant, who had been absent consulting with Admiral Foote, arrived on the field and ordered an all-out assault on the fort, which was captured by nightfall.

After several days of battle, the only course available to the Confederate defenders who had fought their way out was to escape with as many troops and resources as possible to fight again another day. The defeat at Fort Donelson was rather overwhelming to Loreta Velazquez:

> Immediately after the defeat at Fort Donelson, especially, I was greatly depressed in spirit, and it was long before I could shake off the disposition to shudder, and the feeling of intense melancholy, that overcame me to such an extent, that I almost resolved to give up the whole business, and to never allow myself to be put in the way of witnessing anything of the kind again.

She was sick, physically from exposure and fatigue, and mentally from the horrors of battle; it would take awhile to restore her health and spirits. Bob also had been taken sick during the battle. They made their way to Nashville to rest and recuperate.

10

Detective and Spy for the Confederacy

My experimental trip to Washington satisfied me that it was as a detective rather than as a soldier, that my best successes were to be won.
—Memoirs of LORETA JANETA VELAZQUEZ.

After the fall of Fort Donelson, the atmosphere in Nashville was electric with excitement. The southern cause had received a serious setback, and it was time for an agonizing reappraisal of military strategy. Velazquez found herself caught up in the turmoil and felt compelled to return to service sooner than she had planned. She felt she was needed now more than ever before to help prevent further Federal victories. Sending Bob away in charge of a friend, Velazquez reported to General Albert Sidney Johnston and asked for an assignment. She was again assigned to the detective corps.

Not long afterwards, however, she was wounded in the foot during a skirmish, and fearing detection by a surgeon slipped away to join Bob and to rest for a while. For that purpose she made her way to New Orleans and took up quarters at the Brooks House. The city was in turmoil, apprehensive of an attack, and authorities were alert to possible spies in their midst. Thinking she was among friends, Velazquez let her guard down:

> During the eight or nine months I had been wearing male attire, I had . . . seen a great deal of very hard service. My clothing was well worn, and my apparatus for disguising my form was badly out of order; and the result was, that I scarcely presented as creditable a manly appearance as I did upon the occasion of my last visit to New Orleans. . . . [I] had grown careless about a number of little matters that, when attended to properly, aided materially in maintaining my incognito.

Velazquez was thunderstruck when she was arrested on suspicion of being a spy and was taken before the provost marshal. She was outraged by the charge, but feared that if her identity were exposed at this point, her career would be over. Accordingly, she decided to put up a bold front. She would challenge them to prove anything against her:

> I entered a vigorous protest against the whole proceeding to the officer who made the arrest, and I could see, from his hesitating and indecisive manner, that he was in possession of no definite charge against me, and was inclined to be dubious about the propriety or legality of his action. . . . My protest, however, was of no avail.

The provost marshal quickly decided that there were no grounds for holding "Lieutenant Buford" and released him from custody. But the very next evening, Velazquez was again arrested, this time on suspicion of being a woman: "Now what I had so long dreaded was come to pass, and there was nothing to do but to get out of the difficulties which environed me the best way I could."

Taken before Mayor Monroe, she was interrogated and, assuming that she was a woman, he ordered her to change into female apparel. Velazquez demanded that he prove she was a woman. This disconcerted him, she says, but he put her in jail until the matter could be settled. While in jail a reporter interviewed her for a story, indicating that her circumstances had become generally known. She insisted to the reporter that a great mistake had been made.

Her next visitor was a Dr. Root of Charity Hospital, whom she felt knew she was a woman. Giving up the pretense, she confessed to Mayor Monroe, hoping he would release her immediately. To her surprise and disgust, he fined her and sentenced her to ten days in jail instead. (A contemporary news story reports that she was imprisoned for three months; see chapter notes.)

Eventually Velazquez was released: "At length, after long and impatient waiting, I was free once more; and now the problem was to get out of New Orleans as quickly as possible, before I was recognized by too many people." She hit on a plan that would get her quickly back into the army, though on a risky basis. Proceeding to the recruiting office, she enlisted in Captain B. Moses's company, of the 21st Louisiana Regiment. The company started for Fort Pillow next day to join the rest of the regiment.

As a formally enlisted soldier, instead of an independent officer,

her freedom of motion and independence would be severely re-
stricted, so she did not intend to continue in this role for long:

> In this manner I contrived to get clear of New Orleans, but, as I
> had no fancy for going on duty as a private soldier any longer than
> was absolutely necessary . . . my next thought was to resume my
> independent footing at the earliest moment.

Going privately to Brigadier General John B. Villepigue, commanding Fort Pillow, she showed him her commission as an officer,
making up some story to account for her enlistment. Since there
were no vacancies, Villepigue could not assign her the duties of an
officer. Therefore she applied for a transfer to the Army of East
Tennessee, which was "very cheerfully granted." Thus did she
extricate herself from enlisted soldier life and regain her independent status.

After some dalliances at Memphis, "Lieutenant Buford" and
friends were ordered to Corinth where a major battle was impending. Reporting to General William J. Hardee, she participated in
the initial attack at Pittsburg Landing (Shiloh) on April 6th that
overran the Federal camp. Afterwards, seeing her old company
recruited from Arkansas, she received permission from Hardee to
join it and reported to the captain, Thomas C. DeCaulp. They had
known each other in Pensacola during training, and DeCaulp was
delighted to see his old friend "Lieutenant Buford."

Another deeper relationship also existed between the two.
DeCaulp had also known Loreta as the wife of a friend, and when
he had been killed in a training accident, DeCaulp had courted the
widow. They had kept in touch mostly by mail and considered
themselves engaged to be married. What DeCaulp did not know
was that "Lieutenant Buford" and Loreta were one and the same
person.

As plans for resuming the battle commenced, Velazquez looked
around and saw a lot of familiar faces, and down the line saw the
11th Louisiana Regiment commanded by a friend, Colonel Sam
Marks. She looked forward eagerly to going into battle alongside
Captain DeCaulp and among other old friends.

When the battle resumed:

> We had not been long engaged before the second lieutenant of the
> company fell. I immediately stepped into his place, and assumed the
> command of his men. This action was greeted by a hearty cheer from
> the entire company, all the veterans of which, of course, knew me,

and I took the greeting as an evidence that they were glad to see their original commander with them once more.

At the close of the first day's battle the Confederates were successful at all points, but the advantage was not pressed. Velazquez had hoped for a great victory, but was disillusioned by what she observed of the leadership. That night, she reported, "a heavy rainstorm, in the middle of the night . . . drenched everyone to the skin, and seriously disturbed the slumbers of the wearied soldiers."

When the tide turned next day and what had seemed to be victory became defeat, she was furious, and considered giving up altogether. To make matters worse, she had been separated from DeCaulp and Bob had wandered off on the wrong road into Federal camp and disappeared.

> I remained in the woods all night, the roads being perfectly blocked up with the retreating army, trying to shield myself as best I could from the furious storm of rain and hail that came on, as if to add to the miseries which the wretched soldiers of the Confederacy were compelled to endure on their weary march back to Corinth. . . . I managed, however, after the worst of the storm was over, to find a tolerably dry place, where, completely used up by the fatigues I had undergone, I fell into a sound sleep.

Reflecting on events the next day as she headed back to Corinth, Velzaquez feared for the cause. She had experienced defeat for the second straight time, and began to think that plunging into battle might not be the best contribution she could make in the future. Perhaps she should stick to her previous decision and go into secret service instead.

Along the way to Corinth she came across the camp of the 11th Louisiana and stopped to visit. Captain G. Merrick Miller wanted to bury the dead of his company, so she started back toward the battlefield with him to help. While engaged in burying soldiers on the battlefield, Velazquez was knocked down and stunned by a sudden shellburst. Shrapnel severely wounded her in the right arm, which dangled helplessly.

A soldier helped her onto a horse and started back to camp with her, but the pain was excruciating:

> My fortitude began to give way before the terrible physical suffering I was compelled to endure; all my manliness oozed out long before I reached camp, and my woman's nature asserted itself with irresistible force. I could face deadly peril on the battlefield without

flinching, but this intolerable pain overcame me completely, and I longed to be where there would be no necessity for continuing my disguise, and where I could obtain shelter, rest, and attention as a woman. My pride, however, and a fear of consequences, prevented me from revealing my sex, and I determined to preserve my secret as long as it was possible to do so, hoping soon to reach some place where I could be myself again with impunity.

By the time they reached camp, her arm and hand were badly swollen, and her companion had to rip the sleeve of her coat in order to treat the wound with cold water. An ambulance was called, and she was taken to the railroad to be evacuated to the South. But the cars stopped at Corinth for two hours, so she sent for a young surgeon whom she knew and asked him to help relieve her suffering:

> He immediately examined my arm, and, as I perceived by the puzzled expression that passed over his face, he was beginning to suspect something, and guessing that further concealment would be useless, I told him who I really was. I never saw a more astonished man in my life.

Her shoulder was found to be dislocated, her arm cut, and a little finger lacerated. The surgeon dressed the wounds and put her arm in a sling. He urged her to stay in Corinth for treatment, but she persuaded him to obtain travel papers for her so she could press on to Grenada:

> Before the information that a woman, disguised as an officer, was among the wounded on the train, we were, to my infinite satisfaction, speeding out of sight, leaving behind me the camp occupied by a defeated army.

At Grenada she rested for two days, "visited by a great many ladies of the place, who presented me with bouquets, delicacies of various kinds, and bandages for my wound, and who otherwise overwhelmed me with attentions, for which I hope I was duly grateful." But restless and uncomfortable from her wounds, Velazquez had a strong desire to get far away from the army "before the fact that Lt. Harry T. Buford was a woman became generally known."

At Jackson she was too ill to go on, feverish, arm and shoulder inflamed. There, a widow and her daughter took her in and nursed her back to some semblance of health. Gradually she continued on to New Orleans. Once there she saw that the city was about to fall into Union hands, and so put away her uniform and resumed female garb. With the city under Federal occupation, she saw an opportunity for conducting secret service missions as a woman:

> I was very well satisfied to abandon, for a while at least, a soldier's life for the purpose of undertaking work more naturally congenial than campaigning, and for which my sex, combined with my soldierly training, peculiarly fitted me. My experimental trip to Washington satisfied me that it was as a detective, rather than as a soldier, that my best successes were to be won.

To establish her cover, Velazquez worked to gain the confidence of Federal officers in New Orleans by expressing Unionist sentiments, deliberately alienating some of her friends. This enhanced her credibility with the provost marshal and other authorities, who gave her passes to travel through the lines:

> I soon became known as one of the few advocates of the Federal Government in New Orleans, and not only secured myself from molestation, but gained the entire confidence of our new rulers. . . . It was better for me to risk the temporary loss of my friends, in the hope and expectation that vindication of my conduct would come with time, than to risk anything by an incautious word, or even look.

General Benjamin F. Butler, military governor, was her prime target. Ruling harshly, he was handing out severe penalties to spies who were apprehended by Union authorities. Starting a career as a blockade runner, Velazquez carried messages through the Federal blockade to Havana, Cuba, and contacted Confederate agents there. On the return trip, she smuggled in badly needed supplies and drugs. While "running the lines," she pretended to be an English widow in reduced circumstances waiting for money from home in order to return there. She had purchased a passport and other identification papers from an English woman who was sympathetic to the Confederate cause.

Eventually a Confederate officer to whom she had given some dispatches was captured, and the documents were traced back to her. Summarily arrested, she was taken before General Butler who tried to browbeat her into a confession. But the charges could not be proved. Taking refuge in her fake British citizenship, she persuaded the British consul to intervene and was released from prison.

Fearing recapture and exposure she tried to leave the city, but was refused a pass. Paying a fisherman to carry her across Lake Ponchartrain, she made a hurried escape, carrying a concealed six-shooter in case of betrayal. Fleeing to Jackson, Mississippi, she resumed disguise as "Lieutenant Harry T. Buford" and sought more detective or scouting duties, but nothing materialized and she became restless again. Hearing that Bob had escaped from the Federal camp after Shiloh and was in Grenada, she went there and was reunited with him.

Deciding that she could accomplish more in the East, Velazquez headed for Richmond with thoughts of establishing herself as a spy for the Confederate government. She had not counted on the fact that authorities in the beleaguered city were alerted to suspicious-looking strangers. Accordingly, she was quickly arrested on suspicion of being a woman in disguise; her disguise, she said, was "not in good order."

General John Henry Winder, provost marshal general, had a rigorous martial law in effect, and all strangers entering the city were closely watched. Once under observation, she surmised: "Some lynx-eyed detective was not long in noting certain feminine ways I had, and which even my long practice in figuring as a man had not enabled me to get rid of."

"Lieutenant Buford" was unceremoniously deposited in Castle Thunder, one of the major Richmond prisons during the war. But good luck sometimes comes in odd ways. The superintendent of prisons, G. W. Alexander, and his wife befriended Velzaquez and treated her so kindly and considerately that she was induced to tell them her whole story and what her aspirations were in regard to secret service. Although shocked that a woman would take on male disguise, they took a strong interest in her cause, and Alexander interceded with General Winder.

At last, her dream was realized and she received an official assignment in the secret service corps. General Winder immediately put her to a test, sending her off with dispatches for General Earl Van Dorn. However, the "dispatches" were nothing but blank papers and a letter explaining the trick he was putting her through. Then he telegraphed ahead to the provost marshal in Charlotte, North Carolina, to have her arrested when the train stopped there.

Accordingly, at Charlotte a guard took her into custody and demanded to see the papers in her pocket. But Velazquez perceived that the guard was not accustomed to arresting officers, and so refused to acknowledge his authority. The guard showed his orders, which were correct, but she still refused to comply. Instead, she offered to return to Richmond with the papers and report to General Winder. This confused the guard who thought there must be some mistake, and he didn't know quite how to proceed. "Lieutenant Buford" suggested that he send a telegram back to headquarters asking for further instructions. This satisfied the guard that he must be making a mistake, and soon she was released and on her way again; her bluff had worked.

When the package was delivered to General Van Dorn, he read the letter, looked at "Lieutenant Buford," and laughed. "This might be good fun for Van Dorn and Winder," she later wrote, "but I did not particularly admire having been sent all this distance on such a fool's errand, and was very much disposed to resent it." On reflection, she realized that she had carried out her orders and avoided the snares set in her path, and so had reason to be satisfied.

Back at Richmond, Velazquez settled down to carry out assignments for the secret service. All was not well, however. Her arm was still stiff and sore from the wounds, rumors were floating around about her, and she was having trouble with her disguise:

> It seemed to be an impossibility for me now to avoid getting into continual trouble about my disguise. Not only were a number of people fully informed of all the particulars of my career since the outbreak of the war, but it began to be whispered about among the soldiers and citizens that a woman dressed as a man had been discovered, and some highly-exaggerated rumors with regard to my exploits were diligently circulated. My having received a wound . . . appeared to be a particularly attractive episode to the minds of many people; and my performances at that battle were believed, in some quarters, to have been of a most extraordinary nature . . . I was credited with exploits of unparalleled heroism.

Shortly after returning from Van Dorn's headquarters, while on a trip to Lynchburg she was again arrested on charge of being a woman in disguise. Since her notoriety had preceded her, curious crowds gathered to see the Confederate heroine. But Velazquez was not prepared to give up yet:

> My position was a most unpleasant one, and it required very skillful management for me to play the part of a man to advantage. What gave piquancy to the situation was, that, while it was generally believed that I was a woman . . . my visitors were none of them quite sure which sex I belonged to, and all their efforts were directed to solving the mystery.

On one occasion, hearing feminine voices and footsteps approaching up the stairs of the second-floor jail cell, she braced herself for the ordeal:

> During the two years and more I had been wearing male attire, I had not only learned the general carriage of a man, but had picked up a good many little masculine traits, which I had practiced until I was quite perfect in them. . . . When I heard these visitors coming, I stuck my feet up on the window-sill, and, just as they were opening the door, I turned my head, and spat."

This ruse seemed to convince the mother and daughter who had come to lecture her that the prisoner must be a man after all.

Another visitor was a "motherly old lady" who began grilling the prisoner about her gall in pretending to be a man if she were really a woman. When Velazquez offered to reveal her sex to the woman,

> It had an astonishing effect. . . . She got red in the face, her eyes flashed, and, muttering something that I did not hear, she bounced out of the room, leaving me to enjoy a hearty laugh at the comical termination of the adventure.

Finally, with nothing being resolved by local authorities, Velazquez obtained her release from jail in Lynchburg and proceeded to Charlotte, North Carolina. It was now the summer of 1863. Lee was back in Virginia after the battle of Gettysburg, and the impending action was in Tennessee. General William S. Rosecrans was on the march, and General James Longstreet was detached from Lee's army at Richmond to reinforce General Braxton Bragg.

At Charlotte, she met a number of old friends and acquaintances who were awaiting transportation to various points. Velazquez determined to head into Tennessee with Longstreet's forces to join the action and perhaps win some distinction. She managed to talk her way onto Longstreet's train, headed south.

On reaching Atlanta, Velazquez received a number of letters from relatives, for the first time in months. Two were from her father, one from a sister in Latin America, and one from her brother who (she learned for the first time) was serving in the Confederate army in the Trans–Mississippi Department. Her brother was not aware of her male disguise.

At Atlanta she also learned that Captain DeCaulp, whom she had not seen since the battle of Shiloh, was with Van Dorn's army near Spring Hill, Tennessee. Eager to resume the "strange court-ship," she even considered telling DeCaulp the truth. She felt a strong impulse to go to him, and if necessary, abandon army life and resume conventional life as a woman. Her obvious indecision about what she wanted to do, whether to be a soldier or a spy, apparently led her to consider a third alternative.

Heading toward Spring Hill to see him, she fell in with Brigadier General John Pegram's cavalry. En route, she saw "the handsome General Frank Armstrong, an officer for whom I entertained an intense admiration." Unable to reach Van Dorn's camp due to the shifting military situation, Velazquez was forced to change her plans, and turned back to Ringgold, Georgia.

Impatient for action, she decided once more on some free-lance secret service work. She would penetrate enemy lines dressed as a woman and gather information about the strength and disposition of the Union forces. Donning female garb from an abandoned farmhouse, she hid her uniform and other gear in an ash barrel, ate a makeshift meal from leftover supplies, and headed toward the Union lines. Unlike a single soldier in battle, she mused, her present activity depended entirely on her own skill and ingenuity, an individual contest of wits with the enemy; this she found exhilarating. Unfortunately, she felt, spies were generally held in low regard:

> According to all military law, he [the spy] is an outlaw, and is liable to be hung if detected. . . . Nothing has been left undone to render the labors of the spy not only perilous in the extreme, but infamous; and yet the spy is nothing more nor less than a detective officer, and there cannot be any good and sufficient reason assigned for the discredit which attaches to the occupation. (Sarah Emma Edmonds expressed very similar views on the ignoble reputation of spying.)

Using the name "Mrs. Williams" and representing herself as a widow trying to escape the Confederacy to join friends in the North, she asked to see General Rosecrans. After questioning her at some length, he gave her a pass to go north. Making her way to Martinsburg, West Virginia, she checked into a hotel. There she made the acquaintance of a Federal quartermaster. Claiming to be from Cincinnati, she enlisted his help in search of a brother, "Dick," whom she said was missing and presumed killed or wounded.

The little game I was playing with the quartermaster will serve as a very fair specimen of the methods which a secret service agent is compelled to use for the purposes of gaining such information as is desired. A spy, or a detective, must have a quick eye, a sharp ear, a retentive memory, and a talent for taking advantage of small, and apparently unimportant points, as aids for the object in view. . . . Among other things, I had learned the name of a Federal soldier belonging to General [William W.] Averill's command, and I made a mental note of it for future reference . . . my purpose now was to use it as a means of making the Federal officer by my side at the hotel table useful to me.

At her request, the officer went to headquarters and learned that the missing brother had been killed. Feigning tears and acting distraught, she asked where he was buried so that she might visit the grave. He arranged for an ambulance to take them to the gravesite.

My escort proved to be so exceedingly communicative, that before we returned to the hotel, I was informed of the exact number of troops in the neighborhood, their positions, their commanders, where the enemy were supposed to be located, who they were commanded by, the results of the recent conflicts, and a variety of other matters of more or less importance. The man was as innocent and as unsuspicious as a new-born babe, and I could scarcely keep from laughing sometimes at the eagerness he displayed in telling me all manner of things that, had he been possessed of ordinary common sense, he would never have revealed to anyone, much less to a total stranger, with regard to whose antecedents he knew absolutely nothing.

Realizing that the information in her possession would be valuable to Confederate commanders if conveyed to them quickly, she slipped through the Union lines that night and passed on what she had learned to Colonel John S. Mosby's command. Then, "with the extraordinary good luck which so often attends bold ventures," she succeeded in getting back to the hotel undetected.

After another week, Velazquez learned something that induced her to return south to Chattanooga. There she represented herself as a soldier's wife trying to see her husband, and she was allowed to stay within the Federal lines. Returning to the farmhouse where she had concealed her uniform, she found the buildings in charred ruins! After searching through the debris, she managed to find her uniform still intact within the ash barrel where she had concealed it.

Making her way back inside the Confederate lines by crawling through the underbrush, she resumed the guise of an officer. When she tried to present herself as an escaped prisoner from Morgan's command, the officer who interviewed her scanned her papers skeptically. These consisted of her transportation pass and

> the letter to General Polk, which had been given to me in the early part of the war. . . . I was much afraid lest he should suspect something, for I had no mustache, and having become somewhat bleached, was not by any means so masculine in appearance as I had been at one time. I, however, bore his scrutiny without flinching, and he apparently did not know what to do but to receive me for what I appeared to be.

After being fed, and debriefed on what she had learned about the Federal army, Velazquez slept until noon. In the afternoon she borrowed a horse and rode to Dalton, Georgia, where she learned that Captain DeCaulp was sick at Atlanta. She resolved to go there and see him one way or the other. However, quite by accident she reinjured the foot that had been wounded at Fort Donelson, and was so lame that she was sent to Atlanta for medical treatment.

Checking into a hotel, "Lieutenant Buford" was immediately surrounded by a bunch of officers who wanted to know how things were going at the front. After a while she had a quarrel with one of them, a General F., whose drunken and insulting manner she found offensive, but friends persuaded her to go to her room.

That night her condition worsened; her foot was sore and she became feverish. So she was sent to the Empire Hosptial where she was treated first by a Dr. Hammond and then by a Dr. Hay. There she learned that DeCaulp was close by, in Dr. Benton's ward which was adjacent to that of Dr. Hay. Increasingly, she longed to reveal her secret to him and marry him. Meanwhile, she tossed and turned feverishly on her sick bed, taking stock of "the strange life I had been leading."

> I had some understanding now of what the great discoverers, adventurers, and soldiers, who were the idols of my childhood imagination, had been compelled to go through with before they won the undying fame that was theirs, and I comprehended, to some degree, how hard a thing it was to win fame. For myself, I had played my part in the great drama of war with what skill I could command; and, although I had not played it altogether unsuccessfully, the chances that fame and the applause of future ages would be mine, seemed as remote as ever.

Loreta Janeta Velazquez found herself disappointed, frustrated, and in poor health. "I was following a will-o'-the-wisp in striving to gain for myself a great name by heroic deeds," she mused. "I had had enough of this, and . . . it was time for me to exchange my uniform for the attire of my own sex once more, and in good earnest, with the intention of never resuming it again."

In this reflective mood, she recalled vividly a romantic Spanish tale from her youth in Cuba, because of certain resemblances it had to her own experiences. It was called "The Story of Estela."

"The heroines of these old Spanish romances," Velazquez noted, "seem to have a decided fancy for masquerading in male attire, and it is not unlikely that this propensity on their part had some effect in encouraging in me a desire to assume the dress of the other sex for the purpose of seeking adventures."

The fair Estela was beloved by a handsome, rich, and gallant young man, Don Carlos, and was deeply in love with him. Eventually a young and wealthy grandee also fell in love with Estela, and became a favorite of her parents. Don Carlos was forbidden to see her, but with her maid and his page making arrangements for them, they met secretly.

During their secret courtship, Don Carlos's page took sick and died. Not long afterwards, a handsome youth applied for the position of page, and was soon taken into his confidence. The youth, however, was a woman who had fallen in love with Don Carlos and had taken the extreme measure of pretending to be a boy in order to be near him and to try to win his love.

This new page—the female pretender—was soon employed as a messenger between Don Carlos and Estela. Very quickly she realized that Estela stood in her way in her effort to win over Don Carlos, and that her rival must be removed. So she set out to devise a plan that would accomplish that purpose.

An opportunity arose when Estela alerted Don Carlos that her parents were trying to pressure her into a quick wedding with the grandee. Don Carlos realized that, unless he acted decisively, he would lose her, so he persuaded her to elope with him.

The young page, of course, was informed of their plans and quickly decided on her own course of action. With the date of elopement set, Estela wrote a letter to her parents explaining her reasons for avoiding their planned match and announcing her intention to elope with Don Carlos. The page was entrusted to deliver

Estela to a rendezvous with Don Carlos, but instead betrayed the trust by delivering her to Moorish pirates who carried her off to Algiers to be sold as a slave. As a precaution against treachery, however, the pirates forced the page to go with them. Thus Estela learned that her betrayer was a woman, and the reason for her action.

When Estela's disappearance was discovered, the only clue was her letter to her parents. Don Carlos was accused of spiriting her away, and suspected of having murdered her. The grief-stricken Don Carlos was overwhelmed by the accusations. But as time passed and nothing was heard of her, he began to believe that she had been false to him and had run away with the (presumably male) page. Suspicion of him increased and a murder trial was ordered. Don Carlos fled to Italy and joined the army of the emperor Charles V as a common soldier.

Meanwhile, after many strange adventures, Estela managed to make her escape in male disguise and she, too, joined the army of the emperor. In a skirmish thereafter, she had occasion to save the life of the emperor, who—not suspecting her to be a woman— appointed her to an important position in his entourage. In time, she became the emperor's favorite officer and he showered honors on her. But she longed to return to Spain and seek out Don Carlos.

One day Estela was amazed to encounter a soldier in the ranks who reminded her strongly of Don Carlos. After some conversation, she realized that it really was him. Without revealing her identity to him, she befriended him and gradually drew out his story, including the fact that he doubted Estela's honor. Before telling him who she was, Estela wanted to change his opinion of her. She made Don Carlos her secretary, and in almost daily conversation tried to persuade him that Estela might be guiltless. Although he confessed that he still loved Estela despite her behavior, Don Carlos could not be persuaded that there might be an innocent explanation for her disappearance.

At length, Estela learned that the governor of her native city had died, and she applied to the emperor for the position. Her request was granted, and Don Carlos went with her, feeling that he would be safe as part of the new governor's household, or at least he would receive a fair trial. However, when Don Carlos appeared, Estela's parents pressed charges against him. The governor (Estela) promised that justice would be done, and he remained free in her custody.

In the days leading up to the trial, she redoubled her efforts to make him acknowledge that Estela might be faithful after all. Finally he confessed that, deep down inside, he had faith in her and dreamed some day of being reunited with her.

On the day of the trial, Estela sat as chief magistrate with the other judges to hear the case. Witnesses related the story of Estela's disappearance. Her letter announcing her intention of eloping with Don Carlos was produced. The servants who knew about their secret meetings told what they knew. The accused could only deny his guilt.

The governor and chief magistrate (Estela) sternly announced that the only way his innocence could be proved was by the appearance of Estela, but that if she could not be produced, it would be necessary to condemn the accused in view of the weight of evidence. Don Carlos threw himself at the feet of the governor, reminding "him" of confessing privately to his love for Estela, and asking that true justice be done despite the circumstantial evidence against him.

Moved by his entreaties and unable to restrain herself, Estela proclaimed to the assembly that she knew Don Carlos to be innocent and would order his release. A loud murmur of disapproval arose. The governor, commanding silence, then revealed herself to the astonished audience as the lost Estela. She asked for Don Carlos's forgiveness for the trials she had put him through while testing his faith in and love for her. They were married and, of course, lived happily ever after. Don Carlos was appointed governor in place of Estela, who preferred to resume her female identity.

Velazquez notes that the only reason for including this story in the narrative of her personal adventures

> was because it was so much in my thoughts at the particular period of which I am now writing, and because it inspired me to imitate Estela's example so far as to seek to obtain a confession of love from Captain DeCaulp, before I should reveal myself to him. I was filled with an eager desire to hear what he would say of me to his friend, the supposed Lieutenant Buford.

Loreta Janeta Velazquez yearned for a "happy ending."

Stratagems and Wiles

*I have now to tell, not of battles and sieges, but of stratagems
and wiles.*
            —Memoirs of LORETA JANETA VELAZQUEZ.

Captain Thomas C. DeCaulp was delighted to see his old friend
"Lieutenant Buford," who dropped in for a visit unannounced in
Dr. Benton's ward of the Empire Hospital in Atlanta. They had
known each other in Pensacola, and had fought together at Shiloh.
For her part, Velazquez was primed for a resolution of their strange
courtship. She had every intention of revealing her secret to him,
provided she could hear directly from him an expression of his love
for her, in the manner of her fictional childhood heroine Estela.
Ever since her husband's death in a training accident at Pensacola,
she and DeCaulp had stayed in touch, and they considered themselves engaged to be married. But wartime assignments had kept
them apart.

"Lieutenant Buford" found DeCaulp worn and haggard, but
apparently on the way to recovery. During their conversation, he
pulled out her photograph and expressed his love for Miss Velazquez, pointing out that he had not seen her for three years. Loreta
was hard-pressed to choke back her emotions, but she was hesitant
to reveal the truth for fear that he would react negatively to her
masquerade as a male soldier. Should she reveal the truth to him?

Abruptly, she reached over and took the picture of herself out
of his pocket, and asked him whether he was sure he had not seen
somebody like that within three years. She wondered if he would
look at the real thing standing there and suddenly realize the truth.
DeCaulp, puzzled by the question, silently looked at the picture
and then at her, without recognition.

"Well, captain," she finally said, "don't you think the picture of your lady-love looks the least bit like your friend Harry Buford?" DeCaulp, suddenly taken aback, gasped for air; perspiration broke out on his forehead. Grasping her hand, he asked breathlessly, "Can it be possible that you are she?" Anxiously, Velazquez confirmed her identity and asked the astonished DeCaulp, "Will you despise her because she was not willing to stay at home like other women, but undertook to appear on the battle-field in the guise of a man?" To her great relief, DeCaulp replied, "I love you ten times more than ever for this, Loreta."

Assured of his love, Velazquez went into a long explanation of her reasons for acting as she had, and outlined her adventures to him. But realizing that DeCaulp still was very weak and that they both were agitated by the interview, she broke it off, promising to see him again soon. They had agreed to marry, and she was "supremely happy."

After a brief side trip to Alabama on business, she returned next day to the hospital and found DeCaulp out of bed and much improved. Together they went to the Thompson House where she engaged a room and set about preparing the wedding. To avoid gossip and sensation, DeCaulp and Velazquez took Drs. Benton and Hammond into their confidence, telling them the whole story and asking them to witness the ceremony. Loreta obtained a wedding dress, "the main thing being that I should be dressed as a woman when the ceremony took place, for fear of creating too much of a sensation, and, perhaps, of making the clergyman feel unpleasant should I appear before him, hanging on the captain's arm, in my uniform."

Next day they were married in the parlor of the Thompson House by the Rev. Mr. Pinkington, the post chaplain. They looked forward to a pleasant life together after the war. When Velazquez expressed her desire to continue in uniform and accompany her husband into the field (contrary to her previous decision to give it all up), he argued that she had done enough and should now devote herself to their future together. Reluctantly, she assented. After a brief honeymoon, he felt well enough to report for duty, "notwithstanding my entreaties for him to remain until his health was more robust." She felt that he was not as healthy as he should be to face the vigors of army life. But he persisted, and left to report to his command. Before he got there, however, DeCaulp had a relapse, was taken prisoner, and died in a Federal hospital in Chattanooga.

DeCaulp's unexpected death was devastating to Velazquez. She felt that it left her "nothing to do but to launch once more on a life of adventure, and to devote my energies to the advancement of the Confederate cause." Sadder and wiser, she was fed up with her heroic vision and reluctant to go on as "Lieutenant Harry Buford":

> My secret was now known to a great many persons, and its discovery had already caused me such annoyance that I hesitated about assuming my uniform again. . . . I had seen enough of fighting, enough of marching, enough of camp life, enough of prisons and hospitals, and I had passed through enough peril and suffering to satisfy any reasonable human being.

She was weary of war and

> getting out of the notion of subjecting myself to the liability of being locked up by every local magistrate within whose jurisdiction I happened to find myself, simply because I did not elect to dress according to his notions of propriety. . . . On reviewing the whole subject in my mind, I became more than ever convinced that the secret service rather than the army would afford me the best field for the exercise of my talent.

While she had been in the hospital, General Bragg had gained an important victory at Chickamauga (September 19–20, 1863). Lee was successfully defending Richmond. The South was holding on, hoping that antiwar sentiment in the North would turn the tide, or that England or France would intercede on the side of the Confederacy. Though there had been some serious setbacks, the situation was not hopeless.

In the fall of 1863, Velazquez returned to Richmond and called on General Winder and President Davis, seeking a secret service appointment. Neither obliged her, but finally Winder gave her a letter of recommendation to the commanding officer of Confederate forces in the South and West and authorized transportation papers for her. This was not exactly what she had wanted, but at least it opened the door for her to strike a blow for the Confederacy.

At Mobile, Alabama, Velazquez took up residence at the Battle House, where she met a number of officers whom she had known on various battlefields. While there, she received a mysterious note one day asking her to meet the writer on a certain street corner. No reason was given. She hesitated, but decided to go through with it, and was met by a Lieutenant Shorter of Arkansas. He recruited her for an important secret service assignment ("especially," he said, "as you seem to have a talent for disguising yourself") to penetrate enemy lines and deliver a dispatch to a certain party. If interested, she was to meet him next day in Meridian, Mississippi, for final instructions.

At a hotel in Meridian, Shorter informed her that they had captured a spy from Federal General Stephen A. Hurlbut's command who had important papers giving accurate information about the forces and the movements of several Confederate generals. The Confederates proposed to play a counterintelligence game by falsifying the papers to throw the Federal forces off the track. Velazquez was to take the altered papers to Memphis and see that they were delivered to General Cadwallader C. Washburn and convince him that it was accurate intelligence. Also, Shorter had a dispatch for General Nathan Bedford Forrest that she was to deliver to a Confederate agent in Memphis.

Velazquez was given letters of introduction to various Confederates who could assist her along the way, and a password to allow her to communicate with the Memphis agent. At Lieutenant Shorter's suggestion, she impersonated a poor countrywoman whose husband was lost in the war, seeking protection in Federal lines after being badly treated by the rebels. Although her health still was not good, Velazquez found the opportunity appealing and was determined to proceed.

As she approached the Federal lines, Velazquez made contact with the lieutenant in charge of pickets, who would prove to be a valuable—if unwitting—ally. After listening to her story about having papers for General Washburn, the lieutenant personally escorted her on the Memphis and Charleston Railroad to headquarters at Memphis. Since her credibility was greatly enhanced by having a Union escort, she played up to him with flattery, and he seemed attracted to her and looking for a conquest. In answer to questions about her personal life, she told the officer that she was foreign born, had French and Spanish parents, and that her deceased husband had lived in Ohio. Her interest now, she told him, was to return to Europe as soon as possible.

When they arrived at Memphis, the lieutenant engaged a carriage and escorted her to headquarters, where she was ushered in to see the provost marshal. Thanks to the lieutenant's presence, she was not unduly questioned. She told the provost marshal that she was carrying a dispatch and a confidential message from a spy within Confederate lines that she was to deliver personally to General Washburn. However, the general was said to be indisposed and unable to see her. As a last resort she wrote out a note to the general explaining the circumstances and handed over the altered dispatch, expecting the general to contact her later.

Next the lieutenant escorted her to the Hardwick House hotel, where she registered as "Mrs. Fowler." After disposing of the lieutenant by telling him she was tired and needed to rest, asking him to call again in the morning, Velazquez set out to accomplish the other part of her mission. Obtaining some better clothes with the help of hotel personnel, she set out to contact the Confederate agent to deliver the dispatch for General Forrest. Since she had a description of the Memphis agent, Velazquez recognized him on sight and, giving the password, was quickly admitted to his room. She delivered the dispatch, along with verbal instructions from Lieutenant Shorter, and urged the man to get it to General Forrest at once. However, the agent was concerned about imminent movements of Federal troops and asked her to find out what she could at headquarters before he set out on his mission to Forrest's command. To avoid being seen together, they agreed on a means of communicating messages.

While returning to her hotel, Velazquez was startled to see approaching her from the other direction none other than her Federal lieutenant friend, walking along with another officer. "My heart leaped into my mouth when I saw who it was," she said, "but as there was no retreat, I trusted to the darkness and my change of costume, and glided by them as swiftly and quietly as I could, and fortunately was able to gain my room without discovery."

Next morning the smitten lieutenant dutifully called on her and increased his attentions. Since she had pretended to be short of money, he raised some for her, and also helped her obtain better clothes. After a while, other officers and an officer's wife came to call. Velazquez was something of a celebrity, a poor but honest and patriotic woman who had brought important information to headquarters. In casual conversations with her newfound friends, she learned the disposition and numbers of Federal troops and conveyed this information to the waiting Confederate agent, who started at once for Forrest's headquarters. Among other things she had learned that there was a concentration of troops at Colliersville, anticipating an attack in that area, but this left a gap in the Federal line beyond Grand Junction.

A day or two later word was received that Forrest was on a grand raid through western Tennessee. After several weeks, Forrest slipped back past Federal lines into Mississippi, with cattle and other booty. Velazquez felt that her work, in concert with the other Confederate agents, had played an important role in the success of Forrest's raid.

The Federal lieutenant reported back to camp, but returned a day or two later with a 10-day leave and bringing an extra horse for her. While she bided her time, she allowed the lieutenant to escort her around, and went riding with him. They even attended church together. One Sunday at church, she recognized a man in the congregation, in civilian clothes, as a Confederate officer who was in her brother's command. He did not know her as a woman, but had seen her as "Lieutenant Harry Buford." After church she followed the man, with the Federal lieutenant on her arm, hoping to find an opportunity to inquire about her brother. She saw him go to the Hardwick House hotel and, excusing the lieutenant, quickly followed, but the man had vanished.

Later that evening, going to dinner with the lieutenant, she spotted the man in the hotel dining room and maneuvered her escort to a table next to him. Scribbling a note on a card, she directed the lieutenant's attention elsewhere and quickly dropped the note on the floor in plain view of the Confederate officer. He dropped his napkin on top of the card, and stooped to pick it up. The note read: "Meet me at my room, at half past ten o'clock this evening, unobserved. Important." When the man later got up to leave, she turned and gave him a meaningful look to reinforce her message.

That night at the appointed time he showed up at her room, and was perplexed when she promptly identified him as "Lieutenant B. of Arkansas." But at the mention of her brother's name, his face brightened up and he was visibly relieved. From him she learned that her brother had been captured about four months ago and was a prisoner at Camp Chase, Ohio. As a result of this news, she gave up her plans to return to Mobile and decided to go north to visit her brother, and assist him in any way she could. The news was an additional inducement to practice her secret service skills in the North, something she had thought about for a long time. Lieutenant B. gave her names of various Confederate agents or sympathizers who might be in a position to help her.

Her Federal lieutenant suitor was dismayed to learn that Velazquez was leaving. His attentions had been getting more ardent every day, and he obviously hoped for a conquest. She told him she was going to New York, and promised to write him from there. Although disappointed, the Lieutenant obtained a pass and transportation papers for her from General Washburn, and she was on her way.

In Columbus, Ohio, she took a room at the Neil House, then called on the general in command at Camp Chase. Pretending to be a strong Unionist from New York, she asked to visit her "rebel brother." The request was granted and she was given a permit and directed to Tod Barracks. "I found a one-armed major in command," she wrote. "He told me that he had lost his arm in the Mexican war." Her brother was brought in for an emotional reunion, as they had been separated for a long time. Discreetly, the major let them use his private room to talk. Once they were alone she instructed him to refer to her as his "Union sister from New York." She promised to try to arrange his release.

Later, at her hotel, she discovered that Governor John Brough of Ohio was staying there, and she arranged for an introduction. "He took quite a fancy to me," she wrote, "so much so, that he promised to use his influence to obtain a parole for my brother." Governor Brough kept his word, and her brother was released in her custody, with instructions to report first to General George Cadwallader in Philadelphia and then to General John A. Dix in New York City, where he was supposed to stay with her. Then, leaving her brother in New York City, she proceeded to Washington, D.C., to seek spying opportunities for the Confederate cause.

It was now the winter of 1863–1864. Velazquez took stock of the situation. She could see the relative wealth and prosperity of the North, and realized that the South might lose by sheer force of numbers. But the growing antiwar sentiment in the North and the presidential campaign offered some hope, as did strong sentiments against conscription. Draft riots and secret societies for resisting the draft had spread across the North by 1863. She resolved to use her skills in the enemy homeland in any way that would help the cause, even by encouraging political dissension and supporting the antiwar movement.

During this period of her life, Velazquez expressed sentiments very similar to those of Sarah Emma Edmonds, her Union counterpart:

It is impossible for me to reflect upon some of the features of my career as a Confederate secret service agent at the North with anything but regret that I should have been forced by circumstances to do what I did, or to associate with the men I did. [She characterizes her account of those activities as a] plain, unadorned statement of the enterprises in which I was engaged during the last eighteen months of the war.

Velazquez set out to establish contacts with the authorities in Richmond, as well as Confederate agents across the North and in Canada. She also worked on building up her social contacts with Federal officials and officers. Finally her efforts paid off when she obtained an introduction to Colonel La Fayette C. Baker, chief of detectives for the War Department. She described him as having a "wiry frame" and eyes that were a "cold gray. I have felt cold creeps all over me as he looked me straight in the eyes and spoke in that cutting tone of voice he was in the habit of using on occasions."

Since Baker was reputed to be very successful at catching Confederate spies, Velazquez felt she should get to know him and study him. Applying for a position in Baker's service, she expressed bitterness toward the South and claimed to have been treated badly by southerners. She expressed her motives as being both monetary (for self-support) and revenge. Since no position was offered right away, she went to visit her brother in New York City.

In New York she found that her brother was on the verge of being paroled to the South, and Confederate agents were after him to carry some documents. But he was being cautious about it. She contacted the agents and revealed herself to them sufficiently to obtain cooperation, and they asked her to do some work for them. Her brother was then exchanged, and delivered a verbal message to Richmond officials on her behalf.

Working with the New York City Confederate agents, Velasquez honed her skills by undertaking various minor missions. Meanwhile, she kept in touch with Colonel Baker, making it a point to give him some information that would be useful in breaking up fraudulent practices by Federal contractors. Gradually, she gained his confidence while operating right under his nose. Eventually Baker used her services and she became a double agent, maintaining the deception for almost eighteen months.

During the summer and fall of 1864, as Confederate fortunes ebbed, the secret service activities increasingly turned toward "back door" operations out of Canada to confuse and harrass the Federal forces and undermine support for the war. Various plots were hatched, many bordering on desperation measures. Schemes were afoot to raid northern towns, to liberate Confederate prisoners at Johnson's Island on Lake Erie and elsewhere, to organize escapees into a makeshift army, to engage in guerilla warfare and create diversions in the North, and the like. There was even a futile attempt in November to torch New York City and occupy it.

Velazquez was to play a role in the attack on Johnson's Island, and had her instructions from Richmond. Approaching Colonel Baker, she claimed to have information that a noted Confederate spy had been captured and imprisoned in the North. She proposed to go to Richmond and pass herself off as a Confederate to learn not only who the spy was and where he was imprisoned, but also what he and his colleagues might be planning. She knew that this would appeal to him, because the rumors of planned raids on northern prisons were widespread and Baker was concerned about them.

Initially reluctant and skeptical that she could pull it off, Baker finally consented to let her try, warning her that if caught, she might hang. Baker arranged passes for her through Union lines, and once clear of them, she had no problem entering Richmond since she was able to identify herself and her real mission to Confederate authorities. Once there, Velazquez immediately delivered various communications from agents in the North and in turn received information about plans for the northern raids to carry to Canada. On her return North, she was so laden with important Confederate documents that she took a wide detour via Parkersburg, West Virginia, just to play it safe. From there she made her way to Baltimore. While staying at the Barnum's Hotel in Baltimore, she found herself short of funds and ill, and was forced to send for a doctor.

Always resourceful, she obtained some funds from a storekeeper whose name had been given to her in case of emergency, and she made the acquaintance of a young Federal captain at the hotel, telling him a story about her bitterness toward the South. The pliant captain introduced her to General E. B. Tyler, who arranged a pass to New York for her. From Baltimore, she conducted some business in Delaware, rendezvousing with a blockade-runner, and then on to Philadelphia where she took a room at the Continental Hotel. There a communication was received that she quotes, indicating that she was using the cover name "Mrs. Sue Battle." Moving on to New York City, she took lodging at Taylor's Hotel.

Once in New York City, Velazquez learned that some Federal detectives were on her trail, and she feared that Colonel Baker had found her out. Running scared, she set out for Canada carrying letters, orders, packages, and a very large sum of money that would be impossible to account for if it were discovered. At the train depot she spotted a detective following her, but thought she had shaken him until the train arrived in Rochester: "To my infinite horror, he entered the car where I was, and took a seat near me," she later wrote. When the conductor came through, the detective said something to him that she couldn't hear and showed him a photograph. The conductor shook his head, and she heard the detective say, "I'll catch her yet."

Sizing up the situation, Velazquez resolved to talk directly to the detective, hoping to confuse and mislead him. She struck up a conversation, trying to learn how much they knew about her. To her dismay, she found out that they knew quite a bit about her, including the fact that she was on the way to Canada carrying important information and a large sum of money. Something critically important that the detective did *not* know about her was exactly what she looked like.

Upon arrival in Canada, the detective gallantly carried her satchel off the train (documents, money, and all), unaware of its contents. "I took the satchel from him, and thanking him for his attention, proceeded to get out of his sight as expeditiously as I could."

Once in Canada, Velazquez met with agents there, delivering dispatches and participating in long conferences about proposed raids on Federal prisons in the Great Lakes area. Her assignment included a visit to Johnson's Island to alert Confederate prisoners to the planned raids and to enlist their aid in plans to "liberate" them in order to open a "second front" or initiate guerilla activities in the North, the goal being to divert Union forces from southern fronts. In order to accomplish her mission, she needed to exploit her connection with Colonel Baker, so she returned to Washington, "not without many apprehensions."

Velazquez announced herself to Baker as being "just back from Richmond," and was greeted cordially. She told him that she had learned the name of the Confederate spy she had set out to discover on his behalf, some description of him which would help identify him, and also that he was believed to be at Johnson's Island. Playing a dangerous "double agent" game, she fed him a mixture of truth and fiction about what she had learned in Richmond.

It was a very delicate situation. On the one hand, she was working for Baker and his agency as a "trainee" spy, trying to gain his confidence while funneling whatever information she could to him in good conscience, mostly about fraud and corruption by Government contractors. On the other hand, she was trying to exploit her connection with him to gain access into northern prisons while helping to plan the northern raids. "I had much confidence in my own power of reading character and detecting motives," she said. Yet, she never felt sure whether Baker was taken in by her stories, suspected her, or even had definite information about her. It was enough to give her the "creeps."

Next day, Baker approved her proposed trip. She was encouraged to go to Johnson's Island or other northern prisons in order to track down the alleged spy and find out what he was up to, including possible plans for a prison break. It was agreed that she would pass herself off as a Confederate secret service agent intimating that something was afoot as to the rescue or release of Confederate prisoners. Baker was eager to learn whether any escape or rescue plans were in the works.

Baker then confided in her:

> Some of my people are after a spy now who has been travelling between Richmond and Canada, but they don't seem to be able to lay their hands on her. If they don't catch her soon, I have half a mind to let you try what you can do, if you succeed well with your present trip.

"I could not help smiling at the idea of Baker employing me to catch myself," she said.

The presidential elections were now a few weeks away and the Democratic candidate was George B. McClellan, the soldiers' hero. But Velazquez had more hopes for the northern raids than for McClellan's election. She headed west as a secret agent for Baker, via Parkersburg, West Virginia, Cincinnati, Ohio, and finally to Sandusky, Ohio, and the Johnson's Island prison camp. There she spied a young officer who knew "Lieutenant Harry T. Buford." She conferred with him and told him of the liberation plans, but

then reported back to Baker that her spy suspect was not at Johnson's Island. This gave her an excuse to press on to another prison
camp in Indianapolis, Indiana.

Upon arrival in Indianapolis, she found two men from St. Louis
waiting for her, with whom she conferred at length. Her orders
were to gain access to the prison and encourage the prisoners to
try to escape. She gained entry by accompanying a woman known
to the guards who was selling cakes to prisoners. The woman told
the guards that Velazquez was her sister. Inside, she spotted a major
whom she had met in Richmond "but who had never seen me in
female attire." She urged him to help plan a prison break, pointing
out that there were few troops to stop them, and told him the
general plan of trying to raise a guerilla army to harrass the North
and draw troops away from the front.

Then, continuing her double game, Velazquez wrote to Colonel
Baker informing him that the man she was looking for (on behalf
of the Union) was not in the Indianapolis camp, and she now
claimed to have information that he might be at the Alton, Illinois,
prison camp. She told Baker that she proposed to go to Alton, and
if he was not found there she would give up the search. In reality,
she did not plan to go to Alton at all.

Velazquez then called on Governor Oliver P. Morton seeking
employment, using the cover story that she was a widow whose
husband had been killed in the war. While waiting for further orders for secret service, she hoped to establish contacts in Indianapolis and to find new avenues of information for the Confederate
cause. The governor had no jobs to offer, but gave her a letter of
introduction for employment at the Federal arsenal where other
women were employed manufacturing munitions. There she was
given a job packing cartridges. Seeing a golden opportunity, Velazquez plotted to blow up the arsenal, but after about two weeks
decided it could not be done without taking many innocent lives.

Since the volume of her correspondence was beginning to attract
attention at the post office, she waited anxiously for an assignment,
finally receiving money and orders to report to Cairo, Illinois, and
then to St. Louis. Following her instructions, she stopped at Planters' House to learn what she could about Federal movements from
officers using the hotel as headquarters. Playing the role of a widow
in greatly reduced circumstances, Velazquez applied for a job as
chambermaid at Planters' House, but to her chagrin there were no
openings. Snooping around, she was unable to learn much of value,

but did determine the hours during which the officers were least likely to be in their rooms. Lacking any other approach, she determined to surreptitiously enter the rooms in search of information.

Befriending a chambermaid, she managed to steal a passkey and began to pursue her dangerous errand. Slipping into three rooms, she read a number of dispatches of some importance. While leaving the third room, she was almost caught by a bellboy, who turned into the corridor just as she had finished locking the door. Pretending to be lost and confused, she asked the bellboy where the servants' stairway was. He paid little attention to her, and she scurried away in relief.

The information she was able to obtain was forwarded to the proper agent, along with the message that it seemed unlikely she could learn any more at Planters' House. In reply, she was ordered to Hannibal, Missouri, to pick up a package and deliver some dispatches. Here she learned the bad news. The elaborate plan to liberate the Johnson's Island prisoners had failed when the agents were unable to capture the Federal gunboat *Michigan,* a key element of the plot, and the agent who attempted to do so was himself captured. To Velazquez's disgust, the man was carrying papers that revealed the plot, he confessed, and the entire operation came unglued.

> I did not know who was to blame for this failure, but I felt that if all the rest had done their duty as efficiently as I had done mine, success would have crowned our efforts. I, therefore, resolved to return East, and to dissolve all connections with my late co-workers, and with more than half a mind to have nothing more to do with such schemes . . . in the future.

As 1864 drew to a close, Confederate secret service operations took on an air of desperation. With deepening pessimism, the agents in the North still clung to faint hope that they could disrupt the war effort and demoralize the citizens. Velazquez, deciding on a change of pace, took on a new and more lucrative career managing blockade running operations. Ships were loaded with contraband goods from northern cities and Europe, officials were bribed, and cargoes reached southern ports via the Caribbean.

Visiting Cuba once more, she found old acquaintances from 1862 still actively engaged in blockade running. However, she was struck by their "cold-blooded" and "purely pecuniary" attitudes, more concerned that the war might end soon and cut off their source of riches, and seemingly unconcerned about the fate of the Confederacy.

Back in New York City, Velazquez flitted on to other projects, always on the lookout for any opportunity to strike a blow for the cause. She professed to be outraged by the rampant corruption and profiteering in the North, with cynical "war merchants" engaging in all sorts of illegal ventures, but infiltrating these operations made it possible to turn them to the advantage of the South. One of the biggest scandals of all was a ring of thieves and counterfeiters in the Department of Treasury trafficking in bogus Confederate and Federal securities.

Velazquez went to Washington and, after paying a courtesy call to Colonel Baker, contacted a clerk in the treasury who was a known Confederate sympathizer. The man was willing to do anything he could to help, short of risking his personal safety. "He was not the sort of a man I had much liking for," Velazquez noted, "but in the kind of work I was engaged in prosecuting, it did not do to be too fastidious about the characters of one's associates." The clerk gave her an introduction to a very high official who could arrange her entry into the printing bureau; so high up that she was astonished to learn his identity. To him, she proposed a scheme to become involved in the ring and share in the profits, at the same time using the bogus securities to aid the Confederate cause.

Velazquez became the go-between, delivering both real and bogus bonds, currency, and even electrotype plates used to print securities, pilfered from the printing bureau, to brokers in Philadelphia and New York City. The main market for Confederate securities was England. A huge and highly lucrative business was done involving immense sums of money, and she used substantial amounts of her profits to finance continuing Confederate secret service operations.

Finally, when she learned that Colonel Baker was beginning to look into treasury operations, Velazquez quickly severed all connections there, having already accumulated a large sum of money. When Baker tried to expose the treasury ring, he was thwarted by high officials and members of Congress whose attempts to discredit Baker she found "disgraceful." She *knew* Baker's suspects were guilty, she said, because she had been associated with them. She also noted that "during the whole time that the investigation was going on, I was in mortal terror lest Baker should discover that I was implicated."

Velazquez and her associates also took advantage of the widespread, illegal substitute-broker and bounty-jumper operations resulting from the unpopular draft in the latter part of the war. In big cities like New York, immigrants, drifters, and others seized on the Federal offer of bounties to enlist and were paid sizeable sums of money, but then more often than not immediately deserted, only to enlist again elsewhere to make a fast profit. A brokerage ring quickly arose to capitalize on the opportunity for large profits.

Similarly, draft evasion flourished since a man subject to military service could pay a substitute to serve in his place. Fees were determined by supply and demand, and substitute-brokers were in business. The substitutes, too, deserted and repeated the cycle, so that very few actually reached the army. At its worst, the system bred totally corrupt brokers who engaged in kidnapping, drugging, forging of papers, and a long list of other crimes in order to produce a marketable "warm body" for delivery to the army.

New York City was a major haven for the brokers. Early in 1865, Colonel Baker went there to investigate the practices, checking in at the Astor House and concealing his presence to prevent his targets from finding out before he was ready to deal with them. According to Velazquez, he requested her to call on him in the evening at the Astor House and asked for her help in cracking the broker rings. Velazquez gave him some suggestions, later alerting her immediate colleagues to his presence and dropping out of the business, too.

To see for himself how the system worked, Baker arranged to be personally "brokered"—hired to serve as a soldier or to substitute for one. With elaborate use of trickery, he manipulated a large group of the brokers into a position where he could (and did) make mass arrests. But when the news of Lincoln's assassination reached him, Baker returned immediately to Washington, where he played a role in the capture of assassin John Wilkes Booth.

Before that, however, Velazquez had been persuaded to undertake one more Confederate secret service assignment out west, another attempt to free prisoners. Though skeptical about the project, her sentiments for the prisoners induced her to try. Maybe she could at least give them some aid and comfort, she thought. So it was back to Dayton, Ohio, this time dressed as a poor girl looking for housework.

Learning the names of some "copperhead" families (southern sympathizers), she obtained work in a copperhead household. There she was quickly befriended and treated as an equal—even a privileged guest—when she let it be known that she formerly was a person of substance, now reduced to scrabbling around for a living. Gradually, she learned of a network of copperheads who were helping escaped prisoners. They would rendezvous in Cleveland to obtain the means to escape south. By now Velazquez had accumulated almost $150,000, a large portion of which she carried as cash. Heading to Cleveland to help, she was intercepted at Columbus by an urgent dispatch directing her to go to Canada at once. Having no time to take other steps on behalf of the soldiers, she contributed $3,000 for their relief before departing for Canada.

Reflecting the frantic times, her activities became a blur. From her unstated mission in Canada, she headed for New York, then to London to see after the sales of bogus Confederate bonds, which were still profitable even at low prices. Then to Paris, where news of Sherman's march gave the impression the war was almost over, and then to Liverpool. Returning by steamer to New York City, she arrived in the harbor just as news of Lee's surrender reached the ship. "[The news] fairly stunned me," she wrote. Immediately she settled her "secret banking and brokerage transactions" accounts, which again must have been substantial.

Apparently "hope springs eternal," for she refused to believe that Lee's surrender necessarily ended the war; there were other armies that could carry on the fight, she thought. While other Confederate agents in New York City were highly pessimistic, Velazquez "was not disposed to give up while a southern soldier remained in the field." The last remaining hope was the scattered armies in the West. Eager to do what she could to help, Velazquez headed there carrying dispatches for guerilla leader William Quantrill. On the return trip, in Columbus, Ohio, she learned of Lincoln's assassination. Like many thinking southerners, she was deeply concerned about the possible backlash on the South. The unexpected event also disrupted all her plans. She was at a loss as to what to do next.

Returning to Washington, D.C., to confer with her colleagues, Velazquez again met with Colonel La Fayette Baker. To her consternation, he finally enlisted her aid in catching the female Confederate spy who kept slipping through their fingers. Considering the timing of his request, she wondered whether Baker suspected the woman (her) of being in on the assassination plot. The people's mood bothered her; if caught, she could be railroaded as a conspirator. Perhaps, she thought, it would be prudent to leave the country for a while until things calmed down. She had until next morning to decide on his offer.

Next morning before Baker called, Velazquez received a letter from her brother who expected to be in New York City in a few days with his wife and children. He suggested that they all go to Europe together. On the basis of his letter, she decided to accept Baker's assignment as a cover story, but to go to Europe and stay as long as necessary. By now, Joseph E. Johnston's army had surrendered (April 26, 1865) and she was resigned to the fact that the cause was lost, and therefore her mission was at an end. Now she needed to consider her own welfare, and that of her family.

Baker gave her instructions on a general plan for capturing the female agent. "I was astonished to find how much he knew of some of my movements," she wrote. "He and his men must have been on the point of capturing me many times, and they undoubtedly would have done so, had I not had the wit to take the course I did in cultivating his acquaintance."

Velazquez started for New York ostensibly on a search for the female spy, but in reality to wait anxiously for her brother and to get beyond Baker's reach. Before long her brother arrived with his wife, two children, and a nurse in tow, and they had a joyful reunion. One of the children had been named after her. Wasting no time, they left for England on a Cunard Line steamship. From England they went on to Paris where her brother had been educated, visiting the College de France and the medical school where he had studied. Both she and her brother spoke French and appreciated the French culture, so they hired a fancy rig and toured Paris in style, taking in theaters, museums, cathedrals, and monuments.

A side trip to Reims, where Velazquez's childhood idol Joan of Arc had won fame, caused her to observe with some irony:

> [At this time] I was of a more practical turn of mind than I had been a few years before. The romance had been pretty well knocked out of me by the rough experience of real life; and although I was better able to appreciate the performances of Joan of Arc at their true value, somehow they did not interest me to the extent they once did.

The grand tour obviously must have been sponsored by Velazquez's wartime profits, and it continued for some time. They toured Germany, then Poland, and back to Paris, where at the Hotel de Louvre she encountered some Confederate officers who had known "Lieutenant Harry T. Buford." It appears to have been common knowledge shortly after the war ended that "Buford" had been a woman. Without identifying herself to them, Velazquez questioned the officers about "Buford's" career. They praised her valor, but one denounced her for wearing male attire.

The party then toured London, and made a side trip to the factory town of Manchester. By now they were all getting homesick for America, and it was time to decide where they would stay and what they would do. Her sister-in-law wanted to live in Spain, but she and her brother decided to return to the United States. Once they reached New York, however, her sister-in-law persuaded him to move to Mexico. This did not appeal to Velazquez, so they parted company.

The memoirs do not say how much time passed during the European tour. Presumably it was long enough for Velazquez to feel comfortable about dealing with Colonel Baker and traveling openly through the East. The assassination conspirators had been hanged on July 7, 1865, and the country was beginning to emerge from the period of national mourning. The action had shifted away from military conflict to the political arena, President Andrew Johnson and the Congress struggling over Reconstruction issues.

Her Confederate contacts had sternly warned Velazquez about the dangers of going to Washington, but she was stubborn. Fully realizing that Baker must be aware that both she and the female agent under pursuit had vanished, she decided to beard the lion in his den. At the very least, she would have some tall explaining to do. At most, she might be thrown in prison and implicated in the assassination conspiracy. Still, she went to Washington. As it happened, Baker was out of town.

"I do not know to this day," she reported in her 1876 memoirs, "whether he ever discovered that I was a Confederate secret-service agent." (Baker died in 1868.)

Velazquez had decided to tour the old Confederate states and take personal stock of the situation before taking up a new life. As she continued through Richmond, North and South Carolina, and Atlanta, meeting old friends along the way, she found that her reputation had preceded her. Everyone wanted to meet the woman who had served as a male soldier, and she was pleased by their attention and recognition.

Aside from the personal gratification of being praised for her deeds, though, Velazquez found nothing but ruin and despair everywhere in the South. "It is no wonder," she noted, "that at this dismal time, certain ill-advised emigration schemes found countenance with those who saw no hope for themselves or their children but either to go out of the country, or [go far away] to start life anew under better auspices than were then possible [in] the late Confederacy."

New Orleans, her former hometown, she found in a pitiful plight, the desolation sickening, which she attributed to "ambitious and unscrupulous politicians" furthering their own ends. "I longed to quit the scene of so much misery, and fully sympathized with those who preferred to fly . . . and to seek homes in other lands, rather than to remain and be victimized." She felt that most of the emigration schemes, to various Central and South American countries, were started by swindlers.

The exploitation of the people yearning to start new lives, she said, "is one of the saddest and dreariest pages in the history of the country." She was among those earnestly looking for a new home, but she was "street smart"—having observed at close hand all the wartime scams—and unlikely to be taken in by amateurs. Giving up on emigration schemes, Velazquez put the war behind her and went west looking for opportunity.

Postscript

Much of her remaining story, as far as it is presently known, shows her pitted against opportunists and swindlers. Yet, she herself did not hesitate to gain profit toward the end of the war and to use it to travel and explore, for her personal advantage, all over Europe and the western United States.

Whatever her motives, clearly she was personally interested in emigration possibilities and she decided to investigate the 1866 plan for colonization of former Confederates in Venezuela. She and her colleagues were skeptical of the pie-in-the-sky claims made for benefits to be provided by the host country, and she resolved to investigate them personally. Just prior to embarking to Venezuela, she married her third husband, a Major Wasson, who unfortunately, caught "black fever" and died shortly afterwards in Caracas.

The villain of the piece apparently is one "Captain Fred A. Johnston" (his real name apparently was Johnson), whom she denounced in letters to friends in New Orleans, strongly advising against emigration to Venezuela. "My experiences in Venezuela," she said, "convinced me that it was no place for poor Americans to go."

From here on, her memoirs increasingly take on the airs of a travelogue. She goes into great detail about the cultural and natural resources of Venezuela, and she is very interested in its mineral wealth. From there, she goes on to visit her childhood home in the Caribbean, stopping at Havana where she was wined and dined and lauded by Spanish officials who knew of her career as a Confederate solider.

Back in the United States she decided to try her fortunes in the West where everything was up for grabs. Traveling first to Omaha, Nebraska, and then beyond on stagecoach routes, she was exposed to western adventurers and desperados, largely perceived as whiskey-drinking, card-playing, gun-toting fanatics.

In 1868, she married again (her fourth husband), a miner in Nevada. They prospered for a while, but she had a low opinion of her husband's colleagues, and persuaded him to pull up stakes and move to California, where they bought a home in the Sacramento Valley. But her husband had "gold fever," prospecting for a year in Utah, and spending all his money without accomplishing anything. (During this period, her account suggests that they probably were separated for a time.) Then they moved on to Salt Lake City where they stayed for several months, during which she gave birth to a baby boy. She had become disenchanted with the entire milieu of miners and mining, and professed to have learned some lessons, including the fact "that mining speculations are things that people who have consciences should have as little as possible to do with."

From this point on in her memoirs, mentions of her husband became scarcer. She reports seeking fortunes in Colorado, New Mexico, and Texas. While describing a trip down the Rio Grande Valley, she mentions "travelling companions" and a gentleman who is kind to her and her young son, but there is no mention of her husband. In modern terminology, they appear to have been "estranged."

The memoirs of Loreta Janeta Velazquez end abruptly in post–

Civil War Texas. After the memoirs were published in 1876, some book reviews and correspondence exist to partially document her career for the decade of the 1870s. Having squandered her fortunes, she wrote the memoirs (rather hastily, judging by internal evidence) to support herself and her young son. General Jubal Early denounced her as a fraud, even refusing to believe that she was a southern woman.

She wrote to Early on May 18, 1878 (using the title "Correspondent Le Buletin Commercial, Rio de Janeiro, Empire Brazil"), protesting his apparent effort "to injure me and my book." In a plea for sympathy, she told him, "I have had trials enough to have driven almost any proud spirited woman to madness, or to commit suicide . . . and with God's protection I have lived above it all, and all I now ask from you is justice to my *child*. I live for him and him alone."

After about 1880, she literally fades from the pages of history, and no record has been found of her life after that, or of her death. Far from attaining the fame and glory that she originally sought, Velazquez vanished into obscurity.

Strange Facts and Twists of Fate

*She joined a new regiment each time she was discovered in
the previous one and discharged. She was also taken prisoner
by Confederate forces.*
                          —The story of FRANCES HOOK.

Countless stories about female soldiers are recorded as anecdotes
in soldiers' memoirs, diaries, letters, and newspaper reports. Most
often they are passing comments about "oddities" observed in
camp or on the battlefield, and basic information (like names or
regiments or hometowns) that would enable more complete identification are totally lacking. Still, brief as some of the stories may
be, they indicate the presence in both Union and Confederate armies of women who were there to "soldier"—for whatever personal motives—and not merely camp followers or other shallow
opportunists. The stories also broadly portray human nature in all
its facets, including heroism, humor, irony, and tragedy.

Collectively, the stories reveal little-known facts about the war.
Although many *vivandieres* in their fancy uniforms started off as
romantic figures early in the war, they quickly faded from view.
Other women who tried to enlist in male disguise were not sufficiently "masculine" to get away with it for long. Probably there
were more female soldiers early in the war, who were gradually
weeded out or discovered or left the army when their husbands or
boyfriends were killed or wounded.

Still, in 1864 and 1865 we find "survivors": women who had
managed to remain undiscovered until more extreme events (preg-
nancy, serious wounds, or death in battle) disclosed their secret.
We also find many of them to be sergeants or even officers, suggesting that they had above average soldiering skills and leadership

ability. They had competed successfully on equal terms in the male-dominated business of combat warfare.

Occasionally, like "Albert Cashier" (Chapter 2) and "Otto Schaffer," they preferred to maintain a male disguise after the war and were not discovered until late in life. "Otto Schaffer," a hermit farmer in Butler County, Kansas, who had fought in the Union army, was only discovered to be a woman at death.

Too Much Applejack

General Philip Sheridan in his personal memoirs, reporting on camp life in Louisville, Kentucky, in 1863–64, describes the foraging expeditions that were required in order to feed his vast army. In addition to the collection of corn and other supplies, the wagon trains found themselves skirmishing with the enemy, and upon returning to camp reported "intelligence" information about disposition of Confederate forces.

On one such expedition, Sheridan recalls, the colonel in command, Colonel Conrad of the 15th Missouri, reported to him that everything had gone well on the foraging mission, but that he had been mortified by the behavior of two females who had been discovered in the units attached to headquarters. One was an east Tennessee woman who was a teamster in the division wagon train, and the other was a private cavalry soldier in a company attached to headquarters for escort duty. They had become an "annoyance" and contributed to "demoralizing his men" by getting drunk.

"To say that I was astonished at his statement would be a mild way of putting it," Sheridan said, "and had I not known him to be a most upright man and of sound sense, I should have doubted not only his veracity, but his sanity." After verifying the story, Sheridan reported:

> While out on the foraging expedition these Amazons had secured a supply of "apple-jack" by some means, got very drunk, and on the return had fallen into Stone River and been nearly drowned. After they had been fished from the water, in the process of resuscitation their sex was disclosed, though up to this time it appeared to be known only to each other." [Sheridan ordered the arrest of the two offenders of military and male sensibilities, and reports that] the East Tennessee woman was found in camp, somewhat the worse for the experiences of the day before, but awaiting her fate contentedly

smoking a cob-pipe. She was brought to me, and put in duress under charge of the division surgeon until her companion could be secured.

She told the surgeon that she had fled from east Tennessee the previous year, and having adopted male apparel was employed as a teamster in the quartermaster's department. Since she had "coarse and masculine" features, Sheridan was not suprised that she had been able to pass herself off as a man. He was somewhat more perplexed by the "she dragoon" (as he termed the female cavalary soldier) who was caught and brought before him next day.

The cavalry soldier

> proved to be a rather prepossessing young woman, and though necessarily bronzed and hardened by exposure, I doubt if, even with these marks of campaigning, she could have deceived as readily as did her companion. How the two got acquainted I never learned, and though they had joined the army independently of each other, yet an intimacy had sprung up between them long before the mishaps of the foraging expedition. Both were "provided with clothing suited to their sex" and deported beyond army lines.

Female Mannerisms

Despite passing for men in day-to-day soldiering, some young women were detected by their "female mannerisms" and sent home. At the outbreak of the war, there lived in Lake Mills, Wisconsin, a devoted brother and sister team, Mason and Sarah Collins; when Mason made up his mind to enlist his sister decided to do the same. She was physically strong and could easily have borne the hardships of army life. Her brother Mason, won over by her persistence, was a party to the deception. Her hair was cut short and she put on men's clothing.

When the time came to report to camp, she accompanied her brother to the rendezvous of the company, and though she had the appearance of masculinity, her sex was discovered "by her unmasculine manner of putting on her shoes and stockings." So with tears in her eyes, disappointed at her failure to become a soldier, she was obliged to return home, while her brother left for duty without her.

Early in the war the 1st Kentucky Infantry was serving in the Kanawha Valley Campaign in western Virginia. In late July, 1861, a young soldier who had served for three months was discovered to be a woman after arousing suspicion by her manner of pulling on her stockings. In a book about his wartime experiences, newspaper correspondent Albert D. Richardson wrote: "She performed camp duties with great fortitude, and never fell out of the ranks during the severest marches. She was small in stature, and kept her coat buttoned to her chin." Most members of the regiment were from Ohio, where it was originally formed. When the surgeon established that she was a woman of about twenty, she was discharged from the regiment, but sent to Columbus, Ohio, on suspicion of being a spy because of some unspecified remarks she had made. Richardson did not learn what finally became of her.

Mary Smith enlisted in the 41st Ohio "McClellan Zouaves" in male disguise, to avenge the death of her only brother at Bull Run. Unfortunately for her, she was discovered to be a woman at Camp Wood, Cleveland, when she gave an "unmistakable twist to the dishcloth in wringing it out that no masculine [sic] could ever successfully counterfeit."

Mary Livermore, the famous nurse, was visiting the camp of the 19th Illinois one day when a captain asked her whether she noticed anything peculiar about one of the solidiers, whom he pointed out. "It was evident at a glance that the 'man' was a young woman in male attire," she reported, "and I said so." The captain replied, "That is the rumor, and that is my suspicion."

Charles W. Ives, 1st Sergeant of the 95th Illinois, while talking about "Albert Cashier," said that he knew of two other would-be female soldiers dressed in military uniforms who were detected when an officer threw apples to them, and they reached for their (nonexistent) aprons to catch the apples in. (See the notes for Chapter 2 under Rodney G. Davis.)

But the ultimate giveaway was reported in the Maysville, Kentucky, *Dollar Weekly Bulletin*, November 27, 1862: "The sex of a female recruit in Rochester was discovered by her trying to put her pants on over her head."

Female Casualties Discovered

Bell I. Wiley, in his classic book on common soldiers of the Union, *Life of Billy Yank*, reported in a brief summary of female soldiers: "Some of the Union amazons were casualties; at least one was fatally wounded, while another was killed outright." The parallel section about women in the companion volume, *Life of Johnny*

Reb, about common soldiers of the Confederacy, mentions Loreta Janeta Velazquez and her story of being wounded.

Wiley's body count is far too low; in fact, we will never know how many women took their secret with them to their battlefield graves. More than one female soldier reported observing burials of soldiers in male attire that they knew to be female. One such secret was accidentally uncovered 72 years after the burial.

On February 8, 1934, Mancil Miligan was working in his garden on the outskirts of Shiloh National Battlefield Park. When his hoe began turning up what appeared to be human bones, he notified authorities and nine human skeletons were excavated. Pieces of uniform and buttons, in addition to other military gear, allowed identification of them as Union soldiers who had been buried immediately after the battle of Shiloh in April, 1862. The burial site apparently had been overlooked by grave registration units in the confusion of hasty burials. One of the skeletons was that of a woman whose remains were found next to a minie ball that apparently had killed her. The nine bodies were reburied in the National Cemetery, leaving the mystery of her identity and why she was dressed in uniform.

A cavalry soldier in Company B of the 2nd Indiana was discovered to be a woman after 21 months of service, only after being wounded twice. A soldier writing home to his wife noted: "Maybe she would have remained undiscovered for a long time, if she hadn't fainted. She was given a warm bath which gave the secret away." (See Chapter 2.)

After the battle of Gettysburg on July 2–3, 1863, two Confederate female casualties were discovered:

A woman and her husband were found dead at the so-called "high water mark" on the hillside after Pickett's charge on July 3rd. The woman had been noticed because of her young and innocent face, and was thought to be a boy who was being protected by the man. As the Confederates attempted to breach the Union breastworks at the crest of the hill, a flagbearer was shot down. The youth was seen to raise the flag and carry on briefly, before falling in turn under the withering fire, along with the man. They were buried together on the battlefield.

A wounded Union soldier in hospital at Chester, Pennsylvania, wrote home that a Confederate female soldier, who had lost a leg at Gettysburg, was in hospital with them. He found this "romantic" and felt sympathy for her.

As noted in Chapter 2, Mrs. Frances Clayton served with her husband in a Minnesota regiment in Tennessee for nearly a year. She served all duties that the men did in all kinds of weather, including hand-to-hand combat, and was wounded in action. Her husband was killed in the battle of Stone's River, Tennessee. (December 31, 1862 through January 2, 1863).

Other instances of female casualties have been reported in previous chapters. For additional examples, see the "Honor Roll" in Appendix A.)

Exposed by Her Uncle

One young female soldier was able to fool everyone else, but not her own uncle. The story was reported in a Kentucky newspaper, taken from the New Albany, Indiana *Ledger*:

A FEMALE VOLUNTEER   Quite a commotion was created in the Camp of the 66th [Indiana] yesterday afternoon by the discovery of a female volunteer in Capt. Gerard's company. The young lady was among the first to volunteer in the company. She is a resident near Six-Mile Switch, on the Louisville, New Albany, and Chicago Railroad, [and] came into the city some four weeks since, dressed in men's clothes, and volunteered. She conducted herself in the most proper manner after her enlistment, and her sex was never even suspected.

Yesterday her uncle was on a visit to Camp Noble, where he accidentally met and recognized her. She immediately burst into tears on being discovered. She was discharged by Commandant Martin, and, dressed in her soldier clothes, immediately left for home. She belongs to a highly respectable family and we are requested to suppress her name. What induced her to volunteer no one knows.

Real Soldiers Don't Have Babies

Forget mannerisms. If you are pretending to be a male soldier, having a baby definitely will give you away.

John V. Hadley, an Indiana soldier, wrote home to his girlfriend on April 19, 1863, that the "lady soldier" he had previously referred to in the Army of the Potomac had been sent home to her parents after having a baby. A fund had been established in the army to give her boy a military education, and he was inclined to contribute to it. It seems that a line soldier had suddenly given birth to a baby. Apparently her lover had enlisted in a New Jersey regiment, whereupon "she donned the male attire, passed examination, and joined the company with him." She had been with the regiment nearly a year, participating in four battles, and no one had suspected anything right up to the moment of birth.

A Michigan soldier, Private James Greenalch, wrote home to his wife, Fidelia, April 20, 1863, about another shocking circumstance:

> The boys told me to knight [sic] that a regiment that is campt [sic] near us, the 74 Ohio, that an orderly Sergeant in that regiment has got a child, that the sergeant turns out to be a woman with mens cloths [sic] on and has ben [sic] in the regement [sic] twenty months.

Major General William S. Rosecrans, commander of the Army of the Cumberland, was so offended by this event that he directed his staff to issue an order on April 17, 1863, terming it a "flagrant outrage" and directing his subordinates to "deal with the offending party or parties according to law." The delivery of a baby by an orderly sergeant was "in violation of all military law and of the army regulations. . . . You will apply the proper punishment in this case, and a remedy to prevent a repetition of the act."

Authorities at Johnson's Island Federal prison camp on Lake Erie must have been equally shocked when one of the Confederate prisoners, an officer, suddenly had a baby late in 1864. The newspaper story on the event said that the soldier had produced a "bouncing boy." The reporter, with tongue in cheek, said "This is the first instance of the father giving birth to a child that we have heard of. . . it is [also] the first case of a woman in rebel service that we have heard of."

Another "bouncing boy" was delivered by a sergeant of the 10th New York Heavy Artillery, and it was another case of a female soldier who might otherwise have gone undetected. The sergeant was taken sick on the picket line and carried to the hospital, where "he" gave birth early on the morning of March 6, 1865. "For the first three or four days the event created [a] great question among the two regiments as to its parental relations."

Determined to Fight

Some women were so determined to remain in the army that when they were caught (or feared that they might be), they reenlisted in another regiment, sometimes from a different state. The male names they used are seldom known, and some may well have used more than one.

The unnamed female Union soldier at Chickamauga who was sent across the lines under a flag of truce, after being wounded and captured by Confederate forces, told an interviewer that she wanted to stay in the army and planned to reenlist. Also, the female soldier known as "Nellie A.K.," after being discovered and discharged, reportedly tried to reenlist. Who knows how many actually succeeded in reenlisting, and returned to camp life and combat?

The apparent record holder for persistence was Elizabeth ("Lizzie") Compton who is reported to have enlisted at age 14 and served in seven different regiments. "Detected as a woman in each organization, she immediately went elsewhere and reenlisted in a new unit," according to author John W. Heisey. "Her last service was in the 11th Kentucky Cavalry, from which she apparently went back to her home in Ontario, Canada." Since she is said to have served for eighteen months (one source has her serving over a year in the 125th Michigan Cavalry), her disguise must have worked for periods of time. Mary Elizabeth Massey reports that Compton's story only came out after she was wounded in action and forced to quit.

Another major "repeater" was Frances Hook who served as "Frank Miller" in the 66th Illinois Home Guards and 90th Illinois Infantry, and later as "Frank Martin" in the 8th Michigan Infantry (see Chapter 2). She also served in the 2nd East Tennessee Cavalry. According to C. Kay Larson, "she joined a new regiment each time she was discovered in the previous one and discharged. She was also taken prisoner by Confederate forces."

Fanny (or Fannie) Wilson served for two years in the 24th New Jersey Infantry before her sex was discovered during the Vicksburg campaign, and she was discharged. She was sent to Cairo, Illinois, and there killed some time dancing in the local ballet before reenlisting in the 3rd Illinois Cavalry. Once again she was found out and sent home.

Another example of persistence was more humorous than successful. A Cincinnati, Ohio, newspaper in 1864 presented a story taken from the Cleveland *Herald*, about a young woman who said she had lost three brothers in the war, and was determined to enlist and avenge their deaths. The story is excerpted here:

Being too well known in Cleveland she . . . started for Windsor. . . . At this place she donned male attire, had her hair cut short, and when dressed in a new garb, looked the very picture of a boy of about 18, fresh from the country, and paraded the streets of Detroit for two days. She offered herself as a "substitute" to an enrolled man, who took her to four different recruiting offices, where papers were made out; but the "boy" was each time rejected on surgical examination as being "too short," the real state of the case not being explained to the "principal." At last the "boy" started for the Provost Marshal's office to "volunteer." The venerable examining surgeon proceeded to strip the "boy" and was so much astounded at what he discovered that he rushed in alarm from the room and proclaimed the unlooked for sex of the recruit.

The girl was severely reprimanded for her conduct, but declared that she was "bound to be a soldier or die" and was determined to get into the ranks somewhere. She says other girls have got into the army, and she could not see why she should not.

Glimpses of Confederate Officers and Soldiers

A story told by a Union General's orderly at the battle of Atlanta in 1864 sounds suspiciously like a tall tale. As the officers stood watching explosions and columns of smoke rising from the city, they expressed concern about innocent women and children who might be killed. The orderly piped up, saying "the women are the worst of them; one of them put the rope on my neck to hang me." He then told the following story.

At the battle of Peach Tree Creek on July 20th, the orderly was captured and taken before General Hood for questioning, but he refused to talk. About then, a female major with an escort rode up and saluted the general. The "She-Major" wore a cap with feathers and gold lace, flowing pants, a long velvet coat that reached just below her hips, fastened with a crimson sash and partly open at the bosom. She also carried a revolver and sword. Her face was sunburned and somewhat masculine. "Only for her voluptuous bust, little hands, and peculiar airs, I might have taken her to be a very handsome little officer of the masculine gender," said the orderly.

When she asked who the orderly was, General Hood explained that he was a prisoner who refused to talk. She promptly identified him as a spy who had been seen at General Johnston's headquarters masquerading as a scout and giving false information. She offered to take him into custody and deliver him to General Johnston, and General Hood accepted. As they rode off from Hood's camp into the woods, the "She-Major" and her orderly reined in and she accused him of hanging the only man she ever loved. Now she would have her vengeance.

As they tied a rope around his neck and started to fasten it to a tree branch, the frantic prisoner grabbed the rope away and spurred his horse, which leaped and reared. When the "She-Major" pulled out her pistol to shoot him, he kicked her in the face "spoiling her beauty, and giving the dentist a job," sending her sprawling. His horse bounded away, and he made his escape after some further adventures.

The notion of a buxom female wearing an outlandish costume and serving openly as a field officer, especially in the South, is pretty far-fetched. Yet, a few other female Confederate officers have been glimpsed, including Lieutenant Amy Clarke (see Chapter 8) whose story is at least partly documented, though the others were wearing more conventional military attire.

Two British observers traveling through the South reported seeing female soldiers. Fitzgerald Ross, traveling on a train between Augusta and Atlanta, Georgia (no date given), met a female captain whom he learned had taken an active part in the war. And Lieutenant Colonel Arthur Freemantle, on a train between Chattanooga, Tennessee, and Atlanta on June 5, 1863, had a "goodish-looking woman" pointed out to him as a private who had served in the battles of Perryville and Murfreesboro late the previous year. Freemantle's companions told him that she had served in a Louisiana regiment, but had recently been "turned out . . . for her bad and immoral conduct," and that she was not the only woman in the ranks. "When I saw her," Freemantle noted, "she wore a soldier's hat and coat, but had resumed her petticoats."

Reproduced in full is the following story from the Lynchburg, Virginia *Virginian*, October 6, 1864:

A FEMALE CAPTAIN
We find the following in the local column of the Charlotte North Carolina, *Times* of Friday:

ANOTHER BELLE BOYD   A beautiful, dashing lady, in the uniform of a Captain, passed on the Northern train towards Richmond yesterday afternoon. She wore a black belt with a chain attached. She is said to be from Mississippi, and has participated in several hard fought battles, and was promoted on the field for distinguished gallantry. She wore a straw cap, set jauntily on her head, adorned with two rows of miniature gilt buttons. He who seemed to be her traveling companion appeared about forty years of age, and wore the uniform of a Major. She had probably been home on a short furlough, and was on her way back to join her command. There is some mystery yet unravelled about this heroine and her strange career, and which will never see the light till the heart history of a love story is written.

"Moses" Goes to War

Harriet Ross Tubman was born in 1815 (it may have been 1820 as no one knows for sure) to a slave family on the eastern shore of Maryland. She died in 1913, somewhere in her mid- to late-90s, remarkable longevity for someone who was born into poverty and servitude, and who risked everything to escape that fate. Into that long life span she packed several lifetimes of adventure and physical danger, unselfishly for the cause of freedom for her people and victory for the North.

Her grandparents on both sides had come from Africa in chains. She was given the name Araminta, but rejected it and adopted the name Harriet from her mother. About 1844, she was married to a free Negro named John Tubman. About 1849, Harriet Tubman made a break for freedom and escaped to Philadelphia, where she plotted to help other slaves. She was estranged from her husband, and he later remarried. A particularly detailed biography of her early and mid-life is contained in the entry by John Hope Franklin in *Notable American Women*.

The noted black orator and antislavery spokesman, Frederick Douglass, had the highest praise for her. "Excepting [abolitionist] John Brown, of sacred memory," he said to her, "I know of no one who has willingly encountered more perils and hardships to serve our enslaved people than you have." In another tribute to her he said, "The midnight sky and silent stars have been the witnesses of your devotion to freedom and of your heroism."

The latter was an allusion to her role as one of the most famous "conductors" of the Underground Railroad in the years before the war, leading escaping slaves to freedom in safe havens in the North via a secret network of "stations" (or "safe houses") along the way. She was an extremely clever tactitian in these missions, taking elaborate precautions to confuse and mislead pursuers. It was a dangerous business, and Harriet had a price on her head, one time reaching $40,000. She was known as the "Moses" of her people, leading them out of the wilderness, and although a religious person with strong faith in God, she was of the "praise the Lord and pass the ammunition" school of thought. Harriet Tubman carried a pistol, both for self-defense and to insure her sometimes timid charges who might become discouraged. An early book about the Underground Railroad states:

> The discouragement of an individual could not be permitted to endanger the liberty and safety of the whole party; accordingly she sometimes strengthened the fainting heart by threatening to use her revolver, and declaring, "Dead niggers tell no tales, you go on or die."

With strong personal discipline, she personally led the slaves through hostile territory at night and through all kinds of weather, using her intelligence to skirt the dangers and avoid capture. She is attributed with leading more than 300 slaves to freedom in the North. During this same period, she was one of the first black women to speak out for women's rights. She was consulted by John Brown, who admired her, and advised him in planning the famous raid on Harper's Ferry.

As if this were not enough for any one person to contribute, after the war broke out Tubman was recruited by the Union to help in the Carolinas, Georgia, and Florida, and served as a nurse, scout, and spy along these coastal states for more than three years. Under the command of Colonel James Montgomery of the 2nd Carolina Volunteers, she led a corps of black troops on several forays into Confederate territory, gathering valuable intelligence. Despite dialectical differences, she could communicate with local blacks far better than white soldiers could and was able to gain their confidence.

After the war, Brigadier General Rufus Saxton wrote that Tubman "made many a raid inside the enemy's lines, displaying remarkable courage, zeal, and fidelity." The best known raid began on the night of June 1, 1863, up the Combahee River, accomplishing various missions including carrying more than 700 Blacks up river to freedom.

A biography of Tubman by Sarah Bradford notes:

This fearless woman was often sent into the rebel lines as a spy . . . she has been in battle when the shot was falling like hail, and the bodies of dead and wounded men were dropping around her like leaves in autumn; but the thought of fear never seems to have had place for a moment in her mind. She had her duty to perform, and she expected to be taken care of till it was done.

Harriet Tubman returned to her home in Auburn, New York, in 1864, where she lived out her life, but it was not a life of idleness. She continued to help black freedmen begin new lives, and played an active role in advancing women's rights as well as seeking dignity and respect for black women and former slaves. Without a doubt, Harriet Tubman was an extraordinary human being, and probably the most underrated and underappreciated person, of either sex or any race, from the Civil War period.

The Legend of "Mountain Charley"

Always armed with a revolver or two in her belt and a long
sheath-knife in her boot-leg she seemed perfectly able to protect
herself in any emergency.
    —GEORGE WEST, Colorado publisher, 1885.

"Charley Hatfield" was a good soldier. In September, 1862, he had
enlisted in an Iowa cavalry regiment at Keokuk, Iowa. Because he
had good penmanship, "Charley" was detailed to headquarters as
a clerk. When the regiment later took to the field under General
Samuel R. Curtis, Major Charlot, the Adjutant General, requested
that Charley be assigned to his staff.

When General Sterling Price, with a Confederate cavalary force
of about 2,000 men, swept through Missouri in September and
October of 1864, General Curtis gathered his forces along the Big
Blue River near Westport to oppose him. The two armies skir-
mished for several days in mid-October, concluding with the climactic Battle of Westport on October 22nd and 23rd. As a headquarters aide and courier, "Charley" carried orders and messages
all over the command area, often at the front, and was praised by
the commanders for "coolness and bravery."

The first day went poorly for the Union forces, who were routed
from their position, and then spent an anxious night in a council
of war. General Curtis formed a line along Brush Creek in front
of Westport, and the battle resumed at daybreak. At first, the Federals were driven back across Brush Creek, but they counterat-
tacked and it became a see-saw battle. Finally at about noon, the
Confederates were forced to give way. General Price, with his worn
out army, began retreating down the border between Missouri and
Kansas with the Federal forces pursuing him, hoping to destroy

his army. In one of several rearguard actions, Federal cavalary charged across the prairie to attack the Confederates, who turned at bay and formed in line of battle. After heavy losses on both sides, the Federals pulled back.

Among the scores of casualities scattered across the landscape after this battle, some of Confederate General Joseph Shelby's men found "Charley" on the ground alongside his dead horse, weak from loss of blood from a gunshot wound in the leg and a sabre cut in the shoulder. He was taken to an ambulance and evacuated from the field. Dr. Jesse Terry, headquarters surgeon of Shelby's brigade, saw that the diminutive Yankee soldier had fainted and tried to revive him. In the process, he removed the soldier's jacket to inspect the shoulder wound and was startled to discover that the soldier was a woman. Coolly, he dressed the wound and replaced the jacket, saying nothing to the ambulance driver. The leg wound was less serious.

"Charley" finally revived and appeared much better, so Dr. Terry turned his attention to other soldiers, saying nothing to her. Later, out of curiosity, Dr. Terry searched out his unusual Yankee patient. Meanwhile, she suspected that the surgeon who had treated her shoulder wound must have discovered her secret, so she inquired as to his name. When they met again and she anxiously queried him, he quietly replied: "Your secret is safe with me until you are able to tell me your story. There is not time now and this is no place to hear it."

Dr. Terry re-dressed Charley's wounds and gave her some of his rations, after removing the bullet from her leg. Except for some pain, she was in reasonably good condition. Later, during an exchange of wounded prisoners, Charley was freed and transported to Fort Leavenworth, Kansas. While recuperating there she learned that General Curtis had written to the governor of Iowa recommending a promotion for "Charles Hatfield." A commission of 1st Lieutenant came through, along with an assignment as aide-de-camp to General Curtis. "Charley" served until the end of the war, mustering out with her unit at Des Moines. Her story was first published in 1885.

None of this would have been known except for a friendship that had sprung up between publisher George West and a boyish "girl-mountaineer" before the war in Colorado. West had befriended the 22 year-old girl and once protected her from a crowd of drunken, lecherous young men intent on having their way with her. The grateful girl promised to tell him her story exclusively. Next day West received a mysterious message requesting that he saddle her mule and bring it along. He was to meet her in the mountains, and he would have her story if he rode along with her. She was leaving the area suddenly under somewhat mysterious circumstances.

West complied, and met her at the prearranged spot. As they rode along the trail they came to a lonely, deserted cabin, where they stopped and built a fire. There she told him her story, after extracting the promise that he would keep it secret for twenty-five years.

Her real name, she told him, was Charlotte, but she went by the nickname "Charley" even as a schoolgirl in her childhood home back in Iowa. She was happy until her mother died, and at 18 she was left with an uncaring stepfather who only seemed interested that she perform her chores on the old farm. She felt like a slave to him, and looked for opportunities to escape, if only by marrying. But her stepfather discouraged suitors.

"I grew tired of this," she said, "and in an evil hour ran away with a dandified looking young man who was almost a total stranger in the neighborhood." They were married in Des Moines when she was 19 (apparently born in 1840). She loved him, even after discovering that he was "nothing but a gambler and a villain of the deepest cast." His gambling "profession" kept him away from her quite a bit, but she clung to him.

After a little over a year, she had a baby that was born dead. Her husband cruelly chided her for this, struck her, and left her destitute. She then learned that he had gone away with another woman whom he had been seeing throughout their marriage. Her love quickly turned to hate, and she vowed to have revenge on her husband and the "low-down wench." She looked for work to finance her pursuit, and managed to save more than $600 in St. Joseph, Missouri, while engaged in some unspecified "remunerative employment." Suspecting that her husband and his "wench" had gone west, she then followed the emigration of people seeking their fortunes in the Colorado gold rush at Pike's Peak.

For the first time in her life, she told West, she put on male attire in St. Joseph, initially done "in sport." But when her female friends told her that no one would suspect she was a woman, the thought occurred to her that she could better carry out her designs by staying in male disguise. So she bought a mule and started west, across the river, wearing a man's butternut suit. As she crossed the plains she had encountered George West and his party headed to Pike's Peak, and remembered him, though he did not know her at this point.

Along the way she picked up reports of her husband, who had stopped to practice his gambling "profession" here and there, so she knew that she was on the right track. She knew then that she *would* find them sooner or later, but it took all summer. Then, the day before their conference in the secluded mountain cabin in December, 1859, she had succeeded in finding her husband and his paramour.

At this point in her narrative, Charley jumped to her feet excitedly and dashed outside, leaped on her mule, and galloped off across the terrain as if in a state of ecstasy. After a while she came back, calmly, and rode up to West, exclaiming cryptically, "Oh! I wish I could cry!" She told him that he now knew the whole story. "I am so glad you come [sic] out with me, for if you had not I should have been plumb crazy by this time. . . . I don't want to stay in Pike's Peak any longer now, but I have nowhere else to go. You will hear from me bye and bye, if any body does." After she bid him a cheerful good-bye and rode away, West turned and headed back toward his home in Golden, ruminating over what he had heard.

When he had first joined up with her in the mountains, he had noticed a considerable change in Charley's demeanor. Instead of the healthy, vigorous young woman he had known, he was confronted with a "hollow-eyed, pale, cadaverous looking woman, with fully ten years, apparently, added to her age." As they rode along, she occasionally cast an anxious backwards glance.

West does not tell us what he thinks, but his description of her agitated behavior, her haggard appearance, and the fact that she was hastily leaving the area—in conjunction with her excited announcement to him that she had indeed tracked down her husband—all strongly suggest that she had had her vengeance and was fleeing the scene. (Folkloric elements of her story, including the wronged wife seeking vengeance, also appear in other versions of the "Mountain Charley" legend.)

For several years thereafter, West's contact with her was spotty. In the fall of 1860, he received a letter from Charley written in Albuquerque, New Mexico. The following year he chanced to see her in Denver, dressed as a woman wearing a blonde wig and dealing cards in a casino. Finding an opportunity to talk with her discreetly, he learned that she was trying to earn enough money to return to Iowa.

When the Civil War broke out, West served as a Union officer. By 1864, he had been out of touch with Charley for quite a while. During the campaign that fall in Missouri, he found himself in General Curtis's army opposing Confederate General Price. On the evening of the battle of Westport, an orderly approached him with a message to report to General Curtis. En route to Union headquarters, the orderly seized his hand and whispered in his ear, identifying himself as the "Mountain Charley" he had known. West was totally astonished, but recognized his old friend. She told him that she had already served two years in an Iowa regiment without her sex being discovered, and that she had frequently acted as a spy for General Curtis. This was the last time West ever saw her in person.

In January, 1885, George West—having lived up to his pledge of not publishing her story for 25 years—published the story as he knew it up to this point (*Colorado Transcript*, January 14, 1885). His recollection was that when he knew her in the Golden-Pike's Peak area of Colorado, her sex was never concealed. She was simply a boyish woman dressing and acting like a man.

As luck would have it, the article was called to Charley's attention back in Iowa where she had returned. She wrote to him on February 8, 1885, informing him that she had been married for eighteen years (since 1867) and had four children. She sent him a copy of her diary, "kept by me of all the important incidents in my strange life from that hour [when they were separated during the war] until the day I was led to the altar." Her husband, she told West, was someone he had known in Colorado. She gave him permission to use the diary as long as he did not report her current address.

The diary indicated that after leaving Colorado she had been prospecting in the vicinity of Albuquerque until some time in 1862. At Fort Union she chanced across a government wagon train about to start east and signed on as a "mule whacker" headed to Leavenworth, Kansas. She was appointed assistant wagon master, and held a responsible position in the wagon train.

At Leavenworth, she was offered the position of wagon master for the return trip, but declined the appointment. Instead, she returned to her roots in Iowa. But once there, she couldn't face up to resuming her "girl-life." Recruitment for the war was at a fever pitch in Keokuk, where she arrived in September, 1862. She enlisted in an Iowa cavalry regiment (possibly the 4th Iowa Cavalry Regiment). Once enlisted in General Curtis's command, Charley found herself in frequent contact with officers and men of the 2nd Colorado Cavalry and 1st Colorado Battery, many of whom she had known in the Colorado mountains. Because of this, she had to take special precautions to avoid being recognized.

At the peak of the confrontation between Union General Samuel R. Curtis and Confederate General Sterling Price, "Charles Hatfield" volunteered to infiltrate General Price's camp on a spying mission in female disguise. Obtaining female clothing from a kitchen aide, Charley totally fooled her sponsors, Major Charlot and General Curtis, who failed to penetrate his "disguise" as a woman. They were impressed by "Hatfield's" resourcefulness and authorized "him" to undertake the mission.

Shelby's brigade of General Price's advance was bivouacked in the timber on a bluff overlooking the ford of the Big Blue River. Alert pickets on each side were so close to each other that they bantered back and forth during the night. Major Arthur McCoy of General Shelby's staff, while returning to camp from the outposts, came across a sobbing woman. Charley, pretending to be a farm girl carrying eggs from her home in the vicinity, told him tearfully that she had gotten lost and trapped between the two armies and feared for her safety with so many troops in the woods. Major McCoy took her into headquarters to seek permission for an escort to accompany her home.

Once in camp she was startled to recognize several men whom she had known in Colorado before the war. Cautiously, she sold her eggs around the campfire, eavesdropping on conversations as the men roasted chunks of beef over the fire. Just as an officer was assigned to escort her home, a courier arrived with an important message. Shelby barked some orders and the men went into action. Forgotten in all the excitement, Charley backed away into the shadows and watched. As Shelby mounted his horse, she saw a piece of paper fall to the ground. At the first opportunity she scrambled out to retrieve it, retreating quickly back into the shadows.

As the camp broke up and the men dashed off, Charley made her escape back to the river. There her dress made swimming difficult, and she floated downstream kicking her feet to propel her gradually across. Badly chilled by the cold water, she scrambled up the opposite bank and made her way into the Union lines as quickly as possible. The Confederate message she had retrieved gave General Curtis very important information on the disposition of the Confederate forces for the following day.

Later that night, when General Curtis began briefing his subordinates Charley had ridden into West's camp as courier and recognized him.

✳ ✳ ✳

The legend of "Mountain Charley" is a complex story, full of surprise twists and unresolved mysteries. In fact, there may have been more than one Mountain Charley, whose adventures merged into the legend. Two versions of the story, in particular, are similar in content though confoundingly different in detail. The compilers of the story warn in their introduction that the researcher "will be perplexed if he tries to reconcile the facts in each tale . . . with the purpose of compiling the one authentic account of Mountain Charley's adventures."

The autobiography of Mrs. E. J. Guerin, to which George West's story is appended, was originally published in 1861, in Dubuque, Iowa. It tells the story of "Mountain Charley" from her childhood in New Orleans, Louisiana, through the fall of 1860 when she and her second husband, H. L. Guerin, moved away from Colorado and settled in St. Joseph, Missouri. (Her initials were "E. J.," and according to one source cited by the compilers her name had been Elsa Jane Forest. The autobiography describes a childhood marriage to a "Mr. F.")

In this version, "Charley" had given birth to two children by age 15, when her husband, a river pilot stationed in St. Louis, was killed in a quarrel. Some other personal setbacks left her destitute and bitter, and wanting to revenge her husband's death at the hands of a man named Jamieson. After exhausting all her resources and unable to find work as a woman, she hit on a plan: "It was to dress myself in male attire, and seek for a living in this disguise among the avenues which are so religiously closed against my sex."

Jamieson had been arrested, tried, and found guilty, but in subsequent court hearings was released due to some technicality. Charley set out methodically to pursue her aims, first taking a friend of her late husband into confidence and obtaining men's clothing. Next, she placed her children with the Sisters of Charity. Then she cut her hair short, donned male clothing, and practiced acting like a man, at first venturing out only at night. When she attracted no unusual attention, she gained confidence to go out freely in daylight. By her own account, she looked very much like any boy of 15 or 16.

After working as a hand on Mississippi River steamboats for nearly four years, she got a job as a brakesman on the Illinois Central Railroad in the spring of 1854. She was now about 18, and had saved up a considerable sum of money, sending a certain amount weekly for the care and education of her children. At first the conductor she worked for, a middle-aged man, paid little attention to her. But while they were in Chicago he suddenly became attentive and Charley was put on her guard. In fact, something had caused him to suspect that Charley was a woman, and he and a friend were overheard plotting to get Charley drunk to have some sport with her.

When they started to execute their plan, Charley feigned intoxication and "staggered" out, making her escape. She ran to their lodgings, one step ahead of them, grabbed some clothes and her money and fled. Finding a steamship about to embark for Detroit, she rushed on board. She had worked on the railroad for eight months.

She spent some time in St. Joseph and St. Louis, where she donned women's clothes and visited her children almost daily for several weeks. This was a happy period for her, but she was still rankled over the death of her husband and planned to shoot Jamieson down if she ever ran across him. Accordingly, she practiced regularly with a revolver. Periodically she would put on male clothes and wander around the city, mingling with the crowds in hotels or saloons. During one of these sojourns she overheard the name Jamieson mentioned in conversation, turned and recognized him, since she had inquired carefully about his physical appearance. Long pent-up emotions then surged to the surface, and Charley took a long look while struggling to maintain her composure.

"My fingers immediately sought and closed about the butt of my revolver and my thumb spasmodically forced the hammer upwards," she said. She was tempted to draw the revolver and shoot him without warning, but concluded that would be too cowardly, so she bided her time. She had him now; no need to hurry. Idly she wondered what he would feel if he knew that the wife of his victim was sitting nearby, armed and with vengeance in mind.

After a while, Jamieson rose to leave, and Charley quickly followed, trailing him into a gambling establishment. As he proceeded to participate in a poker game, she seated herself in a position to watch him closely. While she watched, she mentally reviewed the circumstances of Jamieson's murder of her husband and the impact it had had on her life.

The poker game continued until long after midnight, whereupon Jamieson emerged a winner. Finally, the party broke up, and Charley followed Jamieson outdoors and confronted him. She began explaining her "mission" to him, and why she was about to kill him, and then drew her revolver and opened fire. Startled, Jamieson jumped back, drew his revolver and returned the fire. Both shots missed the mark, but Jamieson fired again and wounded her in the thigh. She immediately fired again, wounding him in the left arm, whereupon he fled.

It took her six months to recuperate from her wound. Then, in the spring of 1855, she headed west overland from St. Louis with a 60-man wagon train to California, dressed as a man and the only woman in the party. She was now barely 18 years-old and seeking a new life, leaving her children behind. Her log entries describing the western trek, across plains and deserts, include classic descriptions and they have a strong ring of authenticity. Her log entry for October 4th records reaching the Feather River, continuing:

> At this point I met a woman entirely alone. She was mounted on a mule, had a good stock of provisions and was bound on a journey of some fifty miles to reach some friends. She had started for California by the overland route in company with her husband but he had been killed a short time before. She had taken one mule, abandoned the other, and packing as much provisions as she could conveniently, had started alone. She did not seem to think the undertaking as in any way remarkable, and I presume reached her friends in safety.

After reaching the Sacramento Valley, Charley retained her male guise and briefly prospected for gold, then worked in a saloon and speculated in various businesses, including the use of pack mules for delivery of goods and services in the mountains. After a trip back east to visit her children for a few months, she returned to California driving a herd of cattle and leading a wagon train of fifteen men. En route they had a skirmish with some Snake Indians and she received a severe wound in the arm, but shot one Indian and stabbed another.

Back in California, she took up cattle ranching in the Shasta Valley and returned to her mule-packing business in Sacramento. But she had "restless feet," and sold her business and disposed of her cattle ranch and stock and traveled around California sight-seeing, then returned to St. Louis.

Later, seeking new adventure, she went prospecting for gold at Pike's Peak in the spring of 1859. (Note: This would place *both* "Mountain Charley's"—Charlotte and E.J.—in the same place at the same time, if indeed they were two separate people. The two stories overlap here.) After prospecting for about three months with no success, she moved to Denver and went into the saloon business.

Once while riding a mule on an excursion into the mountains outside Denver the following spring, Charley had a chance encounter with Jamieson and there was mutual recognition, according to the autobiography of Mrs. E. J. Guerin. Both immediately drew their revolvers, but she got the drop on him and shot him down. Though severely wounded, he survived and returned to New Orleans, but died shortly afterwards of yellow fever. Before leaving Colorado, however, he publicly revealed her sex, told the story of why she was after him, and absolved her of blame. The story got out and she was suddenly famous.

At some point she married the barkeeper, H. L. Guerin. They sold the saloon, opened a boardinghouse in the mountains, and went into mining. In the fall of 1860, they gave it up and moved to St. Joseph, Missouri. Her autobiography ends there. (Note: In the fall of 1860 the other "Mountain Charley" was prospecting near Albuquerque, New Mexico, and still had the Civil War adventures ahead of her.)

Although the two stories have a number of points in common, it appears that they involve two different people. Or perhaps one or both stories are more folklore than fact, reflecting common elements of western lore. The stories share these features:

Both women apparently were born about 1837 and ran away to get married (one from boarding school and the other from her childhood home). Both experienced the loss of their husband (one murdered, the other running away with another woman). Both went to work to earn money, dressed as men, and followed a villain west (one the murderer of her husband, the other the unfaithful husband who had run off with another woman, and both gamblers). Both tracked down their man, in one case severely wounding him in a gunfight, the other not telling (but possibly killing him). Both did some prospecting for gold, and did stints leading wagon trains (one far more extensively than the other). Both married a second time.

Possibly there was only one "Mountain Charley" who had experiences similar to these, and the variations result from the telling and retelling around campfires until the story became more myth than fact. The weakness of this hypothesis is that the two stories are each "documented," in the sense that one is taken from the Guerin autobiography (at least portions of which are known to be factual), and the other was reported by a journalist based on some personal knowledge and a diary from the principal.

Also, the two stories have many differences when examined in detail, obviously including the Civil War adventures of Charlotte, partially witnessed by George West, but in many other particulars as well. More likely, there were at least two women who went by the name "Mountain Charley," and possibly more as the compilers of the *Mountain Charley* book suggest. The common elements of the stories may be reflections of the times.

As shown in this book, it was not all that uncommon for women of the period to dress as men in order to attain economic freedom and mobility. Prospecting and mining certainly were common activities at the time, and the opening up of the West attracted all sorts of adventurers and settlers. Gambling and saloons were part of the frontier scene.

In a peculiar way, the Civil War was a liberating force for bold or adventuruous women seeking new horizons in the 1860s. It provided opportunities for travel, discovery, and experience on more equal terms with men in the human adventure. Still, it would be a long time before their gains would be consolidated and these opportunities would be freely open to any woman who chose them.

At least, the Civil War was a milestone in women's fight for liberty, for themselves and for the nation.

Notes to
Chapter 1

H. Sinclair Mills, Jr., *The Vivandiere: History, Tradition, Uniform and Service.* Collinswood, NJ: C.W. Historicals, 1988. (General survey of *vivandieres* in the Civil War, including 39th New York and Lizzie Jones.)

Richard Hall, "They All Fought At Bull Run" in *Minerva: Quarterly Report on Women and the Military*, Fall 1991, pp. 48–54.

Frank Moore, *Women of the War; Their Heroism and Self-Sacrifice.* Hartford, CT: Scranton & Co., 1866. (Further reading on Belle Reynolds's story and journal, pp. 254–277; and on Ellen Goodridge and Lieutenant James Hendrick, pp. 532–533.)

George H. Otis, *The Second Wisconsin Infantry.* Dayton, OH: Morningside House, 1984. (Rosters of the regiment, which was at 1st Bull Run, do not show a Lieutenant James Hendrick.)

William C. Davis, *Battle at Bull Run: A History of the First Major Campaign of the Civil War.* Baton Rouge, LA: LSU Press, 1977. (Comment on 1st Rhode Island infantry and three-months regiments, p. 154; 1st Rhode Island in action, pp. 168–173.)

John E. Stanchak, "Tebe, Marie," in *Historical Times Illustrated Encyclopedia of the Civil War*, New York: Harper & Row, 1986, pp. 744–745.

Frank Rauscher, *Music on the March, 1862–65, With the Army of the Potomac, 114th Regt. P.V., Collis's Zouaves.* Philadelphia, PA: William F. Fell & Co., 1892. (Marie Tebe's service at Chancellorsville, p. 68; photograph, opposite p. 187.)

Agatha Young, *The Women and the Crisis.* New York: McDowell, Obolensky, 1959. (Women at Shiloh, pp. 167–170.)

Fred Brooks, "Shiloh Mystery Woman," in *Civil War Times Illustrated*, August, 1978, p. 29. (Remains of female soldier exhumed on battlefield.)

Matthew P. Andrews, *Women of the South in War Times.* Baltimore, MD: Norman, Remington Co., 1920. (Betsy Sullivan, pp. 112–115; Bettie Philips, pp. 120–126.)

Fannie A. Beers, *Memories: A Record of Personal Experience and Adventure During Four Years of War.* Philadelphia, PA: Lippincott Co., 1888. Time-Life books reprint, 1985. (Story of Mrs. Rose K. Rooney, pp. 217–220.)

Arthur W. Bergeron, Jr., *Guide to Louisiana Confederate Military Units, 1861–1865.* Baton Rouge, LA: LSU Press, 1989. (History of 15th Louisiana Infantry. There is some problem with Mrs. Rooney's story of being with this regiment unless she came out with a different unit originally, perhaps with the 3rd Louisiana Battalion that was organized in June, 1861, and later merged into the 15th Regiment when it was organized in July, 1862.)

L. P. Brockett and Mary C. Vaughan, *Woman's Work in the Civil War: A Record of Heroism, Patriotism and Patience.* Philadelphia, PA: Zeigler, McCurdy & Co., 1867. (Arabella Barlow, pp. 225–233; General and Mrs. Ivan Turchin, pp. 770–771.)

Ezra J. Warner, *Generals in Blue: Lives of the Union Commanders.* Baton Rouge, LA: LSU Press, 1964. (General Ivan Turchin, pp. 511–512.)

Ruth L. Silliker (ed.), *The Rebel Yell & The Yankee Hurrah: The Civil War Journal of a Maine Volunteer.* Camden, Maine: Down East Books, 1985. (John Haley's December 29, 1862, diary entry on "Dutch Mary," p. 64.)

Bell I. Wiley, *Life of Billy Yank.* Baton Rouge, LA: LSU Press, 1952. ("Laundress" with Irish Brigade on Antietam battlefield, p. 339.)

Ethel A. Hurn, *Wisconsin Women in the War Between the States.* Wisconsin History Commission, 1911. (Female soldiers and *vivandieres* from Wisconsin, pp. 100–103.)

Mary A. Livermore, *My Story of the War.* Hartford, CT: A. D. Worthington & Co., 1887. (Story of Georgianne Peterman, p. 119, citing the Platville *Witness*, March, 1864. The similarity of names and hometown for Belle Peterson and Georgianne Peterman suggest a possible confusion of one person's experiences, but the two fragmentary stories are considerably different.)

Notes to

Chapter 2

Ted Alexander (ed.), *The 126th Pennsylvania.* Shippensburg, PA: Beidel Printing House, 1984. (Since Frances Day served just under three weeks in the 126th Pennsylvania before deserting, and the identification of the regiment she served in out west is not given, her later record cannot be traced. Additional research may eventually fill in the gaps in her story. The roster of Company F includes the notation: "Frank Mayne, 5th Serg't. Deserted Aug. 24, 1862. Afterwards turned out to be a woman whose real name was Frances Day." Enlistment records in the National Archives indicate that Day was 18 years-old in 1862, with light complexion and light hair. No height is given.)

Rodney O. Davis, "Private Albert Cashier as Regarded by His/Her Comrades," *Journal of the Illinois Historical Society,* Summer, 1988, pp. 108–112. (On Cashier's admission application form for the Soldiers' Home the certificate of a local physician, Dr. C. F. Ross, found "disabilities and weakness of age—with weakened mental faculties." A Soldiers' Home surgeon, Dr. D. M. Landon, certified that Cashier was "incapable of earning his living by reason of his physical disability arising from general debility and infirmities peculiar to senility." Davis includes quotes of C. W. Ives, who also said that he knew of two other women who tried to enlist in the army, but were immediately detected when an officer threw apples to them. "and the girls, dressed in military uniform, forgot and made a grab for their aprons." However, Ives continued, "there was never a doubt about the fellow Cashier.")

John R. Tripp, "The 95th Illinois Faced Illness, Heat and Rebel Bullets in its Three-Year Tour of Duty," *America's Civil War,* January, 1991. (Steamship flotilla to Vicksburg and description of campaigns.)

Pittsfield, Illinois *Republican,* May 14, 1913. (Includes stories of Cashier's capture and escape, and his reputation for aloofness in camp where he tended to sit apart puffing on a pipe, apparently lost in thought. This was overlooked by his comrades "in their admiration for his military bearing and reckless daring.")

J. T. Headley, *The Great Rebellion; A History of the Civil War in the United States*. Hartford, CT: American Publishing Co., 1866. (Assaults on Vicksburg, pp. 167–168.)

Bureau of Pensions, "95th Illinois Infantry," November 12, 1913. (Regimental history summarized in Albert Cashier's pension files.)

Stewart Sifakis, *Who Was Who in the Union*. Facts on File, 1988. (Vicksburg battlefield monument to Illinois soldiers, p. 70.)

Gerhard P. Clausius, "The Little Soldier of the 95th: Albert D. J. Cashier," *Journal of the Illinois State Historical Society*, Winter, 1958, pp. 380–387. (Includes information on 95th Illinois in combat and Cashier's skills in battle and camp.)

Judy Bourne, Dwight, Illinois *Star & Herald*, March 21, 1991. (Interview with Ruth Morehart about childhood memories of Albert Cashier.)

"Woman Who Masqueraded As Man," Quincy, Illinois. *Whig*. (Unsigned and undated article, circa May, 1913, from Illinois Veterans' Home files. Includes reporter interview with Albert Cashier in the Soldiers' Home.)

Illinois Veterans' Home, administrative papers and correspondence related to Albert Cashier's admission to Soldiers' Home and claims on her estate. (A letter dated December 2, 1915, from the estate administrator to a potential heir states, "The doctors and nurses in this institution [Watertown State Hospital] were very fond of her, giving her every attention possible and we were constantly kept informed as to her condition."

John I. Robertson, *Michigan in the War*. Lansing, 1880. (25th Michigan regimental history regarding "Frank Martin.")

C. Kay Larson, "Bonny Yank and Ginny Reb" in *Minerva: Quarterly Report on Women in the Military*, Spring, 1990, pp. 33–48. (Survey of Civil War female soldiers, including Frances Hook.)

Otto Eisenschiml and Ralph Newman, *The American Iliad: The Epic Story of the Civil War as Narrated by Eyewitnesses and Contemporaries*. Indianapolis, IN: Bobbs-Merrill Co., 1947. (Eyewitness accounts of the battle of Stone's River, pp. 291–314.)

Wellsburg, West Virginia *Herald*, October 9, 1863. (Story of Mrs. Frances Clayton. A similar article appears in the Cincinnati *Gazette* of October 2, 1863, taken from the Grand Rapids, Michigan, *Eagle*.)

Minnie D. Millbrook, *Michigan Women in the Civil War*. Michigan Civil War Centennial Observance Commission, 1963. (Bridget Deavers, pp. 30–31.)

Mary A. Livermore, *My Story of the War*. Hartford, CT: A. D. Worthington & Co., 1887. (Livermore refers to her as "Bridget Devens," who was "always fearless and daring, always doing good service as a soldier." She reports that Bridget's husband was a private, pp. 116–119.)

Frank Moore, *Women of the War; Their Heroism and Self-Sacrifice*. Hartford, CT: S. S. Scranton & Co., 1866. (Bridget Deavers, general comments, pp. 110–112; Rebecca Usher letter home, pp. 461–462; on picket duty and at Fair Oaks, pp. 533–535. The apocryphal story of her appearance at Fair Oaks is the only mention found of her being in action with her husband. In all other anecdotes she is operating alone.)

Charlotte E. McKay, *Stories of Hospital and Camp*. Philadelphia, PA: Claxton, Remsen & Haffelfinger, 1876. (Bridget Deavers, pp. 124–126.)

Marjorie Barstow Greenbie, *Lincoln's Daughters of Mercy*. New York. G. P. Putnam's Sons, 1944. (A later book, primarily about the U.S. Sanitary Commission. Greenbie says, "Another soldier nurse was Bridget Devan, an illiterate, tough, brown little Irishwoman whose husband was a non-commissioned officer." pp. 135–136.)

P. H. Sheridan, *Personal Memoirs*, vol. 2. New York: Charles L. Webster & Co., 1888. (Cavalry battle at Five Forks, Virginia, pp. 158–170.)

L. P. Brockett and Mary C. Vaughan, *Woman's Work in the Civil War: A Record of Heroism, Patriotism and Patience*. Philadelphia, PA: Zeigler, McCurdy & Co., 1867. (Mrs. Mary Morris Husband's comments about "Biddy," pp. 772–773.)

George S. May, *Michigan and the Civil War Years, 1860–1866: A Wartime Chronicle*. Michigan Civil War Centennial Observance Commission, 1964. (Postwar dispute between the state of Michigan and the War Department over detention in service of Michigan cavalry brigade, p. 92.)

Notes to

Chapter 3

Franklin Ellis, *History of Genesee County, Michigan*, pp. 63–68. (History of Company F, 2nd Michigan Regiment; description of regiment quoted from New York *Tribune*, June 10, 1861.)

Robert W. Hodge (ed.), *The Civil War Letters of Perry Mayo*. Michigan State University Museum, East Lansing, Michigan, 1967.

George H. Brown, Adjutant General, *Record of Service of Michigan Volunteers in the Civil War, 1861–1865*, vol. 2. "Second Infantry." Kalamazoo, Michigan, 1905.

Alexander S. Webb, *The Peninsula: McClellan's Campaign of 1862*. New York: Charles Scribner's Sons, 1892.

Richard Wheeler, *Sword Over Richmond: An Eyewitness History of McClellan's Peninsula Campaign*. New York: Harper & Row, 1986.

Diane C. Cashman, *Headstrong: The Biography of Amy Morris Bradley, 1823–1904, A Life of Noblest Usefulness*. Wilmington, NC: Broadfoot Publishing Co., 1990. (Chapter 8, "The Hospital Transports.")

Frank Moore, *Women of the War; Their Heroism and Self-Sacrifice*. Hartford, CT: S. S. Scranton & Co., 1866. (Excerpts from Amy Bradley's journal, including quotes about life in the Hospital Transport Service, pp. 415–452. Tribute to Annie Etheridge, p. 513.)

L. P. Brockett and Mary C. Vaughan, *Woman's Work in the Civil War: A Record of Heroism, Patriotism and Patience*. Philadelphia, PA: Zeigler, McCurdy & Co., 1867. (Mrs. John Harris in Hospital Transport Service, including quotes about service on the *Vanderbilt*, pp. 149–160. Vignettes of the Hospital Transport Service, pp. 299–315. Anna Etheridge at Chancellorsville and Spotsylvania Court House, and receiving the Kearny Cross, pp. 749–753.)

George T. Stevens, *Three Years in the Sixth Corps*. Albany, NY: S. R. Gray, 1866. (Surgeon's account of disease during the Peninsula Campaign, p. 74.)

Minnie D. Millbrook, "Michigan Women Who Went to War," in *Michigan Women in the Civil War*. Michigan Civil War Centennial Observance Commission, 1963. (Summary of Anna Etheridge's life and military career.)

Henrietta S. Jaquette (ed.), *South After Gettysburg: Letters of Cornelia Hancock, 1863–1868*. New York: Thomas Y. Crowell Co., 1956. (Views on war, p. 24. Letters mentioning Annie Etheridge, pp. 113, 131, 156, 175–176.)

George H. Brown, Adjutant General, *Record of Service of Michigan Volunteers in the Civil War, 1861–1865*. vol. 5, "Fifth Infantry."

Daniel G. Crotty, *Four Years Campaigning in the Army of the Potomac*. Grand Rapids, MI: Dygert Brothers & Co., 1874; p. 107. (Annie's farewell.)

Notes to

Chapter 4

S. Emma E. Edmonds, *Nurse and Spy in the Union Army: Comprising the Adventures and Experiences of a Woman in Hospitals, Camps, and Battlefields.* Hartford, CT: W. S. Williams & Co., 1864. (Cited as *Nurse and Spy;* Edmonds's memoirs do not mention "Frank Thompson" or her connection with the 2nd Michigan, except for some internal clues. No historical evidence has been found to verify Emma's assertion that, while on secret service missions, she reported directly to senior generals. Allan Pinkerton was McClellan's chief of intelligence, and he used large numbers of men and women as spies.)

1st Bull Run

Nurse and Spy, pp. 41–54.
Horace H. Cunningham, *Field Medical Services at the Battles of Manassas (Bull Run).* Athens, GA: University of Georgia Press, 1968. (The stone church hospital in Centreville where Emma worked is mentioned on pp. 16–17.)

Yorktown

Nurse and Spy, pp. 110–121.
Richard Wheeler, *Sword Over Richmond: An Eyewitness History of McClellan's Peninsula Campaign.* New York: Harper & Row, 1986. (General John Magruder, at Yorktown, is quoted on page 124: "To meet McClellan's force successfully our main reliance is to be placed upon breastworks. Soldiers cannot be expected to work night and day and fight besides. Our Negro force now at work on fortifications is too small to accomplish this object . . . [he calls for "each proprieter" to furnish] one Negro man, with his ax or spade." His description fits exactly the situation reported by Emma.)

Williamsburg

John Robertson, *Michigan in the War, 1861–1865.* Lansing, MI: W. S. George & Co., 1880; pp. 190–192. (Regimental history, including role of 2nd Michigan at Williamsburg and praise for regiment by General Berry and General Kearny.)
Nurse and Spy, pp. 122–137. (On page 126, Emma describes the wounding of "Captain Wm. R.M., of the ___ Michigan," calling him "one of my first acquaintances in the army." This exactly fits documented circumstances of William R. Morse, Captain of the 2nd Michigan, an old friend from Flint.)

Irish Peddler Woman

Nurse and Spy, pp. 147–173.
With reference to the death of Allen Hall, no listing was found for a Major McKee on the staff of General Richard Ewell in *Confederate Staff Officers, 1861–1865,* by Joseph H. Crute, Jr., Derwent Books, 1982.

Seven Pines/Fair Oaks

Nurse and Spy, pp. 173–185. (Emma's account of serving as General Kearny's orderly contains an "error" or slip-up on her part, since the book purportedly was written by a *female* nurse and occasional spy. She describes being in full military uniform and mounted on her captured "rebel" horse while acting as

Kearny's aide. While this is consistent with the true story of "Franklin Thompson," it is not consistent with the story she is telling in the book. That a general like Kearny would *knowingly* employ a female nurse as a battlefield courier stretches the imagination.)

With regard to Emma's story of delivering a message from General Kearny to a General "G" asking for reinforcements, there was no general in III Corps whose last name began with G. There *was* General Willis A. Gorman in II Corps, and General Lawrence P. Graham in IV Corps, both brigadiers. (See Alexander S. Webb, *The Peninsula: McClellan's Campaign of 1862*. New York: Charles Scribner's Sons, 1892; "Troops of the Army of the Potomac Sent to the Peninsula in March and April, 1862," pp. 191–199.)

William Swinton, *Campaigns of the Army of the Potomac*. Secaucus, NJ: Blue & Grey Press, 1988; pp. 121–139. (Reprint edition, originally published in 1866.)

Charles Lanman, *The Red Book of Michigan; A Civil, Military and Biographical History*. Detroit, MI: E. B. Smith & Co., 1871, pp. 316–317. (Roles of Kearny and 2nd Michigan.)

John Robertson, *op cit*. (Regimental history of battle.)

The Seven Days

Nurse and Spy, pp. 207–233. (Incident with J. Robbins, p. 212; Malvern Hill, pp. 223–229.)

Clifford Dowdey, *The Seven Days: The Emergence of Robert E. Lee*. New York: Fairfax Press, 1978.

Jeffry D. Wert, "Seven Days Campaign, Virginia," in *Historical Times Illustrated Encyclopedia of the Civil War*, 1986, pp. 667–668. (Includes casualty figures.)

Notes to

Chapter 5

S. Emma E. Edmonds, *Nurse and Spy*, 1864. (Emma does not report in her memoirs the incident of serious injuries from a fall on a horse, and being cared for by her comrades to avoid discovery in August, 1862.) Specifically, see these pages in *Nurse and Spy*: Secret service mission as female contraband, pp. 261–264; Kearny's death at Chantilly, pp. 265–266. (Emma makes no mention of the thunderstorm and heavy rain, but neither does the regimental history in its brief account of the battle. Like Kearny, she arrived on the field late and probably missed the storm, which had stopped by about 6:30 P.M. Except possibly for the "crackling of dry branches" under foot, her description of the weather and darkness is accurate.); Dying female solider at Antietam, pp. 270–273. (This apocryphal story appears to be in the "too good to be true" category—a woman disguised as a male soldier finding a counterpart on a battlefield dying nobly for the cause, and protecting her secret by privately burying her. If the story is true, however, it has implications for the question of how many female soldiers went undiscovered to their graves, if not to their homes.); Battlefield courier at Fredericksburg, pp. 297–308. (Emma could not have been Heintzelman's battlefield aide since he was no longer a field commander at this time. Her role as orderly for Poe was confirmed after the war by Congressman B. M. Cutcheon, and by Poe in a letter to Cutcheon. Writing to Emma, Cutcheon said: "though you don't remember

Major Cutcheon of the Twentieth, I remember Frank Thompson, an orderly, very well. I saw you almost every day at Fredericksburg and repeatedly during the battle of Fredericksburg." Lansing *State Republican*, June 26, 1900. (Emma's account of Fredericksburg, first published in 1864, is convincingly accurate, comparing very well to the following Commager and Couch references.); Adventures in Kentucky, her final campaign pp. 312–323. (Emma did not, as she reports, go on with the Ninth Corps to Vicksburg. Why she claimed to end her army career there is not known, but may have been to disguise the fact that she actually left the army at Kentucky. Perhaps in 1864 she worried that someone reading her book might make the connection between Emma Edmonds, whose adventures followed the path of the 2nd Michigan, and "Frank Thompson," who had deserted from that regiment in Kentucky. If she stuck too close to the truth, it might give her away.); Illness and leaving the army, pp. 354–360. (Emma's account of the circumstances of her departure from the army is interesting because it contains certain important elements of truth, and provides some psychological insight into her feelings at this time. One can almost imagine her reaching this point of the narrative and struggling to express her motives and feelings at what was a major turning point in her life. Still purportedly at Vicksburg, she comes down with a serious fever, exhaustion, and weakness. Her soldierly qualities had fled, she said, and she found herself giving vent to long pent up feelings, often weeping hour after hour "until it would seem that my head was literally a fountain of tears and my heart one great burden of sorrow. All the horrid scenes that I had witnessed during the past two years seemed now before me with vivid distinctness, and I could think of nothing else." In short, she was experiencing what today would be called "battle fatigue" or "post-traumatic stress disorder," perhaps bordering on a nervous breakdown. Other factors in her personal life may also have been at work. "It was under these circumstances," she continued, "that I made up my mind to leave the army. . . . I sent for the surgeon and told him I was not able to remain longer—that I would certainly die if I did not leave immediately . . . [he] concurred in my opinion, and made out a certificate of disability, and I was forthwith released from further duty as 'Nurse and Spy' in the Federal army." Naturally, it strains the imagination to think that a surgeon would release her while still so obviously ill. She, in fact, deserted from Lebanon, Kentucky, while ill: "The very next day I embarked for Cairo [actually Oberlin, Ohio], and on my arrival there I procured female attire, and laid aside forever (perhaps) my military uniform." She goes on to describe a trip to Washington to rest and recover from fever and fatigue, and to "recruit my shattered health," which happened in real life but at other locations. Except for a few scattered anecdotes, that is the end of her narrative of military life.)

Sylvia G. L. Dannett, *She Rode With the Generals: The True and Incredible Story of Sarah Emma Seelye, Alias Franklin Thompson*. New York: Thomas Nelson & Sons, 1960. (Serious injuries from fall on horse, pp. 192–193; Orlando Poe "affair" and Antietam, pp. 193–198. Dannett suggests that Emma may have had an affair with Colonel Orlando Poe about the time of Antietam. Also, Emma's whereabouts after Antietam until Fredericksburg are unknown. Poe apparently did overstay his leave in Washington during the Antietam campaign, returning to action leading a brigade at Fredericksburg in December. However, Dannett suspects her of consorting with various officers and men without adducing much supporting evidence, even proposing that her soldier friends who cared for her when she was injured *must* have known that "Frank" was a woman.)

Marian Talmadge and Iris Gilmore, *Emma Edmonds: Nurse and Spy*. New York: Putnams, 1970. (Serious injuries from fall on horse, pp. 95–96; Emma at Antietam, Chapter 9.)

Battle of Chantilly

John Robertson, *Michigan in the War, 1861–1865*. Lansing, MI: W. S. George & Co., 1880; pp. 36–37. (Regimental history.)

Jeffry D. Wert, "Chantilly (Ox Hill), Virginia, Battle of," in *Historical Times Illustrated Encyclopedia of the Civil War*, 1986, pp. 129–130.

Charles F. Walcott, "The Battle of Chantilly," in *The Blue and the Gray* by Henry Steele Commager. New York: Fairfax Press, 1982, p. 191. (Walcott reports that the rain had stopped by about 6:30 P.M., and "the atmosphere was thick, and the sky still so heavily overcast, that night coming on prematurely made it impossible to distinguish any object clearly more than a few rods away." Yet the battle continued for a while.)

Fredericksburg

Henry Steele Commager, *The Blue and the Gray*. New York: Fairfax Press, 1982. (Description of the pontoon bridges and Confederate sharpshooters, p. 234.)

Darius N. Couch (Major General, II Corps commander at Fredericksburg), "The Battle of Fredericksburg," in *The Century War Book*. New York: Arno Press, 1978 (reprint of 1894 edition), pp. 165–169. (Couch reported, in part: "The bombardment for the purpose of dislodging the sharpshooters, who under cover of the houses were delaying the bridge-making, was terrific. . . . After the bombardment had failed to dislodge the enemy, the 7th Michigan [and two Massachusetts regiments] of Howard's division sprang into the pontoons, and rowing themselves over drove away Barksdale's sharpshooters. This gallant action enabled the engineers to complete the bridges.")

With 2nd Michigan to Kentucky

Nurse and Spy; After Fredericksburg, Emma records on page 311: "Being desirous of leaving the Army of the Potomac, I now applied to go [to Kentucky] with the Ninth Corps, which was granted." In fact, as Emma acknowledged in an interview in 1884 (Fort Scott, Kansas, *Weekly Monitor*, January 17, 1884), "Frank Thompson" and the 2nd Michigan—which had been transferred to the 9th Corps before Fredericksburg—was ordered west with the corps. The regiment, with its bridgade, moved to Newport News, Virginia, in February, 1863. On March 19th it traveled via Baltimore, Parkersburg, and Louisville to Bardstown, Kentucky. Captain William Humphrey, as new colonel of the regiment (replacing Poe), issued Batallion Order No. 30 at Lebanon, Kentucky, April 25th, which read in part: "Having been commissioned by the Governor of the State of Michigan as colonel of the 2d Regiment Michigan Infantry, I hereby assume command of the regiment from this date." The regiment afterwards, in June, 1863 was sent to reinforce Ulysses S. Grant's army in Mississippi and served with distinction in the Vicksburg campaign that brought Grant to prominence. From there, as part of Sherman's army, it fought at Jackson, Mississippi, and later that year at Knoxville, Tennessee, taking fearful casualties. Among the killed were Lieutenant William Noble and Lieutenant Charles R. Galpin; mortally wounded, Major Cornelius Byington and Lieutenant Frank Zoellener.

The regiment encamped at Blain's Cross Roads, Tennessee, where it stayed until mid-January, 1864. There 198 men reenlisted as Veteran Volunteers. On February 24th, the regiment was ordered to Detroit and given thirty days furlough.

On April 4, 1864 the regiment was ordered east, back to the Army of the

Potomac, taking part in the bloody final Virginia campaigns after Grant was appointed commander in chief of the armies: Wilderness (thirty-eight casualties); Spottsylvania Court House (eleven casualties, Captain James Farrand killed); Bethesda Church (thirty-eight casualties, Lieutenant George S. Williams mortally wounded); Petersburg (June 17th, eighty-six casualties, Captain James Bradley killed; June 18th, eighty-five casualties, Lieutenant Sherman mortally wounded).

During this campaign Colonel Humphrey was in temporary command of the brigade, and other officers, in turn, temporarily commanded the regiment. On October 27th, Captain Frederick Schneider (later a benefactor of Emma Edmonds) was wounded and taken prisoner.

The regiment continued in action around Petersburg, assisting in the siege of that city into 1865, and participating in its capture on April 3rd. Soon after that, Frederick Schneider was paroled and assumed command of the regiment as its final commander. The regiment was mustered out of service on July 29, 1865, arriving in Detroit on August 1st, where it was paid off and disbanded.

The regiment had served from Blackburn's Ford (July 18, 1861) through the Appomattox surrender (April 9, 1865), participating in so many major engagements that there was not room on the battle flag to list all of them! (Regimental history information from John Robertson, *Michigan in the War, 1861–1865, Record of Service of Michigan Volunteers in the Civil War*, 1880, vol. 2; Charles Lanman, *The Red Book of Michigan; A Civil, Military and Biographical History*, 1871; Michigan State Archives records.)

Notes to

Chapter 6

Sylvia Dannett, *She Rode With the Generals*. New York: Thomas Nelson and Sons, 1960. (As Sarah Edmonds's main biographer, Sylvia Dannett says the firstborn in her family was Eliza, followed by Frances and Mary Jane, then Rebecca Sarah, Thomas (who was epileptic), and finally Sarah Emma. The three eldest sisters married and left home. Rebecca Sarah may have died in childhood, Dannett says, since the name Sarah was reused. Information about Sarah and her siblings, pp. 16–26. Sarah Emma's postwar interview suggesting that she "came near marrying a pretty little girl" and other references to "Frank Thompson" escorting female friends around, led Sylvia Dannett to suggest that Sarah Emma was a lesbian, or bisexual. However, the evidence to support this interpretation is lacking. Instead, her interactions with female friends appear to have simply reflected her need for a "cover story" in order to convincingly appear to be male. The same issue arises in regard to Loreta Janeta Velazquez, the southern counterpart of Sarah Emma Edmonds. See Chapters 9–11.)

Betty Fladeland, "Alias Franklin Thompson," *Michigan History*, vol. 42, 1958. (Includes information on Frank Thompson's early Michigan years.)

Marian Talmadge and Iris Gilmore, *Emma Edmonds: Nurse and Spy*, New York: Putnams, 1970. (Includes details about Sarah Edmonds's childhood and escape from her father.)

George S. May, *Michigan and the Civil War Years, 1860–1866: A Wartime Chronicle*, Michigan Civil War Centennial Observance Commission, 1964. (Includes historical notes about origins of 2nd Michigan and other early regiments.)

Franklin Ellis, *History of Genesee County, Michigan*, pp. 63–65 (Background of 2nd Michigan Regiment and Flint, Michigan).

Notes to

Chapter 7

Fort Scott, Kansas, *Weekly Monitor,* January 17, 1884. (Interview with Sarah E. Seelye, including references to Oberlin, Ohio, and *Nurse and Spy.*)

Lansing, Michigan, *State Republican,* June 20, 1900. (Quotes regarding the authenticity of *Nurse and Spy.*)

Sylvia G. L. Dannett, *She Rode With the Generals: The True and Incredible Story of Sarah Emma Seelye, Alias Franklin Thompson.* New York: Thomas Nelson & Sons, 1960. (Includes extensive detail about Sarah Edmonds's postwar life. Emma's selflessness, pp. 241–242; sequel to *Nurse and Spy,* pp. 297–298.)

House Report #820, U.S. Congress, March 18, 1884. (Sarah Edmonds's own statement as well as affidavits of supporters, including her comments on the odium of spying. Also includes text of March, 1884 Kansas City *Times* article reporting her reunion with Captain William Morse.)

Lansing *State Republican,* May 20, 1900. (Colonel Frederick Schneider's quotes about the Seelyes' life in Fort Scott, Kansas.)

Betty Fladeland, "New Light on Sarah Emma Edmonds, Alias Franklin Thompson," *Michigan History,* December 1963, pp. 357–362. (Jerome Robbins and William Boston diaries.)

Ezra J. Warner, *Generals in Blue.* Baton Rouge, LA: LSU Press, 1964. (Biography of Orlando M. Poe.)

Lansing *State Republican,* June 20–21, 1900. (Sarah Emma Seelye's letter to Albert Cowles from Fort Scott, Kansas, August 15, 1883.)

Lansing *State Republican,* June 26, 1900. (Congressman Byron Cutcheon's letter to Sarah E. Seelye, July 16, 1886. After service in the 20th Michigan, Cutcheon went on to command the 27th Michigan and after that was appointed to command the Second Brigade, Second Divisioin, Ninth Army Corps from October 16, 1864, until his resignation on March 6, 1865. After return to civilian life, he successively became a practicing attorney, University of Michigan regent, and four-term Republican congressman. In 1891 he was awarded the Congressional Medal of Honor "for distinguished gallantry" during the Civil War.)

Concerned Citizens for Washington Cemetery Care, *Washington Cemetery Centennial Book, A History of the German Society Cemetery of Houston, Texas.* 1988. (Burial place of Sarah Emma Edmonds Seelye.)

Notes to

Chapter 8

Amy Clarke

Newspaper article from Jackson, Mississippi, reprinted in *Southern Women of the Second American Revolution* by Henry Jackson, Atlanta, 1863.

Maury Darst, "Robert Hodges, Jr., Confederate Soldier" in *East Texas Historical Journal,* vol. 9, #1, 1971, pp. 37–38. (Robert Hodges, Jr., letter home to father. Spelling corrected for clarity.)

Lucy Matilda Thompson

John Mull, "Profile of a Woman Veteran: The Life of Private Bill Thompson, Confederate States of America," *National Women's Military Museum Newsletter*, vol. 1, #1, Spring, 1989.
Joseph H. Crute, Jr., *Units of the Confederate States Army.* Midlothian, VA: Derwent Books, 1987. (Regimental history of 18th North Carolina Infantry.)

Sarah Malinda Blaylock

Greg Mast, " 'Sam Blaylock,' 26th North Carolina Troops," *Military Images,* vol. 11, #1, July–August, 1989.
Joseph H. Crute, Jr., *op cit.* (Regimental history of 26th North Carolina Infantry Regiment.)
Bell I. Wiley, *Life of Johnny Reb.* Baton Rouge, LA: LSU Press, 1978, p. 334. (Cites Clark's *North Carolina Regiments,* vol. 2, as reporting that Moore was a recruiter for Company F, and that Keith Blaylock would only agree to serve if his wife could go with him. Moore agreed to help conceal her true identity.)
National Archives, military records of Mrs. S. M. Blaylock. (Under "remarks" states: "This lady dressed in men's clothes, volunteered, received bounty and for two weeks did all the duties of a soldier before she was found out, but her husband being discharged, she disclosed the fact, returned the bounty, and was immediately discharged April 20, 1862." The bounty was $50.)

Mary and Molly Bell

Mary Elizabeth Massey, *Bonnet Brigades.* New York: Alfred A. Knopf, 1966, pp. 84–85.

Allie McPeak

Simkins and Patton, *The Women of the Confederacy.* Richmond, VA: Garrett & Massie, 1936, p. 72.

Nancy Hart

Simkins and Patton, *op cit.,* p. 77.
Boyd B. Stutler, "Nancy Hart, Lady Bushwhacker," *Civil War Times,* January, 1960, p. 7.
C. Kay Larson, "Bonny Yank and Ginny Reb" in *Minerva: Quarterly Report on Women and the Military,* vol. 8, #1, Spring, 1990, p. 41.

The Nancy Harts (Georgia)

(Materials from Troup Country Archives, courtesy of Randall Allen.)
Randall Allen, "The Nancy Harts," *TCHS Newsletter,* June, 1987.
Mrs. J. Brown Morgan, entry in *Dictionary of Georgia Biography,* vol. 2.
"LaGrange Sent Nancy Harts to Battle During War of '64," LaGrange, GA, *Daily News,* January 19, 1937. (Quotes from Mrs. Thaddeus Horton about target practice, marksmanship, patrolling of streets, and the standoff with Federal cavalry.)
Clark Johnson, "The Nancy Harts Were Gallant Ladies," LaGrange, GA, *Daily News,* undated. (Roster of Nancy Hart officers.)
"Confederate WAACs," LaGrange, GA, *Daily News,* circa 1942.
Eleanor Orr, "LaGrange WAACs 82 Years Ago," LaGrange, GA, *Daily News,* May 23, 1943. (Quotes about the attire of the Nancy Harts.)

Notes to

Chapter 9

C. J. Worthington (ed.), *The Woman in Battle: A Narrative of the Exploits, Adventures, and Travels of Madame Loreta Janeta Velazquez, Otherwise Known as Lieutenant Harry T. Buford, Confederate States Army.* Hartford, CT: T. Belknap, 1876; Childhood fantasies, p. 42; In combat at 1st Bull Run, pp. 95–106. (Lending credence to her story are numerous examples throughout the book of Velazquez being thwarted or frustrated, failing to get her way. She constantly goes down blind alleys and experiences more "defeats" than victories. These tend to contradict the notion that she was merely trying to tell a good yarn and make herself out to be a heroine for profit. One such example is her effort to obtain a promotion from General Jackson at the conclusion of the battle. She reports disgustedly, "[instead] he gave me a recommendation to General Bragg for a recruiting commission. This I did not care about, for I thought that I did not need his permission or his aid to do recruiting duty." pp. 105–106.); Battle of Ball's Bluff, pp. 115–125. (Although her general description of the battle and the units engaged is accurate, Velazquez in one place reverses the names of the commanders of the 13th and 18th Mississippi regiments, is one day off in the date of the battle, and makes a flagrant error of omission. Standing on top of the bluff looking down into the Potomac River, she reports that it was "very wide." Instead, there is a relatively narrow channel between the foot of the bluff and Harrison Island, a long, elliptical land mass that divides the river into two channels and dominates the view from the top of the bluff. She fails to mention it at all.); Spying excursion in Washington, D.C., pp. 126–143; Detective corps in Tennessee, pp. 143–152; Fort Donelson, pp. 161–173.

1st Bull Run

William C. Davis, *Battle at Bull Run: A History of the First Major Campaign of the Civil War.* Baton Rouge, LA: LSU Press, 1977. (Jubal Early at Bull Run, p. 228 et seq.)

Newton Martin Curtis, *From Bull Run to Chancellorsville: The Story of the Sixteenth New York Infantry Together With Personal Reminiscences.* New York: G. P. Putnam's Sons, 1906. (Curtis was a captain commanding a company of the 16th New York at 1st Bull Run, and rose to the rank of major general. He includes the following comment about the inexperienced military commanders at 1st Bull Run, to be found on page 44: "It is probable that in no battle of modern times, in which thirty-five thousand men were engaged, was there so small a number of officers educated in the science and art of war; nor was there a battle which was the nursery of so many who came to great prominence in the profession of arms, as those who rose from the mob-like forces which contended at Manassas.")

Battle of Ball's Bluff

Byron Farwell, *Ball's Bluff: A Small Battle and its Long Shadow.* McLean, VA: EPM Publications, 1990. (Includes this graphic description of Harrison Island to be found on page 37: "From the top of the bluff one can look across a narrow stretch of the river to Harrison's Island, 500 acres of flat, wood-fringed farmland shaped like a huge dolphin caught in the Potomac, a great stationary fish in a river too small for it to move." For a description of the retreat down the bluff and the slaughter of soldiers trying to escape in boats, see p. 109–117.)

Joseph Dorst Patch, *The Battle of Ball's Bluff*. Leesburg, VA: Potomac Press, 1958. (Includes official reports and eyewitness descriptions, among the latter one by Oliver Wendell Holmes, then a lieutenant in the 20th Massachusetts Regiment, who was wounded in the battle.)

Fort Donelson

J. T. Headley, *The Great Rebellion; A History of the Civil War in the United States*. Hartford, CT: American Publishing Co., 1866, pp. 262–274.

M. F. Force, *From Fort Henry to Corinth*. New York: Charles Scribner's Sons, 1881, pp. 33–65.

Notes to
Chapter 10

C. J. Worthington (ed.), *The Woman in Battle*, 1876. Memoirs of Loreta Janeta Velazquez. (Excerpts in this chapter include additional examples of her not particularly telling a "good story," but instead revealing her as confused and indecisive about what she should do, and recounting her numerous disappointments and failures. On balance, this tends to support the interpretation that she was trying to give an honest account of her experiences, rather than consciously trying to deceive anyone for some ulterior motive.); Jailed in New Orleans, pp. 177–181; Enlistment in 21st Louisiana Regiment, pp. 181–182. (We are not told what story she gave General Villepigue about her enlistment, but it must have been a good one! She almost certainly would have been vigorously questioned about enlisting under false circumstances and misleading the authorities, and not so readily and cheerfully transferred away without any inquiry. There is also the mystery of her alleged commission papers, referred to here as "this document." Who authorized the commission, and at what point? How did she manage to preserve this paper through all her adventures? Did General Villepigue consult with Captain Moses or check on her New Orleans identity before authorizing her transfer? The Velazquez narrative leaves many puzzles unexplained.); Battle of Shiloh and aftermath, pp. 200–230. (The drenching rain on the first night is reported in several memoirs, and General Ulysses S. Grant in his account of the battle reports being discomfited by the rain as he tried to sleep under a tree. See U. S. Grant, "The Battle of Shiloh: The Union Side," *Century War Book*, 1894, p. 53); Blockade running and arrest in New Orleans, pp. 232–267; Arrests in Richmond and Lynchburg, pp. 272–287. (A report on the arrest, in Richmond, of a woman in Confederate uniform using the name "Lieutenant Bensford" appears in the Lynchburg *Daily Virginian*, July 4, 1863, taken from the Richmond *Enquirer*. She told authorities her name was "Mrs. Alice Williams" (a name used elsewhere by Velazquez) and that her husband was in the Federal army. A related article appeared in the Richmond *Whig*, June 19, 1863, taken from the Jackson *Mississippian*. It reports the presence in the city, recently arrived from New Orleans, of Mrs. Laura J. Williams, a former resident of Arkansas, who had served in the Confederate army as "Henry Benford" and whose husband was in the Union army. The article also reports several incidents in her army career that resemble, but do not always totally agree with, statements in her memoirs. These are discussed elsewhere. The *Official Records*, series 2, vol. 8, p. 936, includes 1865 correspondence referring to a "Miss Alice Williams" who served in the Confederate army as "Lieutenant Buford."

Research conducted at the Jones Memorial Library in Lynchburg, Virginia, by

Staff Researcher Lewis H. Averett failed to find any record of the Velazquez/ Buford arrest in contemporary local newspapers. Mr. Averett located a transcribed news article from the Lynchburg *News* on "Lynchburg in the '50s" mentioning that the jail was upstairs on the second floor of the City Market with the mayor's office, confirming that detail from the memoirs.

Professor Stuart Sprague of Morehead State University, Kentucky, located an article in the Louisville *Daily Journal*, October 9, 1861, reporting the arrest in Lynchburg of a "Mrs. Mary Ann Keith" of Memphis, Tennessee, who had registered at the Piedmont House as "Lieutenant Buford" and who was "rigged out in a full suit of soldier's clothes." She was sent to Richmond for a further hearing. Mr. Averett reports: "The Piedmont Hotel, formerly the Lancaster House, was located . . . across from the Virginia and Tennessee Railroad depot."); Through Georgia and Tennessee, pp. 288–293. (Upon leaving Lynchburg and heading to Atlanta and Tennessee, Velazquez does not explain how or why she is suddenly detached from General Winder's secret service corps and able to go where she pleases. Nor does she explain how her family knows to address letters to her in Atlanta, or whether they have some other address for her from which mail was being forwarded. In any case, her visit to Atlanta obviously was on the spur of the moment and the city was not one of her regular haunts. Serious questions remain unanswered about the accuracy of this portion of her Memoirs.); Spying behind Union lines, pp. 294–309. (Includes her views on the negative reputation of spying.); Atlanta hospital, pp. 310–325. (*Generals in Gray*, by E. J. Warner, lists fourteen Confederate generals whose last name begins with "F." Though some had Atlanta connections, none stands out as an obvious candidate to have been the drunken "General F" of her narrative.)

Arch Fredric Blakey, *General John H. Winder C.S.A.* Gainesville, FL: University of Florida Press, 1990. (Biography of Winder, including his years as prison commander and provost marshal of Richmond during the Civil War.)

James Parton, *General Butler in New Orleans*. New York: Mason Brothers, 1864. (Detailed description of New Orleans under Federal occupation in the Civil War. Reference to Mayor John T. Monroe, p. 311.)

Arthur W. Bergeron, Jr., *Guide to Louisiana Confederate Military Units, 1861–1865*. Baton Rouge, LA: LSU Press, 1989. (As reported by Velazquez, the 21st Louisiana Regiment did go to Fort Pillow at this time; Bernard Moses was captain of Company D; Colonel Sam Marks did lead the 11th Louisiana at Shiloh; Captain G. Merrick Miller was commander of Company I; Frank Armstrong was colonel of the 3rd Louisiana and later a brigadier general cavalry commander in 1863.)

Notes to

Chapter 11

C. J. Worthington (ed.), *The Woman in Battle*, 1876.

Atlanta hospital and marriage, pp. 326–338. Franklin M. Garrett, historian at the Atlanta Historical Society, provided the following information about Civil War Atlanta in a personal communication, June 12, 1990: Thompson House most likely was the Atlanta Hotel located just north of the railroad station, whose proprietor was a well-known Atlantan named Dr. Joseph Thompson. The Empire Hospital was a converted hotel near the railroad station at Pryor and Alabama Streets. The names of the doctors could not be verified, and they probably were wartime transients rather than natives.

Velazquez states that the battle of Chickamauga, September 19–20, 1863, occurred while she was in the hospital, so that Captain DeCaulp's capture at Chattanooga would have been sometime after that. Yet a register of prisoners of war in the National Archives lists DeCaulp as being captured at Chattanooga on September 14, 1863. This is one of several examples of her getting dates of events wrong, or out of sequence. More importantly, there are major discrepancies between her story and what the official records say about DeCaulp. These are discussed elsewhere.); Richmond and secret service, pp. 339–379. She asks for secret service assignments, but gives no explanation for her previous abrupt departure from the service to go off free lancing. Nor does she mention, on this trip to Richmond, calling on her friends Major and Mrs. Alexander.

Concerning the captured spy and her mission to Memphis, General Stephen A. Hurlbut, in 1863, was in garrison at Memphis commanding xvi Corps. General Cadwallader C. Washburn commanded three divisions of xvi Corps. Except for some occasional minor misspellings, such as Quantrell for Quantrill, Velazquez is highly accurate about the locations, positions, and activities of the prominent people she names. In this section, she also correctly names the governor of Indiana, Oliver Morton.

Forrest's raid into western Tennessee took place December 11, 1862–January 3, 1863, well before the time period she gives for her spying mission. See *Historical Times Illustrated Encyclopedia of the Civil War*, pp. 270–271. (Another example of events not reported in their proper sequence.); Camp Chase and on to New York City, pp. 379–382. (Her reference to the one-armed major in Tod Barracks at Camp Chase is a striking confirmation of this part of her memoirs. The prison itself was little known (see Knauss reference, below). Researcher Jennie Zeidman, with the help of the Columbus Civil War Round Table, located an obscure reference in the Delaware, Ohio, *Gazette* of August 24, 1863, to the "one-armed major" John W. Skiles of the 88th Ohio who commanded Tod Barracks. As a result, his military records were obtained from the National Archives, showing that he served both as commander of Tod Barracks and provost marshal of Columbus, and toward the end of the war as commander of the "Draft Rendezvous" in Columbus.

Velzaquez correctly gives the names and location of the two generals to whom her paroled brother was to report in Philadelphia and New York City.); Spying at the North as double agent, pp. 383–453. (Her physical description of La Fayette C. Baker was accurate; see Leech reference, below. General Erastus B. Tyler was commander of Baltimore defense. See Ezra J. Warner, *Generals in Blue*, Baton Rouge, LA: LSU Press, 1964, p. 515.); Treasury ring and bounty jumpers, pp. 464–498. (Her account of the broker rings in New York City compares very favorably to Baker's own story (see reference below). She talks knowledgably about how the brokers operated and describes accurately Baker's own undercover activities, suggesting that she did have inside knowledge of both.); Missions to west and war-end activities, pp. 499–518. (Velazquez gives no reason for or explanation of her sudden diversion from Ohio to Canada, nor of which Canadian city was involved. If it was Montreal, this might have special significance. See Headley reference below.); Touring Europe with brother and family, pp. 519–530; Confederate colonies in South America, pp. 531–561. (Her apparently carelessly written memoirs are Velazquez's worst handicap when it comes to credibility. Yet, analysis of the historical record on the colonization of Venezuela shows clearly that she must have been there and really played a role in the affair. According to a scholarly publication in 1960, the Venezuela colonization plan "is probably the least known." (See reference, below.) Therefore it is of exceptional interest in evaluating the reliability and veracity of Velazquez since it provides independent documentation of the story she gives in her memoirs. Her account of the Venezuelan expedition dovetails extremely well with the 1960 historical study.

In her typical sparse style, she describes in the memoirs abruptly marrying one of the passengers (her third husband), a former Confederate officer, a Major Wasson, just before setting off on the schooner *Elizabeth* for Venezuela. This seemingly impulsive act is not particularly justified, other than by the fact that he was "fine-looking" and "a strong attachment sprang up between us" (page 539). The Confederate Centennial Studies report, listing the fifty-one passengers aboard the *Elizabeth*, includes the names of "Mr. and Mrs. John Wasson" (page 51). Overall, the comparison between her account and the 1960 study is quite remarkable, strongly suggesting that she was a real participant in the planned exodus.)

William H. Knauss, *The Story of Camp Chase*. Columbus, OH: The General's Books, 1990. A reprint of the 1906 edition. (Camp Chase served as a rendezvous for newly forming Union regiments and for paroled Union prisoners, the Confederate prison compound originally being secondary and constructed to hold only 450 inmates. As the war dragged on, the prison population peaked at about 8,000 in 1863. "It is remarkable that in all the official reports and records of 1861–65 of the Governor of Ohio, his Adjutant General, or his subordinate officers no mention is made of the Confederate prison at Camp Chase except a brief reference made in 1861 by Gov. William Dennison." page 122.)

Margaret Leech, *Reveille in Washington, 1860–1865*. New York: Harper & Brothers, 1941. (An in-depth study of events in the nation's capital during the war. Describes Baker as "a lean, muscular, taciturn man, with . . . cold, searching gray eyes. (page 148). Includes passing mention only of scandals in the Treasury Department (page 317), but several references to bounty brokers and La Fayette Baker's activities.)

La Fayette C. Baker, *Spies, Traitors and Conspirators of the Late Civil War*. Philadelphia, PA: John E. Potter & Co., 1894. (Bounty jumpers in New York City, pp. 249–275.)

John W. Headley, *Confederate Operations in Canada and New York*. New York: Neale Publishing Co., 1906. (Includes chapters on Confederate efforts to free prisoners in northern prison camps late in the war. A possible connection to Velazquez's story appears in Chapter 36, reporting on Confederate officers imprisoned in Montreal after the raid on St. Alban's, Vermont, October 19, 1864. On page 376 it reports: "Mrs. ____, a widow only 24 years old [Velasquez was born in 1842 and would have been 22 years old], employed by the Confederate Government for secret service in the Northern States, had come to Montreal and called on the prisoners at the jail." She volunteered to obtain badly needed documents for the prisoners' defense from Richmond, and did so. "She declined to accept from Col. Jacob Thompson any compensation whatever for her services or expenses." She was said to be from Kentucky. After the war, she had visited Frankfort, Kentucky, and the legislature took a recess of fifteen minutes in her honor, and gave her an ovation.

After forty years, when the book was written, the grateful survivors had forgotten her name, but one had obtained a photograph of her at the jail. The photograph is reproduced opposite page 376, and the young woman bears a *strong* resemblance to the engraving of Velazquez that appears in her memoirs. An effort was made, without success, to determine the name of the woman who was honored by the Kentucky legislature.)

James D. Horan, *Confederate Agent: A Discovery in History*. New York: Crown Publishers, 1954. (Three-fourths of the book deals with Confederate secret service operations in the North late in the war, headed by Thomas Henry Hines, with activities often planned in and executed from Canada. In a section on Union counterspy Felix Stidger, Horan reports that in the summer of 1863, Stidger went to St. Louis "where he saw the beautiful Madam Valesque [sic], the Confederate spy whose black eyes bewitched passes from Union generals." (page 106). Also includes chapters on the Johnson's Island prison camp attack, St. Albans raid, and the attempt to burn New York City.)

Alfred J. Hanna and Kathryn A. Hanna, *Confederate Exiles in Venezuela.* Confederate Centennial Studies #15. Tuscaloosa, AL: Confederate Publishing Co., 1960. (Further evidence of Velazquez's involvement in the colonization expedition is reported on pages 23–24: "On January 5, 1867 the New Orleans *Picayune* reported that 'Mrs. Mary de Caulp has appeared as agent for the Southern states for a Venezuelan emigration company. . . . During the War she fought for the Confederacy as Lieutenant Bufort [sic] until her sex was discovered. Bufort was a member of a Texas cavalry regiment. She was arrested by Butler, escaped to Richmond and claimed she went to Europe as a purchasing agent for the Confederate Government.' This woman was Loreta Janeta Velasquez, a New Orleans girl of Cuban extraction.")

Jubal Early–Loreta Velazquez correspondence, Tucker family papers, Southern Historical Collection, Chapel Hill, North Carolina. (Includes May 18, 1878 letter from Velazquez to General Jubal Early care of Congressman W. F. Slemons, as copied by Early; Letter drafted by Early to Congressman W. F. Slemons, but never sent, May 22, 1878; Letter from Early to Congressman John Randolph Tucker, May 26, 1878. For additional background on the correspondence, see Sylvia D. Hoffert, "Madame Loreta Velazquez: Heroine or Hoaxer?" in *Civil War Times Illustrated,* June 1978, pp. 24–31.)

Notes to

Chapter 12

Introductory

The story of "Otto Schaffer" is based on notes provided by Dr. Stuart Sprague, Morehead State University, Kentucky, from Record Group 94 in the National Archives.

Sheridan's female soldiers

Philip H. Sheridan, *Personal Memoirs.* New York: Charles L. Webster & Co., 1888; vol. 1, pp. 253–255.

Female mannerisms

Ethel Alice Hurn, *Wisconsin Women in the War Between the States,* Wisconsin History Commission: Original Papers No. 6, 1911, p. 103. (Regarding Sarah Collins.)

Albert D. Richardson, *The Secret Service, The Field, The Dungeon, and the Escape.* Hartford, CT: American Publishing Co., 1865, p. 175. (Regarding a 1st Kentucky Infantry female soldier.)

Cleveland *Plain Dealer,* September 10, 1861. (Regarding Mary Smith.)

Mary A. Livermore, *My Story of the War.* Hartford, CT: D. A. Worthington & Co., 1888, pp. 113–114.

Female Casualties

Bell I. Wiley, *Life of Billy Yank,* Baton Rouge, LA: LSU Press, 1971, p. 339.
Bell I. Wiley, *Life of Johnny Reb,* Baton Rouge, LA: LSU Press, 1978, p. 335.

Fred Brooks, "Shiloh Mystery Woman," in *Civil War Times Illustrated*, August, 1978, p. 29.

Fanny J. Anderson, "The Shelley Papers," in *Indiana Magazine of History*, June, 1948, p. 186.

Herbert L. Grimm and Paul L. Roy, *Human Interest Stories of the Three Days' Battles at Gettysburg*, Gettysburg, VA: Gettysburg Times and News Publishing Co., 1927, p. 18. (Regarding man and wife killed at Gettysburg.)

Gregory A. Coco, *On the Bloodstained Field*, Hollidaysburg, PA: Wheatfield Press, 1987, p. 40. (Regarding female soldier who lost leg at Gettysburg. Author cites letter of Thomas Read, Company. E, 5th Michigan, August 20, 1863, in University of Michigan Library.)

Wellsburg, West Virginia, *Herald*, October 9, 1863. (Regarding Mrs. Frances Clayton.)

Exposed by Her Uncle

Owensboro, Kentucky, *Monitor*, August 20, 1862.

Soldiers Giving Birth

James I. Robertson, Jr., "An Indiana Soldier in Love and War: The Civil War Letters of John V. Hadley," in *Indiana Magazine of History*, September, 1963, pp. 237–238. (Report of Army of Potomac soldier in New Jersey regiment who had a baby.)

James Greenalch, letters home to wife, Fidelia. *Michigan History*, June, 1960, pp. 237–238. (Report of 74th Ohio sergeant who gave birth.)

Bell I. Wiley, *Confederate Women*. Westport, CT: Greenwood Press, 1975, p. 142. (Report of Confederate officer who gave birth in prison. Author cites Sandusky, Ohio, *Register*, December 12, 1864.)

"They Also Served," in *Civil War Times Illustrated*, August, 1978, p. 41. (Editor cites George W. Ward, *History of the Second Pennsylvania Veteran Heavy Artillery*, p. 133. That unit is the second of the two regiments alluded to in the quote.)

Determined to Fight

Mary E. Massey, *Bonnet Brigades*. New York: Alfred A. Knopf, 1966, pp. 80–84. (Regarding female soldier captured at Chickamauga and "Nellie A.K." who wanted to reenlist, and Fanny Wilson who did.)

John W. Heisey, " 'Ladies' in Our Wars," in *AntiqueWeek*, May 29, 1989, p. 12b. (Regarding Elizabeth Compton and Fanny Wilson.)

New York *Sun*, February 10, 1901. (Article about female soldiers, including Frances Hook and Fanny Wilson. Notes provided by Dr. Stuart Sprague, Morehead State University, Kentucky, from Record Group 94, National Archives.)

Cincinnati *Dollar Times*, August 11, 1864. (Story of the unsuccessful recruit. Notes provided by Dr. Stuart Sprague, from the National Archives.)

Glimpses of Confederate Officers and Soldiers

B. A. Botkin, *A Civil War Treasury of Tales, Legends, and Folklore*. Secaucus, NJ: Blue & Gray Press, 1985, pp. 396–400. (The "She-Major." Excerpted from David P. Conyngham, *Sherman's March Through the South*. New York: Sheldon & Co., 1865, pp. 194–197.)

Francis B. Simkins and James W. Patton, *The Women of the Confederacy*.

Richmond, VA: Garrett & Massie, 1936, pp. 80–81. (Ross and Freemantle anecdotes.)

Arthur J. L. Freemantle, *Three Months in the Southern States.* Edinburgh and London: William Blackwood & Sons, 1863 (Time-Life replica edition, 1984), p. 174.)

Lynchburg, Virginia, *Virginian,* October 6, 1864; p. 1 (Story of female captain on train.)

"Moses" Goes to War

Eric Foner and John A. Garraty (eds.), *Reader's Companion to American History.* "Tubman, Harriet" entry. Boston, MA: Houghton Mifflin Co., 1991.

John H. Franklin, "Tubman, Harriet" entry in *Notable American Women.* Cambridge, MA: Belknap Press of Harvard University Press, 1971.

Wilbur H. Siebert, *The Underground Railroad From Slavery to Freedom.* New York: Macmillan Co., 1898. (1968 reprint edition by Peter Smith, Gloucester, MA.)

William S. McFeely, *Frederick Douglass.* New York: W. W. Norton & Co., 1991. (Tribute to Harriet Tubman, p. 263)

Jean M. Hoefer, "They Called Her 'Moses' "; in *Civil War Times Illustrated,* February, 1988, pp. 36–41.

Notes to
Chapter 13

Fred M. Mazzulla and William Kostka, *Mountain Charley or the Adventures of Mrs. E. J. Guerin, Who Was Thirteen Years in Male Attire.* Norman, OK: University of Oklahoma Press, 1968. (Basically reports two stories which I have labeled "Charley I" and "Charley II." Charley I served in the Civil War, Charley II flourished just before the Civil War.)

Charley I

Enlistment and battle of Westport, pp. 82–111; Wounded in action and sex discovered, pp. 100–109; Story told to George West, pp. 72–75; Charley's 1885 letter to George West, pp. 79–81.

Charley II

Male disguise to avenge husband, pp. 18–28; St. Louis encounter with Jamieson, pp. 28–36; Wagon train West, pp. 37–53; Skirmish with Indians, p. 54.

Herman Hattaway, "Westport, Missouri engagement at," in *Historical Times Illustrated Encyclopedia of the Civil War.* New York: Harper & Row, 1986, p. 816.

D. Alexander Brown, "The Battle of Westport," in *Civil War Times Illustrated,* July, 1966, pp. 4–11, 40–43.

Emerson Hough, *The Passing of the Frontier: A Chronicle of the Old West.* New Haven, CT: Yale University Press, 1918. (A rich depiction of activities on the western frontier in the latter part of the 19th century.)

Joseph H. Crute, Jr., *Confederate Staff Officers.* Powhatan, VA: Derwent Books, 1982. (Captain A. C. McCoy is listed as a staff officer of Brigadier General Joseph O. Shelby.)

APPENDIX A

Honor Roll of Female Soldiers
(w) = wounded in action; (k) = killed in action

Alphabetical by Female Name

ANDERSON, Charlotte ("Charley Anderson") of Cleveland, Ohio. 60th Ohio Infantry. Discovered to be a female, January 18, 1865, at City Point, Virginia, interviewed by Provost Marshal General Marsena Patrick and returned home four days later.

BARLOW, Arabela Griffith (Mrs. Francis C.). 61st New York Infantry. Campaigned with husband in the field and served in the Sanitary Commission.

BELL, Mary ("Tom Parker") and BELL, Molly ("Bob Martin"). Confederate female soldiers arrested in the fall of 1864 in General Jubal Early's command in the Shenandoah Valley as suspected "camp followers" after serving for two years. Spent three weeks in Castle Thunder, Richmond, then sent home to Pulaski County, Virginia, still in their uniforms.

BLAYLOCK, Malinda (Mrs. S. M.). Enlisted as "Samuel" in 26th North Carolina Infantry to serve with her husband. Later engaged in guerilla activities.

BROWN, Harriet. Enlisted as "Harry" in Illinois regiment. Not discovered for three months. Arrested at Union depot in soldier's uniform en route from Lexington, Kentucky, to Chicago. Put in hospital to serve as nurse.

BROWNELL, Kady (Mrs. Robert S.). 1st and 5th Rhode Island Infantry regiments. Served with husband who was orderly sergeant. Color bearer at 1st Bull Run. Daughter of regiment in 5th.

BURNS, Mary ("John" Burns). 7th Michigan Cavalry. Enlisted to be with boyfriend; discovered in about two weeks and sent home.

CLALIN, Frances. Said to be in Missouri or Maine Militia Cavalry, but not traceable to either of these units. Photos from Boston Public Library.

CLAPP, Sarah A. 7th Illinois Cavalry. Maiden name Chardrock. Claimed to be assistant surgeon and surgeon in 7th Illinois Cavalry.

CLARKE, Mrs. Amy (w). Served in General Braxton Bragg's command in Mississippi–Tennessee. Enlisted with husband, and continued in service after he was killed at Shiloh. She was later wounded and captured, and her sex discovered; sent into Confederate lines in a dress. ("Anna Clark"—almost certainly the same person—was reported to have served as Confederate private "Richard Anderson" with her husband Walter in the 11th Tennessee infantry. Husband killed at Shiloh.)

CLAYTON, Mrs. Frances Louisa (w). Enlisted in a Minnesota regiment to be with husband. She was wounded and her husband killed in the battle of Stone's River, Tennessee.

COLLINS, Sarah. Wisconsin soldier, enlisted with brother but detected by her mannerisms and sent home.

COMPTON, Lizzie (Elizabeth) (w). 125th Michigan Cavalry. When wounded and sex detected, claimed to have enlisted at 14 and served eighteen months in seven different regiments, "leaving one and enrolling in another when fearing detection."

COX, Lucy Ann. *Vivandiere* for 13th Virginia Regiment.

DAY, Frances (k). (Sergeant "Frank Mayne") served in 126th Pennsylvania Infantry. Later mortally wounded in a battle while serving with a different regiment in the western theater.

DEMING, Mrs. L. L. daughter of regiment, 10th Michigan Infantry.

DEAVERS (DIVERS/DEVAN), Bridget. Served in 1864–1865 Virginia campaigns, allegedly with 1st Michigan Cavalry.

EDMONDS, Sarah Emma ("Franklin Thompson"). Served for two years in 2nd Michigan Infantry as soldier, spy, and nurse.

ETHERIDGE, Anna. Served as daughter of the regiment with 2nd Michigan Infantry in Army of Potomac, and later with 3rd and 5th Michigan regiments, for a total of three years.

EWBANK, Hannah. Served as daughter of the regiment with the 7th Wisconsin Infantry.

GOODRIDGE, Ellen (w). Served with boyfriend James Hendrick in an early Wisconsin regiment. Went on skirmishes and raids, and was wounded in action.

HART, Nancy. Virginia. Served as guide for Jackson's cavalry. Once captured, escaped by shooting captor.

HENRY, Margaret. Captured by Federals near end of war with another female soldier in Confederate uniform, and imprisoned at Nashville.

HINSDALE, Jane. Regimental nurse in 2nd Michigan Infantry. Enlisted with husband Hiram H. Taken prisoner after 1st Bull run while helping the wounded and searching for missing husband. Escaped and took information on Confederate movements to authorities in Washington, D.C.

HODGERS, Jennie ("Albert Cashier"). 95th Illinois Infantry. Only woman known to have served complete three-year term of enlistment disguised as man, maintaining male disguise well after the war.

HOOK, Frances (w). ("Frank Martin"). Served in 90th Illinois, 2nd East Tennessee Cavalry, 8th Michigan. Joined a new regiment each time discovered in previous one. Once taken prisoner.

JENKINS, Mary Owen. Served in 9th Pennsylvania Cavalry.

JONES, Annie. Alleged consort of Custer and other officers in D.C. area camps. Said to have served as scout and spy.

JONES, Lizzie. Served as daughter of the regiment in 6th Massachusetts Infantry.

KIRBY, Mrs. William. Husband and son in Confederate army. She smuggled weapons through Federal lines at Baton Rouge, Louisiana; caught, convicted as spy, imprisoned on Ship Island. Died there near end of war. Son killed at Gettysburg, husband survived.

LILLYBRIDGE, Annie (w). Detroit. Served in 21st Michigan Infantry. After Battle of Pea Ridge found shot in arm, taken to Hospital in Louisville. Swapped discharge with Joseph Henderson to reenlist.

MARCUM, Julia. Female soldier from Kentucky. (No other details known. Source: Ida Tarbell letter in National Archives.)

MCCREARY, Mary (Mrs.). Served as private with husband in Company H, 21st Ohio, but after several months "found herself in a delicate condition," obtained leave from the colonel, went home, and never returned.

MILLER, Charley. Served in 18th New York Regiment as "drummer boy" using name "Edward O. Hamilton." Preferred to live as male since childhood.

MOORE, Madeline. Joined army to be with boyfriend, was elected lieutenant and served in West Virginia under General George B. McClellan, and later at Bull Run.

MURPHY, Mary Ann. Served as "Samuel Hill" in Company B, 53rd Massachusetts, with brother Tom.

NILES, Mrs. Elizabeth A. Fought in Civil War beside her husband in 4th New Jersey. Died October 4, 1920 at age 92.

OWEN(S), Mary (w). From Huntingdon (or Montour) County, Pennsylvania. Served eighteen months, fought in three battles and wounded twice. When she returned home she claimed to have been married to the man with whom she had enlisted. He was killed and she wounded in same battle.

PETERMAN, Georgianne. From Ellenboro, served two years as a "drummer boy" with 7th Wisconsin.

PETERSON, Belle. Young country girl who lived near Ellenboro. Enlisted in a Wisconsin regiment probably late in 1862 and "served in the army for some time."

PHILIPS, Bettie Taylor (Mrs. W. D.). When with her husband in 4th Kentucky Infantry (Confederate), cared for wounded on battlefield, part of famous "Orphan Brigade." Arrested, held as spy at Nashville.

REYNOLDS, Mrs. Belle. Served with her husband, a lieutenant in 17th Illinois Infantry. Traveled with regiment, saw combat while under fire at Shiloh.

ROONEY, Rose (Mrs.). Served with 15th Louisiana Infantry. Braved battlefield shot and shell in order to care for the wounded. Later a hospital matron in New Orleans for soldiers' home.

SEABERRY, Mary Y. From Columbus, Ohio, served in Company F, 52nd Ohio as "Charles Freeman" until "sexual incompatibility" was admitted, November 10, 1862.

SMITH, Mary. Enlisted in 41st Ohio Infantry, McClellan *Zouaves*, to avenge death of only brother at Bull Run. At Camp Wood, Ohio, found out to be a woman by her mannerisms.

SULLIVAN, Betsy (Mrs.). Battlefield nurse with Company K, 1st Tennessee Infantry (Confederate). Served with husband, John Sullivan, and shared the hardships of army life with the regiment.

TAYLOR, Sarah. Served as daughter of the regiment with the 1st Tennessee Regiment.

TEBE, Marie (w). "French Mary" served in 27th Pennsylvania Infantry ("Washington Brigade") which was at 1st Bull Run, and the 114th Pennsylvania Infantry as *vivandiere*. Frequently under fire as battlefield nurse, wounded in action, awarded medal for gallantry.

THOMPSON, Ellen P. L. Served in 139th Illinois Infantry Regiment.

THOMPSON, Lucy Matilda (w). ("Bill Thompson"). At 49, followed her husband, Bryant Gauss, into the Bladen Light Infantry (Bladen County, North Carolina), 18th North Carolina Regiment. Wounded at 1st (or 2nd) Bull Run and again during siege of Richmond. Husband wounded three times and eventually killed. She lived to be 112 years old.

TUBMAN, Harriet. Pre–Civil War "Moses" in "Underground Railway." June 1862–1865 commanded scouts and river pilots for Union forces in South Carolina, including spying missions. In June, 1862, led 150 Black troops in a raid. Later participated in other raids, carrying a musket.

TURCHIN, Mrs. General John B. 19th Illinois Infantry. Went to war with husband. On march into Tennessee in the spring of 1862 (then) Colonel Turchin was taken seriously ill and was carried in ambulance. She assumed command of the regiment. Later served as battlefield nurse, frequently under fire.

VELAZQUEZ, Loreta Janeta (w). ("Harry T. Buford"). Served as independent officer in Confederate army, and as "detective" and spy in secret service.

WILSON, Eliza. Served as daughter of the regiment in 5th Wisconsin Infantry.

WILSON, Fannie (or Fanny). Served eighteen months in 24th New Jersey Infantry Regiment before sex discovered during Vicksburg campaign. At Cairo, Illinois, danced in local ballet, reenlisted in 3rd Illinois Cavalry.

WISE, Mary E (w). Served for two or more years in the 34th Indiana Infantry Regiment. Wounded in action three times before having to quit military service.

WRIGHT, Mary. Arrested in Confederate uniform and imprisoned at Nashville with another female soldier, Margaret Henry, near the end of the war.

Alphabetical Index by States

Arkansas

Loreta Janeta Velazquez claimed to have raised a regiment or battalion called the Arkansas Grays that traveled to Pensacola, Florida, for training. Fought in several battles.

Georgia

Female militia as "home guard" during Sherman's "march through Georgia," training with weapons, wearing uniforms, and having a confrontation with a Wisconsin cavalry regiment late in the war.

Illinois

Harriet Brown enlisted as "Harry" in Illinois regiment, served in Kentucky. Not discovered for three months. Arrested in uniform while en route from Lexington, Kentucky, to Chicago. Pressed into hospital service as nurse.

At Battle of Lookout Mountain, Tennessee, November 24, 1863, an Illinois woman was one of eighteen scouts sent out to reconnoiter General Braxton Bragg's position; served as attaché in General Francis P. Blair, Jr.'s, XVII Corps during operations into Georgia, North Carolina, and South Carolina.

3rd Illinois Cavalry. Fannie Wilson disguised as male, discovered and discharged for second time, having been caught in another regiment after eighteen months service.

7th Illinois Cavalry. Sarah A. Clapp.

17th Illinois Infantry. Mrs. Belle Reynolds served with her lieutenant husband, saw combat, given a major's commission by governor.

19th Illinois Infantry. Female soldier discovered by her mannerisms.

19th Illinois Infantry. Madame John B. Turchin once took over command of regiment when her husband became seriously ill, constantly under fire as battle-field nurse.

63rd Illinois Infantry. Female soldier discovered with the regiment on board the steamer *Leni Leoti* at Smithland en route for Nashville.

66th Illinois Home Guards. Frances Hook served as "Frank Miller."

90th Illinois Infantry. Frances Hook.

95th Illinois Infantry. Jennie Hodgers ("Albert Cashier") served full three-year term without being discovered.

116th Illinois Infantry. "Kate" discovered dressed as a man serving on picket duty.

139th Illinois. Ellen P. L. Thompson served as female soldier.

Indiana

A woman was arrested in Indianapolis wearing a soldier's uniform. She was jailed until evening, then sent home to Winchester, Indiana.

Cavalry soldier wounded twice, fainted. When given a bath was found to be a woman, after twenty-one months of service.

Mary E. Wise served two or more years in the 34th Indiana Infantry regiment.

Female soldier discovered serving in Captain Gerard's company of the 66th Indiana Infantry regiment.

Iowa

"Charles H. Williams" (female name unknown) served in the 2nd Iowa Infantry with her lieutenant boyfriend.

"Charles Hatfield" served in Iowa cavalry as an orderly for General Samuel R. Curtis's adjutant, and as spy behind enemy lines.

Mrs. Jerusha Small served as battlefield nurse with 12th Iowa Infantry.

A female soldier serving in the 14th Iowa Infantry shot herself after her sex was discovered in April, 1863.

Kansas

"Otto Schaffer," a farmer from Butler County who had served in the Civil War, found to be a woman upon death.

Kentucky

Female private in 1st Kentucky Infantry discovered to be a woman by her method of pulling on her stockings.

Louisiana

Loreta Janeta Velazquez served in 21st Louisiana Infantry.

Maine

"Dutch Mary" served with husband in 17th Maine Infantry, drilling with men and caring for wounded.

Massachusetts

Lizzie Jones served as a daughter of the regiment in 6th Massachusetts Infantry.
Mary Ann Murphy served as "Samuel Hill" in 53rd Massachusetts Infantry.

Michigan

Bridget Deavers served as battlefield nurse in 1st Michigan Cavalry.
Sarah Emma Edmonds served as soldier, spy, and nurse in 2nd Michigan Infantry.
Jane Hinsdale served as nurse in 2nd Michigan Infantry, once captured by enemy.
Anna Etheridge served as a daughter of the regiment and battlefield nurse in the 2nd, 3rd, and 5th Michigan infantries.
Mary Burns enlisted (as "John") in 7th Michigan Cavalry, but was discovered in about two weeks.
Frances Hook served in the 8th Michigan Infantry.
Anny Lillybridge served in the 21st Michigan Infantry.
Elizabeth Compton served in the 125th Michigan Cavalry.

Minnesota

Unidentified Minnesota girl claimed two years of service before being wounded.
Mrs. Frances Clayton wounded in action with a Minnesota regiment at Stone's River, Tennessee.

Missouri

Frances Clalin allegedly served in a Missouri militia cavalry regiment in Federal service.
"John Williams," Company M, 17th Missouri Infantry, was discovered to be a woman.

New Jersey

Female soldier in a New Jersey regiment who had been in four battles with her husband was discovered when she gave birth, and was sent home.
Fannie Wilson, from New Jersey, served eighteen months before being discovered during Vicksburg campaign.
Mrs. Elizabeth A. Niles, who served with her husband in 4th New Jersey Infantry, died in 1920 at age 92.

New York

Drummer boy "Edward O. Hamilton" in 18th New York Infantry was a girl who had preferred to act as a male since childhood.
The 39th New York Infantry ("Garibaldi Guard") had at least six *vivandieres* who dressed in red, blue, and black costumes.
The 40th New York Infantry reportedly had a female lieutenant colonel (source: Ida Tarbell letter in National Archives).
Arabella G. Barlow served with her officer husband in the 61st New York Infantry during the 1862 Peninsula Campaign, at Gettysburg, and in the siege of Petersburg, also acting as a nurse on and near the battlefield.
A female soldier identified only as "Nellie A.K." enlisted with her brother in the

102nd New York Infantry, until discovered and discharged near Chattanooga, Tennessee.

North Carolina

Lucy Matilda Thompson served as "Bill Thompson" in 18th North Carolina Infantry.

Malinda Blaylock posed as "Samuel" to serve with her husband in the 26th North Carolina Infantry.

Ohio

Mary McCreary served in Company H, 21st Ohio Infantry.

Mary Smith enlisted in 41st Ohio Infantry to avenge only brother's death at 1st Bull Run. Sex discovered at Camp Wood, Ohio, September, 1861 by female mannerisms.

Mary Y. Seaberry served as "Charles Freeman" in Company F, 52nd Ohio Infantry.

Two women served three years in 59th Ohio Infantry.

Charlotte ("Charley") Anderson served in 60th Ohio Infantry. Discovered to be female and sent home to Cleveland by provost marshal of Army of Potomac.

Female sergeant in 74th Ohio Infantry gave birth, after twenty months of service.

Pennsylvania

Female using name "Charles Martin" served as drummer boy in a Pennsylvania regiment. Was in five battles.

Mary Owen Jenkins served in 9th Pennsylvania Cavalry.

Marie Tebe served in 27th and 114th Pennsylvania Infantry regiments.

"Charles D. Fuller" (female name not known) served in 46th Pennsylvania Infantry.

Frances Day ("Frank Mayne") served in 126th Pennsylvania Infantry.

Rhode Island

Kady Brownell served with husband, Robert, in 1st Rhode Island Infantry as color bearer at 1st Bull Run, and in 5th Rhode Island as a daughter of the regiment.

Tennessee

Tennessee teamster with Sheridan in Shenandoah Valley discovered to be a woman when she got drunk and fell in a river.

Sarah Taylor served as a daughter of the regiment in 1st Tennessee Infantry.

Frances Hook served in 2nd East Tennessee Cavalry (Union).

Anna Clark served as "Richard Anderson" in Confederate 11th Tennessee Infantry. (See Amy Clarke.)

Virginia

Mary and Molly Bell ("Tom Parker" and "Bob Martin"). Confederate soldiers from Virginia arrested by Federals in the fall of 1864 after two years of service.

Nancy Hart served as a cavalry scout for "Stonewall" Jackson.

Lucy Ann Cox served as a *vivandiere* in 13th Virginia Infantry.

Wisconsin

Ellen Goodridge served in an early Wisconsin infantry regiment with boyfriend, Lieutenant James Hendrick.

Eliza Wilson served in 5th Wisconsin Infantry as a daughter of the regiment.

Hannah Ewbank served in 7th Wisconsin Infantry as a daughter of the regiment.

Georgianne Peterman served two years in 7th Wisconsin Infantry as a "drummer boy."

Sarah Collins enlisted with brother, Mason, from Lake Mills; detected as a woman by mannerisms.

Other Union References

A female soldier in Sheridan's command (name and state of origin unknown), with a female teamster from Tennessee, got drunk, fell in a river, discovered to be female when rescued.

Unnamed "stout and muscular" female solider in her 20s wounded at Chickamauga (September 19–20, 1863), captured, released under flag of truce. Had been with regiment a year.

"Woman in man's dress, taken prisoner..." and released under flag of truce just before 2nd Bull Run (August 30, 1862). She had been serving in Sigel's command (1 Corps in Pope's Army of Virginia).

A "laundress" (*vivandiere*?) attached to Irish Brigade (New York and Massachusetts regiments) advanced with troops at Antietam, stood with them in the fight and "swung her bonnet around and cheered on the men."

Bell I. Wiley reports two female soldier casualties in Union army: one fatally wounded, the other killed outright. (The first probably a reference to Frances Day.)

Unknown female soldier killed at Shiloh (April 6–7, 1862).

Cincinnati, Ohio, newspaper reported on January 6, 1862, the discovery at Bacon Creek, Kentucky, of a female soldier from Cincinnati in uniform. Upon her pleading, officer did not report her and she stayed in service.

Other Confederate References

Englishman Fitzgerald Ross, traveling in the United States during the war, met a female captain on the train between Augusta and Atlanta, Georgia, who was said to have taken an active part in the war. (*A Visit to the Cities and Camps of the Confederate States*, 1863.)

Female captain in uniform seen traveling on train between Charlotte, North Carolina, and Richmond, Virginia, in October, 1864. Said to be from Mississippi, fought in several battles, field promotion for gallantry.

Female Confederate major allegedly seen serving in General Hood's command at the Battle of Atlanta.

A Confederate officer imprisoned on Johnson's Island (Sandusky Bay, Ohio, on Lake Erie) gave birth to a baby boy the first week of December, 1864.

Two Confederate female casualties at Gettysburg, July 2–3, 1863.

Female Confederate cavalary soldier taken prisoner and presumed to be a spy.

(*Note:* Casualties among these unknown female soldiers included three killed and three wounded.)

APPENDIX B

RESEARCH NOTES

Introduction

Research for this book began with the names of two dozen or so women alleged to have fought in the Civil War, three core books about Sarah Emma Edmonds (including her memoirs, *Nurse and Spy*), and the memoirs of Loreta Janeta Velazquez, *The Woman in Battle*. There was a lot of information about two of the women, and only sketchy information about the rest. My search for additional information led to research in state archives and historical societies (with the invaluable help of a number of local researchers; see acknowledgments), and attendance at numerous Civil War shows over a 3 year period, from Gettysburg to Baltimore to Harpers Ferry to Richmond, browsing through books and documents and augmenting my personal library.

The more I searched, the more names were found along with new information (usually minimal) about additional female soldiers; it is likely that many others escaped my attention. I was able to fill in more details about several of the women only with great difficulty and by persistent searching of memoirs, diaries, and regimental histories, and by questioning various librarians and archivists. With one notable exception, the information did not fall in my lap.

Issues of Credibility and Authenticity

As I familiarized myself with the literature about women in the war, including the views of postwar reporters and commentators, it became clear that women who took part while wearing dresses were considered "noble," but women who disguised themselves as men were thought to be of dubious moral character. In 1867, L. P. Brockett and Mary Vaughan opined that "those who . . . donned the male attire and concealed their sex, are hardly entitled to a place in our record, since they did not seek to be known as women, but preferred to pass for men." In 1959, Agatha Young considered it "utterly impossible" that the sex of the female soldiers who dressed as men was not known to their male comrades.

Both of the main protagonists in this book have been controversial, especially Loreta Janeta Velazquez. But until relatively recently Sarah Emma Edmonds also had her detractors. Because of this, I took special pains to check the biographical and historical records on both women to determine whether their stories could be believed, in whole or in part. If it were to turn out that they were *not* credible, my story would have to be at least partly an exposé. I did not want to be a party to reporting fiction as fact, or to help to develop a mythology about women in the Civil War. So, as part of my research I undertook a critical appraisal of their stories, as well as checking the others for factual accuracy as much as possible.

Sarah Emma Edmonds

In the reference cited above by Agatha Young, she added that the stories of women successfully disguising themselves as men in the ranks was "beyond credibility," making it clear in a footnote that she had Sarah Emma Edmonds primarily in mind: "[Her] adventures as she relates them are not believable and it seems clear that her story is of more interest to the clinician than to the historian." (It should be addded that Sylvia Dannett's extraordinary, groundbreaking biography of Sarah Emma Edmonds was not published until the following year, providing ample documentation of the basic truth of Edmonds's story.)

My research included visits to the Michigan State Archives to examine the records of the 2nd Michigan Infantry Regiment, among other Michigan-related information, and checks with librarians and archivists in Flint, Michigan (home of the 2nd); Hartford, Connecticut; Fort Scott, Kansas; Houston, Texas; and elsewhere. Returning to primary sources used by Sylvia Dannett, I was able to confirm the accuracy of her reporting and to be impressed by the scope and depth of her research, though I do not always agree with her interpretations or opinions. Most importantly, I was able to sort through the factual and fictional elements of Edmonds's story.

At the heart of the problem is the fact that, in *Nurse and Spy* (1864), Edmonds deliberately disguised the truth in a number of places, to avoid identifying herself as "Frank Thompson," since the war was still going on and she had deserted. Some spinoff writings about her, to this day, accept *Nurse and Spy* at face value and perpetuate some of the apocryphal anecdotes. (In my summaries of her book, I have left out some anecdotes that seem farfetched or likely to be part of her "cover story," and tried to stick as closely as possible to the better documented portions.)

As pointed out in the chapter notes, Edmonds (calculatedly, intuitively, or otherwise) included ample "reality" in the form of verifiable historical facts in *Nurse and Spy*, mentioning Captain William M. (Morse) and J. (Jerome) Robbins of the 2nd Michigan, among others. Describing the aftermath of the battle of Seven Pines/Fair Oaks, she reports (on page 192) the names and regiments of two mortally wounded soldiers encountered on the battlefield: William C. Bentley of the 2nd Rhode Island, and Francis Sweetzer of the 16th Massachusetts. As an afterthought, having reviewed her book many times, I requested the military records of the two men at the National Archives and learned that they indeed had been killed in that battle. Additionally, Edmonds gave colorful—and accurate—descriptions of major battles in which she participated (also, in 1864, using the expression "landscape turned red" in reference to Antietam).

The clincher in the case of Sarah Emma Edmonds, however, was that when she decided to seek a pension and "came out of the closet" in the 1880s to reveal that "Frank Thompson" was a woman, she was able to get confirmation of her military service from a large number of eyewitnesses. "Frank" had been very visible in camp as a mail carrier, and was widely known and liked throughout the brigade. Even the Jerome Robbins diary with its hints of scandal adds proof that she really did serve in the ranks. Congressman Byron Cutcheon's testimony about seeing "Frank" on the battlefield at Fredericksburg provides additional proof.

Although *Nurse and Spy* is a mixture of fact and fiction, it primarily is based on a hard core of fact and is essentially a true story. By her own account, some of it is not strictly true, but was all either experienced or observed by her. Some of the fictionalization appears to have been deliberate in order to keep her secret, while other portions might be outright embellishment. We may never know (for example) if "Lieutenant V." was a real person, part of her fictional cover story (as I think), or simply embellishment. In a number of cases, people she identified only by a last initial (including "General G." and "Chaplain B.") have not been identifiable, though the contextual information probably should have permitted identification.

Late in life, Sarah Emma Edmonds Seelye was working on a sequel to set the facts straight, but unfortunately it was never published and the manuscript has been lost. The information available establishes beyond a shadow of a doubt that she served in the ranks and in combat, and deserves the recognition she has received. In addition, though unrelated to the foregoing, she lived an exemplary postwar life.

Loreta Janeta Velazquez

Far more controversial was Velazquez. Patricia L. Faust, in the *Civil War Times Illustrated Encyclopedia of the Civil War*, said "[she] chronicles an unbelievable series of adventures with more characteristics of fiction than of fact . . . it is the least credible of the Civil War spy literature."

Francis B. Simkins and James W. Patton in *Women of the Confederacy* wrote, "The only person impressed with the valor and worth of Loreta Janeta Velazquez was that woman herself . . . the stories of her adventures have an air of the tawdry and the unreal."

A more balanced appraisal, and one that I agree with in most respects, was made by Stewart Sefakis in *Who Was Who in the Confederacy*: "Little in her work can be even circumstantially supported. Yet there may be an element of truth. She may have done some of the things she claimed, but this will never be definitely known due to her penchant for exaggeration."

In preparing this book, I made a substantial effort to check the factual accuracy and credibility of her story, and found that a *lot* in her work could be "circumstantially supported." The memoirs are rich in descriptive detail of people, places, and events, including many verifiable names and unit designations. I tried to check as large a sample as possible of this information, though much more could be done with time. (In fact, I intend to continue this research.) My effort covered the following elements, which will be discussed in turn: battle scenes and circumstances; people; Thomas C. DeCaulp; places; the Arkansas connection; postwar emigration scheme; Jubal Early's criticisms.

Much of what I learned in specific instances is included in the chapter notes. All had to be evaluated in light of her own proviso in her preface to *The Woman in Battle*: "The loss of my notes had compelled me to rely entirely upon my memory; and memory is apt to be very treacherous, especially when, after a number of years, one endeavors to relate in their proper sequence a long series of complicated transactions. Besides, I have been compelled to write hurriedly, and in the intervals of pressing business [of] earning my daily bread." She goes on to say forthrightly that she badly needs the money she hopes the book will bring her.

Upon closer analysis, the biggest flaws in the book are that she tends to state facts out of their proper historical sequence, and that the book appears to have been written rather hastily and somewhat carelessly! Her proviso can be taken (as

I take it) to be a *partially* legitimate excuse for some garbled facts or date and sequence errors; but it also could be taken as an all too convenient excuse to cover up errors committed while concocting fiction for personal gain and trying to pass it off as fact. The issue, as I see it, is to evaluate whether the errors the book contains can be explained convincingly as resulting from careless mistakes and faulty memory, or whether the evidence points more toward outright fabrication.

To study the credibility of her battlefield descriptions, I read several reports of the battles of Ball's Bluff, 1st Bull Run, Fort Donelson, and Shiloh, including eyewitness accounts, and compared them point by point with her story. Although her accounts sometimes were very general, they fit well with authentic accounts by others, sometimes down to details of weather or unusual occurrences. The most glaring error—or instance of faulty memory—was her failure to take notice at all of Harrison Island, which dominates the view from Ball's Bluff, in her account of that battle.

Almost invariably, Velazquez correctly reported the names, unit designations, official positions, and other details of the numerous people she mentions in her memoirs. One exception is her story of trying to reach General Earl Van Dorn's command at a time, in her story, that he had already been killed (Jubal Early makes note of this "error" too). However, this could be an excusable error based on faulty memory, plausible due to the amount of elapsed time.

One of the most puzzling facets of her book is the story of her longtime romance with, and ultimate marriage to, Captain Thomas C. DeCaulp of Arkansas. She reports very specifically on page 337 that he was a native of Edinburgh, Scotland, who had studied medicine in England and France, and had emigrated to the United States in 1857. His father was of French descent and his mother English. In 1859 he had joined the U.S. Army, but when the war broke out "he came South" (she does not say where he was living in the North) and offered his services to the Confederacy. She knew him as a friend of her first husband in Pensacola, Florida, a training area for Confederate soldiers early in the war.

Among other lines of inquiry, I requested the military files on Thomas C. DeCaulp from the National Archives, and was pleased and surprised to quickly receive a substantial file on him. At first glance this seemed to be a very strong confirmation of her story, but on closer examination it raised more questions than it answered. Though there is some overlap between her story and the official records, including DeCaulp's capture at Chattanooga in the fall of 1863, a surprising discrepancy exists.

The National Archives records showed Thomas C. DeCaulp enlisting in the 1st Arkansas Mounted Volunteers on July 29, 1861, as 3rd corporal. The unit later became the 3rd Arkansas Cavalry. DeCaulp was promoted to 2nd lieutenant on May 26, 1862, and 1st lieutenant on July 25, 1862, whereas Velazquez's account has him as captain in command of the Arkansas battalion at Shiloh on April 6, 1862. DeCaulp was wounded in the legs and captured at Corinth on October 2, 1862 (October 4th according to Collier; see below), and paroled by November. He was sent to a general hospital (city not named) on May 14, 1863, where he apparently stayed for some time with an unspecified illness. The time period would coincide roughly with her visit at the Atlanta hospital.

Then there is the major discrepancy. After they are married, in her story, he returned to active duty, was taken sick, and died in a Federal hospital in Chattanooga a few weeks after their September marriage. The official records show DeCaulp being captured at Chattanooga on September 14, 1863, and then either on that same date or on October 15th (contradictory information in files) deserting the Confederate army and returning to his home in Philadelphia! (Collier reports the desertion date as September 21st just after the battle of Chickamauga.) Additional information in the files suggests that he had been impressed into Confederate service against his will, deserted, and later fought under the assumed name "William Irwin" in a Union regiment and was married to the daughter of an English admiral by the name of Rosche.

I also consulted Calvin L. Collier, author of *The War Child's Children* about the 3rd Arkansas Cavalry (which contains references to DeCaulp) and other works on Arkansas units in the Civil War. He very kindly provided background information and answers to various questions. He disagrees with the implication in a letter in the National Archives file that DeCaulp was a northerner impressed into Confederate service who then deserted, but instead states that after his capture he was recruited to become a so-called "galvanized Yankee," to go west and fight Indians, thus obtaining his freedom. In a personal communication dated March 21, 1991, Collier added:

> DeCaulp could not have been either at Pensacola or the battle of Shiloh. [At the time of Shiloh] DeCaulp was doing patrol duty in northeast Arkansas. . . . Her statement that DeCaulp was in central Tennessee in the summer of 1863 is correct. . . . He deserted on September 21, 1863 during the Chickamauga action and it is most unlikely he was ever in a Confederate Hospital in Atlanta. . . . I believe it most unlikely that DeCaulp was some kind of "agent" or "mole" [a possibility I had raised—RH]; he was just a straight deserter for personal reasons of his own.

I have thought of a few theories to explain the discrepancy between her story of his death at Chattanooga and all the other records showing that he did not die, but was captured and served in some capacity for the North. None is entirely satisfactory, and all require much more research on critical points. Perhaps, (a) she knew (or knew of) DeCaulp and used part of his history, with some embellishments, in creating her "fictional" memoirs. (This is, to some degree, supported by Calvin Collier's expert knowledge about Arkansas units and DeCaulp's personal career). Or, (b) she found out that DeCaulp had gone North and abandoned her, and was too embarrassed to report that, and so wrote him out of her life and declared him "dead." Or, (c) DeCaulp, as a "double agent" took advantage of her, deserted her, but arranged for her to be notified of his "death" and she was taken in. The latter two interpretations would be truly ironic, but cannot be supported at present except by assuming that DeCaulp *was* impressed into Confederate service against his will, as the fragmentary information in the National Archives suggests, and used the situation to his advantage as best he could until the opportunity arose to desert.

Unless future research turns up evidence to support alternative interpretations, the "evidence of the files" (though some of it is confused and contradictory as to details) tends to support the interpretation that—at least in this part of her memoirs—Velazquez mixed fiction with fact in some unknown but significant proportions. Although there *was* a Thomas C. DeCaulp who served in an Arkansas unit, and whose history overlaps her version of the story, and who was in some of the places at some of the times she reports, major discrepancies remain between her memoirs and the official records.

To check the accuracy of place descriptions and local people, I contacted the Atlanta Historical Society about her descriptions of that city, and researchers in Richmond and Lynchburg, Virginia, and Columbus, Ohio (the site of Camp Chase), about her adventures in those places. As indicated in the chapter notes, her descriptions were accurate insofar as could be determined. A passing reference she made indicated that the Lynchburg jail, where she had been detained, was on the second floor. With some difficulty, this proved to be true after persistent research on my behalf by Lewis H. Averett of the Jones Memorial Library staff.

The most striking "hit" of an obscure fact in her narrative was unearthed by a friend and colleague, Jennie Zeidman, when she obtained confirmation that the officer in charge of Tod Barracks at Camp Chase, where Velazquez reported visiting her Confederate prisoner brother, was a "one-armed major" just as she had reported. Also, the prison camp at Camp Chase was not widely known and would not have been an obvious choice for someone creating a fictional account.

Unfortunately, more research of a similar nature remains to be done for other cities where Velazquez spent time, especially in New Orleans (her childhood home and "home base") and Louisville, Kentucky, where there may be an important clue as to the authenticity of her spying adventures in the North (See "Kentucky Mystery Woman," following).

The Arkansas connection reported by Velazquez I checked with some historical and geographical research. She reports crossing over the river from Memphis to Hopefield, Arkansas, and taking a train to a small way station, recommended by the conductor, called Hurlburt Station, to recruit soldiers for the Confederate army. She recruited a battalion of soldiers which she called the "Arkansas Grays" and took them downriver to New Orleans, and on to Pensacola for training.

Calvin Collier determined that Hopefield did exist, and was the railroad terminal on the Arkansas bank of the Mississippi River opposite Memphis. The railroad spur was only some eighty miles long, from Hopefield to White River, but no place called "Hurlburt Station" could be found on contemporary maps. The tracks were torn up sometime in 1862 to supply "iron clad" for the C.S.S. *Arkansas* that was later in action at Vicksburg. The only Arkansas Grays on record was a unit recruited from the Arkadelphia area, much farther west than the area she describes.

The story of her postwar involvement in a Confederate scheme for emigration to Venezuela (and other South American countries), was strongly confirmed, as reported in the notes of Chapter 11. Again, this demonstrates that significant portions of her memoirs are essentially true, and that instead of feeling compelled to an "either-or" conclusion as to the authenticity of her overall story, we need to examine the various elements of it and determine what the evidence is, pro and con. It is not exactly a radical idea to think that some portions of her story may be entirely factual, and her basic experiences more or less as reported, while some portions are "tailored" or even "fabricated" for self-serving reasons.

General Jubal Early in 1878, two years after the publication of *The Woman in Battle*, took serious issue with Velazquez about the book, stating that she was "a mere pretender." (May, 1878 correspondence in Tucker family papers, Southern Historical Collection, Chapel Hill, North Carolina.) His arguments against the authenticity of her memoirs were complex, ranging from the general to the specific. In my judgment, they included both trivial arguments based on an idealized concept of southern womanhood, and sound arguments that legitimately raise serious questions.

Upon reading her book, Early found "several inconsistencies, absurdities, and impossibilities in it which I thought proved beyond all question, the writer of it to be a mere pretender." After meeting her face-to-face, Early said: "Her appearance and voice are those of an American woman, and bear no resemblance to those of a cultivated Spanish lady. If she is really Spanish in origin, then her associations with camp life have thoroughly Americanized her." He was "satisfied that she had not written the book of which she proposed to be the author, or that it had been very much changed and improved in style by her editor."

Early goes on to specify reasons for his conclusions, and, without considerably more information to go by, some of his arguments are difficult to refute. Among his more cogent arguments are that:

1. She fails to give the name of her first husband who, allegedly, was a U.S. Army officer who resigned to go into Confederate service and whose records could have been checked. (That *is* the description given, according to her story, of her *second* husband Thomas C. DeCaulp.)

2. Her description of recruiting troops in Arkansas depicts her as acting without any state or Confederate government authority, and she seems to appoint non-commissioned officers on her own, and to pay for all the expenses of transferring the battalion from Arkansas to Pensacola, Florida, without any explanation of how she came to have the money to do so.

3. On a trip north in June, 1861 she reports taking a train from Columbia, South Carolina, bound for Richmond, passing through Lynchburg, Virginia, en route. Early is correct in stating that this could not be true, because there was a gap in the railroad between Greensboro, North Carolina, and Lynchburg until 1870. (On the other hand, this could be a simple failure of memory.)

4. Her statements about flitting from one army to the other in the Confederacy defy his knowledge and experience and seem unlikely from his perspective. (It is quite true that a regularly commissioned officer could not have done this, but she claimed to be an "independent." Even so, some of her abrupt changes of command raise a lot of questions.)

Judging by the copy of a letter from Velazquez to Early that he "introduced in evidence," he is correct that the person who wrote the letter (which was loaded with spelling and grammatical errors, and a few incomplete sentences) could hardly have been the author of her alleged memoirs, unless she had a lot of help from the editor. Quite possibly C. J. Worthington, the editor, was the primary writer, based on information provided by her, and he may have taken some liberties. Also, the entire question of her alleged Spanish background via Cuba rests solely on her word as of now.

My overall impression of *The Woman in Battle* is that if she was trying to "tell a good story," she was not very good at it and there is no reason (other than the purely mercenary) to think that she would try out such a seemingly farfetched story unless she thought it was true. She goes down one blind alley after another and has failure after failure, including some disastrous experiences. She debunks her own early romanticism and expresses cynicism about the glory of war and decries the corruption of the human spirit by wartime opportunists. Hers is not a tale of derring-do and wondrous achievements. In fact, it tracks the mood and spirit of the war from the Confederate standpoint very well. I get the strong sense that she was trying to be thorough and complete in her memoirs, and that her memory for details and sequences of events failed her at times, but that can't be the whole story.

Moreover, certain key portions of her memoirs have been authenticated, so we know it is not entirely a work of fiction. The fact that she did serve in male uniform as "Lieutenant Buford" (or "Benford," in some accounts) also is established. The ultimate question, which only additional research can answer, is: How much of "Lieutenant Buford's" career (and her spying career) is fact and how much fiction? And why the mix? Did she perhaps, like Sarah Emma Edmonds, have some reason to conceal the truth in some sections of the book?

Continuing Problems and Mysteries

Some of the unresolved problems and mysteries may eventually yield to research, while others are unlikely ever to be resolved.

A search was made by a genealogist for prewar records of Anna Etheridge's life, with no success.

If Sarah Emma Edmonds Seelye's manuscript which was intended to be a sequel to *Nurse and Spy* could be found, it would clear up the remaining questions about her wartime activities.

What became of Loreta Janeta Velazquez? Where and under what circumstances did she die? What records about her might be found in New Orleans, or Havana, or other cities involved in her story? What is the *real* story of Thomas C. DeCaulp?

Who was Frances Clalin and what was her story? Why does one source list her as serving in a Missouri militia cavalry unit that did not exist, and another as serving in a Maine cavalry unit where no record of her can be found?

Why is it seemingly impossible to trace any personal history of Bridget Deavers either before the war, or after it when she allegedly served with the U.S. Cavalry out west? Yet, a number of reliable sources reported meeting her or serving with her during the war.

Who was the woman killed at Shiloh and buried in Union uniform? Who were the Confederate husband and wife killed at Gettysburg and buried on the battlefield? In fact, who were the many other women for whom we have only a male name or no name at all?

Who was the Kentucky mystery woman who was honored by the legislature after the war for aiding Confederate prisoners in Canada, whose name the veterans could not recall later, and whose photograph bears a striking resemblance to the engraving of Loreta Velazquez in *The Woman in Battle*?

Information Invited

Anyone who has information from published sources not cited in this book, or unpublished diaries, letters, or documents bearing on these unresolved questions or adding information to the stories of the women reported here, is invited to address the author c/o: Paragon House, 90 Fifth Avenue, New York, NY 10011.

APPENDIX C

2nd Michigan Infantry

The 2nd Michigan Infantry Regiment was mustered into service on May 25, 1861, at Fort Wayne, Detroit, and was sent to the defense of Washington, D.C., one of the first western regiments to arrive. Among the women with the regiment were:

- Sarah Emma Edmonds (Private "Franklin Thompson")
- Anna Etheridge, daughter of the regiment
- Jane Hinsdale, regimental nurse

The original regimental officers were:

- Colonel Israel B. Richardson (Later promoted to brigadier general, brigade commander, and division commander in the Army of the Potomac. Mortally wounded at Antietam, September 17, 1862.)
- Lieutenant Colonel Henry L. Chipman (Appointed captain, regular army, May 11, 1861; colonel, April 15, 1864, commander of a black infantry regiment. Served for the entire war, and postwar military service until February 1, 1887.)
- Major Adolphus W. Williams (Commissioned lieutenant colonel, March 6, 1862. Wounded in action three times in the 1862 Peninsula Campaign. Appointed colonel of 20th Michigan Infantry, July 26, 1862. Disability discharge, November 21, 1863).

Colonels of the 2nd Michigan

The following men were commissioned as colonel of the 2nd Michigan in succession:

- Israel B Richardson (April, 25, 1861)
- Orlando M. Poe (September 16, 1861)
- William Humphrey (April 25, 1863)
- Edwin J. March (September 30, 1864)
- Frederick Schneider (March 18, 1865)

At various times, the following men were acting regimental commander during the temporary absence of the colonel: Lieutenant Colonel Louis Dillman; Major Cornelius Byington (mortally wounded at Knoxville, Tennessee, November 24, 1863); Captain John V. Ruehle, Jr.; Captain James Farrand (killed in action at Spottsylvania Court House, Virginia, May 12, 1864); Captain John L. Young (killed in action at Petersburg, Virginia, July 30, 1864); and Captain John C. Boughton.

APPENDIX D

Selected Bibliography

Antonia Fraser, *The Warrior Queens*. New York: Knopf, 1989.

Jessica Amanda Salmonson, *Encyclopedia of Amazons: Women Warriors from Antiquity to the Modern Era*. New York: Paragon House, 1991.

Tim Newark, *Women Warriors*. London: Blandford, 1989.

Norma L. Goodrich, *Priestesses*. New York: Franklin Watts, 1989.

Lucy Freeman and Alma H. Bond, *America's First Woman Warrior: The Courage of Deborah Sampson*. New York: Paragon House, 1992.

Ellen R. Jolly, *Nuns of the Battlefield*. Providence, RI: Providence Visitor Press, 1927.

George Barton, *Angels of the Battlefield: A History of the Labors of the Catholic Sisterhoods in the Late Civil War*. Philadelphia, PA: Catholic Art Publishing Co., 1898.

H. Sinclair Mills, Jr., *The Vivandiere: History, Tradition, Uniform and Service*, Collinswood, N.J.: C.W. Historicals, 1988.

Septima M. Collis (Mrs. General Charles H. T. Collis), *A Woman's War Record*. New York: G. P. Putnam's Sons, 1889.

Mary A. Gardner Holland (ed.), *Our Army Nurses*. Boston, MA: B. Wilkins & Co., 1895.

John R. Brumgardt, *Civil War Nurse: The Diary and Letters of Hannah Ropes*. Knoxville, TN: University of Tennessee Press, 1980.

Index

About the Author

Richard Hall is author of *Uninvited Guests* (Aurora Press, 1988), an overview and analysis of the UFO mystery, and numerous other writings on that subject. He has worked as an abstractor/indexer, science writer, and technical editor in the Washington, D.C., area for more than thirty years on a broad range of scientific and political topics, including environmental issues. He has an avid interest in the Civil War, as well as gardening, nature, feline companionship, and equine prognostication, being a founding member and *Magister Velocitatis Equinae* of the "Church of Equine Velocity."